WOMEN AND THE
GENESIS OF CHRISTIANITY

WOMEN AND THE
GENESIS OF CHRISTIANITY

BEN WITHERINGTON III

Edited by Ann Witherington

CAMBRIDGE
UNIVERSITY PRESS

Published by the Press Syndicate of the University of Cambridge
The Pitt Building, Trumpington Street, Cambridge CB2 1RP
40 West 20th Street, New York, NY 10011-4211, USA
10 Stamford Road, Oakleigh, Victoria 3166, Australia

First published 1990
Reprinted 1992

Printed in Great Britain at
the Athenaeum Press Ltd, Newcastle upon Tyne

British Library cataloguing in publication data
Witherington, Ben
Women and the genesis of Christianity.
1. Bible N.T. Special subjects: Society. Role of women
I. Title   II. Witherington, Ann
225.8′30542

Library of Congress cataloguing in publication data applied for

ISBN 0 521 36497 3 hardback
ISBN 0 521 36735 2 paperback

WG

This book is dedicated to my wife, Ann, my co-worker and life partner whose skills in editing, formatting, typing, and criticizing my ideas and efforts have made this book and the previous two monographs it is based on possible. She embodies those same virtues, talents, and faith that we find in the various first-century Christian women discussed in these pages.

CONTENTS

Contents

Contents

ACKNOWLEDGEMENTS

To date I have written two SNTS monographs: *Women in the Ministry of Jesus* (Cambridge University Press, 1984) and *Women in the Earliest Churches* (Cambridge University Press, 1988). The first book was based wholly and the second one partly on my doctoral work at the University of Durham, England, under the direction of the Reverend Professor C. K. Barrett. My deepest gratitude goes to him as both teacher and friend.

My wife, Ann, was primarily responsible for the final draft of this book. While I transliterated and edited the technical material, it was she who rewrote the material into its present form for the general public.

Much of the financial support for my earlier works was provided by A Fund for Theological Education, based in Marshall, Texas, under the leadership of Dr. Ed Robb. This present volume has been prepared while teaching at Ashland Theological Seminary, Ashland, Ohio. I would like to acknowledge the support of both institutions.

I would also like to acknowledge the editorial and production assistance of all those at Cambridge University Press, especially Ulrike Hellen, who helped with the editing of each draft of this condensed version of my first two monographs, and Alex Wright, for seeing the project through to its publication.

Finally, my thanks go to Bill and Laura Kollar who took time from their busy schedules to proofread the final draft.

PREFACE

Women and the Genesis of Christianity condenses my two previous monographs, *Women in the Ministry of Jesus* and *Women in the Earliest Churches*, in order to make them accessible to a wider audience that is not familiar with the technical jargon of New Testament studies, or the Greek, Hebrew, and various other languages needed for New Testament research.

In order to achieve this goal I have left out a great deal of the technical discussion and detailed footnotes found in the previous two works, especially in regard to matters of textual criticism, grammatical details, and the historical plausibility of this or that narrative. Those wishing to pursue such matters are advised to consult my two monographs. Much of this work is the synthesis of the ideas of a great many people besides myself, and their work is liberally cited in the monographs. I regret having to now leave out so much of the deserved citation.

In addition, I have transliterated the Greek into English, and then explained its probable translation in the course of the discussion. Further, when citing articles or books that have Greek words in their titles, I have transliterated these as well.

In this work I intend to discuss all the crucial New Testament data involving women, but since the subject is "Women and the genesis of Christianity," I have not gone beyond the canonical period as I did in the last chapter of *Women in the Earliest Churches*. It is hoped that the reader will gain a new perspective on the part women played in the beginning days of the most remarkable movement in human history.

The author of Ecclesiastes knew what he was about when he said, "Of the making of books there is no end" (12.12). Indeed, it can be said that this applies especially in areas of interest to contemporary

Preface

readers such as, for instance, the study of women and the Bible. In the wake of various movements in the twentieth century, especially in Western nations, that have led to women having more freedom in regard to voting rights, choice of vocation, and educational opportunities, it is not surprising that women's religious roles have been written about extensively.

What is surprising is how seldom the subject of women and the Bible has been fully addressed in such books even by those who are perfectly capable of doing so. What we actually find when we survey the available resources is: (1) purely popular books written by those who are not historical and/or biblical scholars, and thus are incapable of assessing the real historical issues the Bible raises; (2) purely technical books, impenetrable to the average reader, that cover only a portion of the data; and (3) books written by those who are so passionately traditionalist or feminist in their approach that their personal interests and biases skew the interpretation of the data, or tend to lead the writer to highlight only that portion of the material which favors his or her own views on matters such as women's roles in the Church, and especially the question of women's ordination. Sadly, most of these last sort of books are forms of propaganda, attempting to claim either Jesus or Paul or the New Testament writers as a whole for one's own cause. Usually, such books shed more heat than light on the subject.

There is both room and a need for a book written *by* a biblical scholar and historian, but written *for* a more general audience and written *after* all the detailed scholarly historical research has been done. This book distils most of my earlier research and, I hope, presents it in a form that will prove useful to the general public. I openly admit that during the fifteen years I have studied women and their roles both in the Jesus movement and in the early Church, my own views have changed on various important matters, and I am under no delusion that what is presented here will be seen as the final or definitive word on the subject of women in the beginning of Christianity. I do hope that my readers' curiosity will lead them to read on and to seek out the more technical studies behind this book.

I should also add that I am a committed Christian who takes seriously the canonical authority of the whole of the Bible for the Church. This study would not have been undertaken if I were not

xii

convinced that the New Testament in particular has something
vital to say about women and their roles in society in general
and in the Church in particular, even today. I believe that the
Bible must be allowed to have its say. It must be carefully read;
all of the relevant data must be considered; and historical and
practical judgments should then be made on the basis of a patient
hearing of the sources. This is, of course, no new view for the
Christian Church. Furthermore, Western society in general has
historically agreed that the Bible does have something relevant
to say about pressing personal and ethical issues in any and every
era.

Certainly, the Bible has been one of the most formative of all
books in the West in regard to views about a whole host of subjects
including male – female relationships, the family, sexual morality,
and women's roles and functions in various fields including religious
ones. The Bible has been the basis of our law codes. It has shaped
our view of the nature and structure of such important institutions
as marriage and the family. It has established the very pattern
of our work week and informed our view of work in general.
Western codes of honor, civility, and hospitality have all grown
out of the Bible, as have the majority of Western charitable institutions. The Bible in general and the New Testament in particular
have shaped our view of what good government should look like,
as well as our views on the proper relationship of Church and
State. Indeed, it has fundamentally shaped our views on good
and evil, the natural and the supernatural, and the real and the
unreal. Even for those who may have little or no connection with
what has been called organized religion, the Bible's views on
women and their roles may prove illuminating, not least because
in the West we live in societies that have been shaped in so many
ways by that Bible.

For those who read this book carefully, it will perhaps be surprising
to discover how "the more things change, the more things stay
the same." Jesus and his followers lived in a culture that was
excessively patriarchal, but there were various reform movements
about and one of them was early Christianity. Living as we do
in an era when many of the basic assumptions of a traditional
patriarchal approach to life and work are again being challenged

and various attempts at reform are underway, it is interesting to see *how* Jesus and Paul among others set about reforming the social structures of their day. It is very clear from the New Testament that the Kingdom Jesus and the early Christians believed they were bringing in was not a *purely spiritual* one, if by that is meant one which has no bearing on basic social relationships and conditions. Jesus and the early Christians were indeed interested in the redemption of whole persons, not merely souls, and this entailed a certain reformation of the patriarchal structure of society, so that for Christians the family of faith rather than the physical family became the basic unit of social identity and identification. I would suggest that it was in part because Christianity was not just another social movement, that it has not merely endured but has grown as a movement of worldwide impact over the course of its nearly twenty centuries of existence.

There are a host of areas on which the historical study of the New Testament material dealing with women and their roles has a bearing. One may consider, for instance, women's studies in general, which is becoming an ever more popular field for research at colleges and universities, especially in the West. It has been rightly recognized that in the West those who seek to do women's studies without at least incorporating in it a study of the impact of biblical material do so at their peril, in view of the impact of the Bible on society as a whole. Or again, the modern feminist movement, which has some of its roots not only in the Christian Church but also in various Christian social action movements, has a need to understand and explore its biblical roots. Or again, in regard to the vexed issue of women's ordination in various denominations including the Church of England, if purely emotional or prudential or political factors are not to dictate the course the Church will take, then biblical data will have to be assessed and duly weighed.

I am convinced that by analogy much of what Jesus and the early Christians said and did and the principles by which they operated are still applicable today. This is especially true for the Church as it seeks a more equitable approach to male – female relations in general and the roles of women in the Church in particular. I also believe that all of us, *if* we ignore the biblical data, would be impoverished in our attempts to understand human sexuality and relationships. Thus, this book should be seen as an invitation to all who have any interest in why we as men and women live as we do in modern society to consider the relevance and effect that the New Testament has had and perhaps should have on our society.

PART I

WOMEN IN FIRST CENTURY CULTURES

1

WOMEN IN JUDAISM

No study of women in the New Testament can be undertaken without first looking at the larger historical context in which the events of New Testament history took place. This chapter describes the prevailing attitudes about women, their status and roles, in Israel before and during the New Testament era. We can mention only selected portions of the relevant data, but it appears that the information given is representative of the period.

When discussing first-century Palestinian Jewish women, the problem of dating the material immediately confronts us. Much of the rabbinic literature is of an unknown date, since it is not identified with a particular rabbi or school. Thus, we will rely primarily on information found in the Mishnah, a collection of oral traditions which explain and expand upon the law or legal material found in the Old Testament. These oral traditions were certainly in existence before the Mishnah was written down (codified) around A.D. 200. Information from other Jewish writings, such as the Talmuds and midrashes, are used when they seem to summarize attitudes that prevailed throughout the era of early Judaism.[1]

Social life

There can be little doubt that the family was the exclusive sphere of influence for Jewish women in the first century A.D. This limiting of a woman's sphere of influence is partly attributable to Jewish marital customs of that day. One must bear in mind the extraordinary power a father had over his daughter, and a husband over his wife. The laws of inheritance, betrothal, and divorce were heavily biased in the male's favor, with only a few checks and balances (such as the wife's ''divorce price'' and a daughter's ''right of

3

maintenance''). A woman was passed from her father to her husband's sphere of authority, usually without being consulted. Since a woman changed families when she married, she could not be expected to preserve the family name or keep property in the same family. For this reason, the laws stated that she was entitled to ''maintenance'' rather than inheritance in most cases. That Rabbi Ishmael can bemoan the poverty of Israel's women is perhaps an indication of how hard and rare it was for a woman to inherit property.[2]

When a girl was underage (under twelve years), she had no right to her own possessions, and the fruit of her labor or anything she found belonged to her father. If she was sexually violated, compensation money for the indignity was paid to the *father*. Though a girl could not refuse a marriage arrangement made by her father, she could express her wish to stay in the home until puberty, and she was within her rights to refuse any arrangement made by her mother or brothers after her father's death and before she was twelve and a half years old. Once she was of age, a girl could not be betrothed against her will. Considering the early age of betrothal and marriage, it would be rare indeed for a woman to have acquired an inheritance prior to marriage, or to have reached an age when she could refuse a marital arrangement made by her family.

A woman's security in her husband's family was limited by the fact that the husband could divorce her if she caused an ''impediment'' to the marriage. This privilege to divorce was rarely extended to the wife. A husband could divorce his wife without her consent for reasons ranging from her unchastity, to her burning a meal, or to finding another woman fairer than his own wife. A wife's security was also threatened in some cases by the fact that polygamy was permitted in New Testament times as it was in Old Testament days. While monogamy for economic and moral reasons was the common practice, the Mishnah does record cases of, and rules for, a man betrothed to two women.[3]

In spite of these limitations it would be wrong to assume that a Jewish woman had no respect or *rights* in Jesus' day. Jewish writings reiterate in various places the Old Testament rule that the mother is to be honored equally with the father. In Exod. 20.12 we read: ''Honor your father and your mother ...'' (note the father is

4

mentioned first), while in Lev. 19.3 we read "Every one of you shall revere his mother and his father ..." (note the mother comes first). Thus, it was deduced that they were to be revered equally, indeed honored as God is honored. The Talmud instructs a man to love his wife as himself and to respect her more than himself.[4] A further example of a woman's rights is that while normally it was the man or the man's family who started the betrothal process, a woman was in some circumstances said to be able to betroth a man on her own initiative.

In the family, the wife's duties included grinding flour, baking bread, washing clothes, breast-feeding the children for eighteen to twenty-four months, making the beds, working with wool, and washing her husband's face, hands, and feet. The extent of a wife's household duties depended on how many servants she brought into the marriage. As regards child-bearing duties, Rabbi Johanan ben Baroka said that the commandment to be fruitful and multiply was aimed at the wife as well as the husband, though this was probably not a majority opinion and we usually read that this commandment was required only of the man.[5]

The husband's duties were equally extensive. Whereas a man had an *obligation* to provide for his wife, he had a *choice* over whether or not to provide for his slaves. Thus, a wife was not treated as property. The marriage contract bound the husband to provide food, clothing, and material needs for the wife, and she could demand these things before a court. Responsibilities of the husband also included fulfilling his connubial duty, redeeming his wife from foreign captivity, and providing shelter. Unlike a man, a woman was said to have a *right* to sexual pleasure. Indeed, the School of Hillel said that a man had not fulfilled Gen. 1.28 until he had both a son and daughter, whereas the School of Shammai conceded that two sons would fulfill one's duty.[6] Considering the importance of a son to a Jew who wished to pass on his name and heritage, it was rare for a father to prefer his daughters.

With few exceptions, a woman could not divorce her husband, while a husband could divorce his wife practically at will so long as he could afford to pay his wife a pre-arranged sum known as the dismissal price. There were, however, situations and ways in which she could precipitate a divorce. If a husband refused to consummate the marriage, was impotent, had an unpleasant occupation, had leprosy, was unable to provide support, or if he was to be separated from her for a long time, then she could sue for divorce in the courts. A woman could leave her husband and return to her parents' home, thus precipitating a divorce in most cases. Though a woman could not normally pronounce the ''formula of divorce'' which finalized the act, she was able to write her own bill of divorce and its validity depended on her. Thus, while technically only a husband could initiate a divorce, and a bill was only valid if written specifically for the woman, a woman did have means of legally ending a marriage. It should be added that divorce was frowned upon by most rabbis.[7] Also, in Jewish law, unlike early Greek and Roman law, a husband was never allowed to take the life of his wife if she was an adulteress.

An Israelite woman was allowed to hold property in her own right, as discoveries at the Dead Sea have shown. She was also allowed to inherit property, though male heirs had precedence over her. If she remarried, her property remained her own, though her husband had a right to use it. This was especially true of a wife's slaves. Both the Schools of Shammai and Hillel agreed that a woman could sell or give away any of her inherited property prior to her betrothal. The School of Shammai adds that she could sell it after betrothal as well.

In addition to rights of *inheritance*, a woman also had a right to *maintenance* from her father's or husband's resources. Indeed, if a man died leaving only a little property, his daughters had a right to maintenance before his sons could inherit, even if this meant that the sons had to go without. This was also true of a widow who remained with her former husband's household.

Spiritual life

A certain spiritual significance was assigned to a woman's presence or role in the home; as Rabbi Jacob says, ''One who has no wife remains without good, and without a helper, and without joy, and without blessing, and without atonement.''[8] Even more dramatic is the comment by Rabbi Phineas ben Hannah that a woman has an atoning force not inferior to the altar if as a wife she remains within the domestic seclusion of her family.[9] The spiritual influence of the mother in the home is perhaps indicated by the fact that the rabbis

6

considered a child a Jew *only* if his mother was a Jewess. The rabbis' appreciation of a woman's potential spiritual influence is also shown by a saying which points out that if a pious man marries a wicked woman he will become wicked, but if a wicked man marries a pious woman, she will make him pious.

It was in the home that the training began which equipped Jews for participation in the synagogue or Temple services and, in the case of men, for religious leadership whether as a scribe, rabbi or priest. It was a cause of debate whether and how much a woman should teach or be taught Torah even in the home.[10] Although Rabbi Eliezer says that teaching one's daughter Torah is teaching her "lechery" (or extravagance), his opinion is said to be a minority one.[11] Support for this verdict can be found in several places. Rabbi ben Azzai says, "A man ought to give his daughter a knowledge of the Law," and Mishnah Nedarim 4.3 reads, "He may teach scripture to his sons and daughters."[12]

On the other hand, negative remarks about wives cannot be ignored. Mishnah Kiddushin 4.13 tells us that a wife is not to teach her children, perhaps a result of the fact that women were exempt from studying Torah. Nevertheless, women are said to be expected to know the holy language, and it was also inferred from Exod. 19.3 that women accepted Torah before men. There are even cases of women being taught the oral law and being consulted on its fine points. Rabbi Meir's wife, Beruriah, is well known in this regard. Possibly the maidservants of Rabbi Judah the Prince received similar training, for there are instances where they gave some scholars enlightenment on rare Hebrew words in the Bible. Imma-Shalom, sister of Rabbi Gamaliel II and the wife of Rabbi Eliezer, was prominent enough to have some of her sayings recorded in the Talmud. Finally, Rabbi Nahman's wife was said to vex him continually because of her expertise in Jewish matters. Though these examples are exceptional, they do show that even when Judaism was beset with the problems of foreign occupation and influence, when there was a tendency to protect and confine Jewish women and children to preserve important traditions, some women were able to become learned in both oral and written law and tradition.[13]

Women were allowed to take Naziritic vows (see Num. 6.1–21) during and after Jesus' time, as the example of Queen Helena of

Adiabene (a Jewish convert from Mesopotamia) demonstrates. We are told that women could bring sacrifices to the Temple; even a suspected adulteress' offering is not refused. Mishnah Zebahim 3.1 says that women could legally slaughter the animals for sacrifice, even those designated for the Most Holy Things – sacrifices used for special feast days or unblemished sin offerings. There are cases recorded where women were allowed to lay hands on their sacrifice, despite the fact that Mishnah Menahoth 9.8 says they cannot. Even more significant is that some women, with a priest's aid, were able to ''wave the meal offering in the air,'' an act of offering the wheat sacrifice to God normally performed by a priest.

A woman of priestly stock (a descendent of Levi or Aaron) had certain priestly rights and privileges in regard to the offerings. Women were obligated to light the candles at the Feast of Dedication because they too benefited from the ending of the Seleucid persecution.[14] Though women were limited to their own court in the Jerusalem Temple, it is not certain when the practice of having special galleries for women in the synagogues began, though apparently they existed in Trajan's time (early second century A.D.).[15] We know that such popular feasts as the Feast of Tabernacles took place in the women's court.

Babylonian Talmud Megillah 23a tells us that women were qualified to be among the seven who read Torah in the synagogue, though it appears that after New Testament times and perhaps before that they were expected to refuse. Further, there are no known examples of women reading in the synagogues during Jesus' time. In the domestic observance of the Sabbath, women were responsible for preparing the dough offering and lighting the Sabbath lamp. Women were required to say the Tefillah, the eighteen benedictions, the table blessings, and to maintain the Mezuzah on the doors of their homes.

From the above evidence we may conclude that at least in theory a woman's position and privileges in regard to the Jewish cult during and beyond New Testament times differed little from their status and rights in Old Testament times with two important exceptions. First, a separation of women and men in the Temple and synagogue was introduced after Old Testament times, and secondly, perhaps women were not allowed to read Torah in the assembly by New

Testament times. The Old Testament's high regard for women's religious rights seems to have been preserved legally in the rabbinic literature with notable exceptions.

In order to understand why a woman was restricted in regard to place and function in the Temple one must bear in mind the ordinances of Lev. 15. According to these rules a priest had to be holy and ritually clean at all times in order to offer the sacrifice. Thus, the exclusion of women as priestesses in the cult was because of their "uncleanness" during their monthly menstrual period, and not because of any rabbinic prejudice aimed directly at women. Women's exclusion from cultic office on these grounds also meant that since they could not be depended upon to be ritually clean on every occasion, they were not even eligible to participate in those ordinances of the Law which were periodic in nature, such as certain feasts, daily appearances in the synagogue to make a quorum, periodic prayer, etc. This is probably why we read in Mishnah Kiddushin 1.7, "The observance of all the positive ordinances that depend on the time of year is incumbent on men but not on women, and the observance of all positive ordinances that do not depend on the time of year is incumbent both on men and women."[16]

The evidence concerning Jewish women's roles in religion indicates that by and large the religious privileges and functions they had were those they could participate in at home. The biblical rules in Lev. 15 and their rabbinic interpretations restricted a woman's participation in the Temple rituals. Further, certain views about propriety appear to have taken away her theoretical right to read the Scriptures in the synagogue even in Jesus' day.

2

WOMEN IN HELLENISTIC SETTINGS

Greece

Within the general patriarchal framework which was present at least to some extent in all of Greece's city-states and colonies from Homeric times (*c.* 700 B.C.) through the age of the Roman Empire, one finds a diversity of roles and views of women that goes beyond the confines of early Judaism. There was a great deal of difference, however, between being a woman in Athens, Sparta, or Corinth.

Athens

Athens was a city of contrasts in regard to the status and roles of women. It is impossible to generalize about their positions because apart from common prostitutes and slaves, there were three categories of women: Athenian citizens, concubines, and companions.

Concubines are probably the smallest and least important group for our discussion. They occupied the middle ground between legal wives and companions. Their relationship to an Athenian male citizen was recognized by law, and if the concubine was an Athenian citizen her children would be free, though not legitimate members of the family of her male partner – unless he chose to give them such status. Finally, concubines had no dowry and their main function was to care for the personal, especially sexual, needs of their male partners. In this way, a male Athenian citizen could limit his legitimate heirs without limiting his sexual activities.[1]

It is fair to say that although female Athenian citizens were respected as wives and mothers in the classical period (before Alexander the Great [356–323 B.C.] who initiated the age of Hellenism), their position on the whole was little better than that

10

of Jewish women in the same period. Certainly the women of Attica, the region surrounding Athens, led a more sheltered and subordinate existence than women anywhere else in Greece. By Hellenistic and Roman times these views were still in existence, though less strongly held because of the liberalizing influence of Macedonian and Roman occupations.[2]

The historian Thucydides (*c.* 400 B.C.) spoke not only for his classical generation but also for those succeeding in Attica, when he had his hero Pericles remark that the glory of the woman is greatest "of whom there is least talk among men, whether in praise or in blame."[3] Athenian citizen-women were married usually at fifteen or sixteen years of age, and up to this time they were said to have seen little of the world and inquired about nothing. Once an Athenian citizen-woman married she usually lived in a separate and guarded chamber, not unlike some upper-class Jewish women in New Testament times. It is doubtful, however, that these matrons were never allowed out of those chambers. Citizen-women were appreciated chiefly as a proper means to a legitimate male heir.[4] Even the practice of leaving unwanted daughters on a hillside to die was known in New Testament times. In contrast to Spartan practices, Athenians severely limited a matron's rights to acquire or retain any personal property apart from her dowry.[5] If one bases one's views of a woman's position in Athens solely on the position of Athenian citizen-women, one can well understand why Thales (*c.* 400 B.C.) was grateful, "that [he] was born a human being and not a beast, next a man and not a woman, thirdly, a Greek and not a barbarian."[6]

The companions, being foreign women, had no civic rights; however, this also meant that they had few civic restrictions. They were not allowed to manage public affairs, or to marry citizens, or to usurp citizen-women's positions. Beyond this they were virtually allowed a free hand.[7] Many famous Greek men, including Plato, Aristotle, Epicurias, Isocrates, and Menander, had female companions. Because of the frequent sexual liaisons involved, the term soon became synonymous with courtesan. Yet it would be wrong to assume that these women were simply harlots. In order to be a good companion for intelligent and important men, many of them studied the arts, philosophy, and politics. In fact, they were said to be "the only educated women in Athens."[8]

Apparently, companions were allowed to participate in the religious cults, for there are cases of some being initiated into the secret Eleusinian rituals as early as the fourth century B.C. This may be attributed to the fact that the Athenians tried to raise the Eleusinian cult to the status of the common cult of Greece.

Note that within its own social framework Athens was a city of contrasts in regard to women's positions and rights. On the one hand, we have seen that Athenian matrons who had the rights of citizens and the right to legal marriages were in most other regards disenfranchised. On the other hand, companions who had no civic rights nor the right to marry an Athenian citizen could be educated and become objects of much of the affections of Athenian men. It is not surprising that in Athens there was a shrine built, not to the matrons, but to the companions and their patron goddess, Aphrodite.

Little can be said concerning an Athenian woman's religious and legal status. A young woman's primary means of contact with the outside world was through her participation in various religious processions. At seven she could carry the mystical box; at ten she could grind the flour for the patron goddess' cakes; and at fifteen she could carry the sacred basket. Citizen-women were allowed to participate in some of the cults but so were the companions. In regard to her legal status, it appears that an Athenian citizen-woman was not allowed to be a valid witness in Athenian courts except possibly in homicide cases.

Sparta

If one takes a cursory glance at the references to Spartan women in Greek literature it is possible to draw the erroneous conclusion that women were liberated to a great extent in that part of Greece. Certainly in comparison to Athenians, Spartan women occupied a position of more freedom and influence but this difference is only relative, for even Spartan women were not equal to their male counterparts. Lycurgus, traditional founder of the Spartan constitution, set the pattern for the future of women's roles in Sparta when he established special eugenic laws or breeding programs. Thus, "All the legislation that relates to women has one sole object – to procure a first rate breed of men."[9]

12

The Spartans felt it necessary to educate and train women to be strong, brave, and resolute so that their sons would have a similar character, ideal for military service. From the earliest times, Spartan women were involved in gymnastics, wrestling, festivals, rudimentary educational schemes, offering sacrifices and, in general, they mingled freely and competed openly with men. This not only prepared them to be good mothers, but also afforded the men an opportunity to choose a proper mate. The darker side of this selection process was that the weaker women would be detected in various contests and prevented from marrying for fear of producing weak children. It is in light of the Spartan belief in eugenic principles that one should evaluate the relative freedom of Spartan women.

Women of Sparta are often praised in the inscriptions for their prudence, discretion, and true love of their husbands (Sparta having virtually a monogamous society). Spartan women did not usually eat with their husbands, most of whom were soldiers and ate with their regiments. Further, a woman's sons were taken from her when they were of age and ready for military instruction. This left mothers with a great deal of free time, and they were allowed to do whatever they pleased within legal and moral bounds. For instance, some women, once they had been good mothers and with their husband's permission, occasionally played a role in public life. That women were involved in public building projects or activities in the general interest, and were known to have held public office, indicates that they had money and were able to avail themselves of what the law and their husbands permitted. However, this is not to say that Spartan women were equal to Spartan men.

The divorce laws, for instance, gave men more freedom than women. Childlessness was a ground for a man to divorce his wife and take another. Perhaps most representative of a Spartan woman's true position and her famed fidelity are the following words spoken to a man proposing an illicit relationship. "When I was a girl, I was taught to obey my father and I obeyed him. When I became a wife, I obeyed my husband; if then, you have anything just to urge, make it known to him first."[10] The Spartan woman, like her Jewish counterpart, was subordinate to her father or husband, yet she had greater civil and property rights than a Jewish woman, and probably also greater security since polygamy was not a viable option in Sparta.

13

In her freedom of movement and physical and educational training, she compared favorably with a Jewess and also with an Athenian matron. In regard to her religious position, as elsewhere in Greece, Spartan women often participated in the cults and had official roles.[11]

Corinth

Little can be said of the family life or legal status of Corinthian citizen – women, but probably their position was even more compromised than Athenian women since Corinth was infamous all over the Mediterranean as the city of courtesans and companions. Of the religious status of Corinthian women and women who lived elsewhere on the Grecian mainland, other than Sparta and Ionia, we have more information.

If the companions were enshrined at Athens, they were incorporated into the very fabric of Corinthian public life. The historian Timaeus (c. 300 B.C.) tells us that many companions were dedicated to prayer in the temple of Aphrodite and for the salvation of Corinth from Persia. They were present regularly whenever the city offered sacrifices to this goddess. Being a port city, Corinth may have been more lax morally than other parts of Greece, but its difference from Athens in the freedom it bestowed on its companions was a difference of degree, not of kind. Both companions and free citizen-women were allowed to be devotees and administrators in some of the Corinthian cults.

It appears that Corinthian citizen-women had greater freedom and earned greater respect than their Athenian counterparts. There were separate festivals involving sacrifices in which freeborn Corinthian citizen-women participated and were honored. These women were noted for their boldness as well, for at one point they defended a particular sanctuary against the attack of Spartan men. It was not only Corinthian women who had vested interests and important roles in the religious cults; rather this was one of the few features of life that women from all over Greece shared in common.

Cultic roles of Grecian women

On an island off the coastal town of Troecenia in Argolis, a young girl served as an official in a temple of the god Poseidon. This is noteworthy because usually women were active only in the cults of goddesses. Women, however, were almost always the organs of divine inspiration and prophecy in Greece, and in the cult of Apollo only women were allowed to perform this office. The prophetess of Apollo was called a Pythoness and was expected to be a free-born Delphian widow who had faithfully ''tended the fires'' in the temple and given oracles in her home region.

Women also led the processions in the ''mysteries'' or secret rituals, though there was a male overseer. In the cult of Despoina there were apparently places, such as Megalopolis, where women had free access to the cult while men could only enter once a year. Women were prominent particularly in orgiastic rites, such as the Bacchanalia, and even young girls could be initiated into the Dionysian mysteries. In general, however, women were followers of the goddesses, and when associated with the temples of the gods their activities were limited.[12]

Conclusions

Despite all the above, Pseudo-Demosthenes (*c.* 340 B.C.) seems to sum up the common view concerning Greek women from Homeric to Roman times when he says, ''Mistresses we keep for the sake of pleasure, concubines for the daily care of our person, but wives to bear us legitimate children and to be faithful guardians of our households.''[13] Though it is probable that Grecian women gradually gained more freedom during the Hellenistic and Roman periods, and it is likely that most Grecian women compared favorably to Jewish women, they compared poorly to women of neighboring Macedonia and Asia Minor.

Macedonia

The bulk of our evidence about the women of Macedonia and Asia Minor is inscriptional and relates mainly to women who were wealthy or of royal lineage. Nevertheless, the evidence is pertinent because

Lydia of Acts 16 was apparently a well-to-do business woman who assumed an important role in the Christian community in Macedonia. Such a social position and religious role was not uncommon for women in Macedonia or Asia Minor.

It is common knowledge among classics and New Testament scholars that many women in Macedonia from the Hellenistic period onward had a great deal of influence and prominence. The following statement is typical:

If Macedonia produced perhaps the most competent group of men the world has yet seen, the women were in all respects the men's counterparts. They played a large part in affairs, received envoys, and obtained concessions from them for their husbands, built temples, founded cities, engaged mercenaries, commanded armies, held fortresses, and acted on occasion as regents or even co-ruler ...[14]

Macedonian men would frequently name cities after their wives because they admired and respected them. For example, Thessalonica was named by Casander (c. 358–297 B.C.) after his wife, Thessalonice, daughter of Philip. In the same area we have evidence of a woman being given inheritable civic rights in order to honor her. There were women politarchs (officials) in Thessalonica. Both men and women in Macedonia could evidently be money earners for there are cases of tombs erected for a husband and wife paid for out of their common earnings. Not only private admirers, but also public bodies, erected monuments to notable women. We often find inscriptions to Macedonian wives which refer to them in warm terms.

One must take into account such Macedonian queens as Arsinoe II (c. 316–270 B.C.) who ruled with distinction in Egypt, as well as Eurydice (337–317 B.C.) or Olympias (mother of Alexander the Great) who ruled in the homeland.[15] Their rising status and importance is evidenced by the fact that from Arsinoe II onward the queen's head always appeared on the coins with her husband. These queens were notable for their love of culture and were known to have written poems to famous personalities and to have corresponded with scholars such as the physicist Strato. Apparently, these Hellenistic queens also had an influence on Macedonian women who were not of royal blood, for we are told, "From the Macedonian courts (relative) freedom broadened down to the Greek home."[16]

16

Some women founded clubs and took part in various social organizations. Freedom and education in Macedonia, though available to all women in theory, could only be grasped by a few who could afford not to work. Undoubtedly, most women continued in their traditional roles without education or mobility, but at least the door was opened in Macedonia, and this had a great effect on Asia Minor and Egypt as Hellenization spread.

Asia Minor

Asia Minor and the nearby Aegean Isles bear more resemblance to Macedonia than to Greece in the roles they gave to women. Whether one looks in records of public offices, charities, or cults, women appear as regular participants in large cities and small towns, on the mainland and the islands.

There were women serving in the temple precincts of Artemis in Ephesus, and rigid rules of chastity were applied to them. Stratonice, wife of Antiochus I (324–261 B.C.), built and enriched many temples, such as the Temple of Apollos at Delos and Syrian Atargatis at Hieropolis. As in Athens, women led the cult worship of Dionysus on the island of Kos. Nonetheless, even in the Dionysian cults of Asia Minor, the women who celebrated the rites had a male overseer to make certain that all was done properly.

Women were allowed to hold public and cultic offices in Asia Minor which elsewhere were held only by men. Aurelia Harnastia, according to one inscription, was a priestess of Hera, a demiourgos (high magistrate), and at one point even a chief priestess. Aristodama, a priestess of Smyrna, was so well known that she was given honorary citizenship in Thessaly. Further, a woman's dowry remained her own in Asia Minor, though a husband had a right to its use in a somewhat similar fashion to the Jewish practice. After her husband's death, a woman could do as she wished with her possessions.

The prominence and rights of Asia Minor women are perhaps a result of the growth and spread of the cult of Isis into the region from Egypt, a country where women were allowed unprecedented freedom. A further factor was probably the Hellenization of Asia Minor during and after the time of Alexander the Great. Donaldson is surely correct when he says:

17

Especially in Asia Minor did women display public activity. Their generosity took the most various forms even to bestowing considerable sums on each citizen in their own cities. They erected baths and gymnasia ... presided at the public games or over great religious ceremonies ... and they paid the expenses incurred in these displays. They also held priesthoods and several of them obtained the highest priesthood of Asia – perhaps the greatest honor that could be paid to anyone.[17]

3

WOMEN IN ROMAN SETTINGS

Balsdon, in his important study on Roman women, remarks: "At no time did Roman women live in the semi-oriental seclusion in which women lived in Greece."[1] Nonetheless, he adds, "Complete equality of the sexes was never achieved in ancient Rome because of the survival long after it was out of date of a deep-rooted tradition that the exclusive sphere of a woman's activity was inside the home ..."[2] Both statements are fundamentally correct; thus, we should not measure Roman women's freedom by any yardstick other than the relative one of how they fared in comparison to their female contemporaries in the Mediterranean world. To anticipate our conclusions, a Roman woman compared favorably to her Athenian or Palestinian counterparts; however, there is reason to question whether they were better off than women in Macedonia or Asia Minor.

Social life

As was the case in various parts of Greece, one has to specify a class or group of Roman women when discussing whether Roman women were freer than Greek women. If one is discussing the Roman matron, then she appears to be freer, better educated, more highly respected, and more influential than matrons of the Greek mainland. On the other hand, though there were prostitutes in Rome, we do not find the phenomenon of educated companions in any significant numbers in the Eternal City. Because of the lack of evidence, we can say little about the women of the plebeian and slave classes. Thus, we will be limited mainly to an examination of Roman women of the patrician class and, as a result, the picture of Roman women we obtain from the evidence is not complete in depth or breadth.[3]

In order to understand a Roman woman's position in a first-century Roman family we must consider how the situation had changed since ancient times. In ancient Rome the authority of the father was as great as that of a Jewish father in the context of early Judaism. A Roman father had the power of life and death over his children and wife, and his right to slay his child, particularly a daughter, existed at least until the last century B.C. During the Republic, the five hundred years preceding Christ, the power of a husband or father was evident from procedures involved in a marriage arrangement. The father "sold" his daughter into the hand of her husband by a form of marriage known as *coemptio*. Livy remarks that during the Republic, "Our ancestors permitted no woman to conduct even personal business without a guardian to intervene in her behalf; they wished them to be under the control of fathers, brothers, husbands ..."[4]

The *coemptio* form of marriage began to be replaced even as early as 300 B.C. by a freer form of marriage. Though married, the woman, as far as property rights were concerned, remained primarily in the control of her father, and after the age of twenty-five was nominally subject to the supervision of her guardian or tutor. Legally, a woman could extricate herself from this looser form of marriage without much problem. By the time of the Empire, beginning about 27 B.C. when Augustus was proclaimed Emperor, the *coemptio* form of marriage was non-existent, having been replaced by less-restrictive forms. Further, the role of the guardian had lost its importance. By the time Hadrian came to power in A.D. 117, the guardian was deemed to be totally unnecessary. Both men and women were able to end a marriage on the flimsiest of excuses and life-long marriage became the exception rather than the rule among the aristocracy.

In upper-class society, marriage was an obligation for all women, except the Vestal Virgins (whom we will discuss later) and women over fifty. Amongst the aristocracy, marriages were frequently made and broken for financial or political reasons. Women were allowed to initiate marriages from late Republic days onward, but not to refuse a marriage unless they could prove their proposed husbands were morally unfit. It is doubtful that girls aged twelve to fourteen, the normal age of marriage, could or would refuse a marriage under any circumstances.

We know that by the standards of antiquity matrons were well educated. Even among the poorer families, both daughters and sons went to school, while in richer families both had tutors. A girl's education ceased when she married, while a boy, who usually did not marry before seventeen to eighteen, went on to study with philosophers and rhetoricians outside the home for an additional three to four years. After this, the boys were expected to find a mate. Unlike many other cultures in the Mediterranean, Romans saw the education of women not as an extravagance, but as a way to enhance a woman.

Despite their education Roman women were not allowed to vote or hold public office even in the age of the Empire, though they were often deeply involved and highly influential in affairs of state and matters of law. Examples of this were two famous Fulvias, one of whom was involved in the Catiline conspiracy, while the other helped Mark Antony by being his agent in Italy and commanding one of his armies when Octavian besieged it. Some matrons, such as Maesia, had special gifts for pleading a case and were acquitted on their own court testimony.

Perhaps those matrons who had the greatest influence for good or ill in the political realm were the wives of the Emperors, such as Caesar Augustus' Livia and Claudius' Messalina. Augustus often consulted Livia when he needed good advice. She was known to be an excellent administrator in her own right, managing a personal staff of over one thousand, and property holdings in Asia Minor, Gaul, and Palestine. She was the first priestess in her husband's cult when it began after his death.

In the home, matrons also wielded great influence and power. They were not homemakers in the ordinary sense; indeed, though they bore sole responsibility for the home, they usually assigned tasks to the servants. Meanwhile, they went to market, to recitals and festivals, to the games, or stayed at home and supervised their children's education. Though in the Republic it was usual for a woman to nurse her children, by the time of the Empire it was common for a matron to allow a female servant to nurse or raise the children. Most matrons did spend the majority of their time in the home, however, and even in the Empire they were expected to cultivate the time-honored domestic practices of spinning and

21

weaving. Augustus was fond of wearing wool items made by his wife and daughters as an advertisement for his plan of re-establishing "old-fashioned" ideas. Until the second century B.C., matrons were required to bake bread, but by the time of the Empire it was a poor house indeed where a wife had to perform the household chores which her counterpart in Greece would be expected to do. When we consider how seldom the husband might be home, especially if he was in the army, we can understand why the matron was often the family's *de facto* head and business manager.

Little is known about the status and roles of freed women and slaves in Rome apart from comments made by upper-class writers and politicians. What we know of customs and conditions in Rome does give us some indirect information. Most freed women were shop-keepers, artisans, or domestics, while some were known to be physicians, commercial entrepreneurs, brick makers, and perhaps even owners of brick-making or ship-building operations. Financially, it seems that some freed women were secure, for they could afford respectable burial places. Others remained in the service of their mistresses rather than become one of the free poor. In some respects it was better to be a slave than a free-born poor woman, since slaves were often treated well and even educated in the essentials so that they could read to their matrons and their matrons' children. Cato (*c.* 234 – 149 B.C.) tells us that it was the responsibility of the female housekeeper to keep the hearth clean, to hang a garland on the hearth at the *kalends* (each new Roman month), to keep a supply of cooked food on hand, and not to visit the neighbors too often. Though the evidence is not vast, it is fair to say that freed women and female slaves in Rome were in a better position than their counterparts in Greece, since Rome had the more liberal property laws and since a female slave of a Roman matron could acquire a rudimentary education and even money if she was a good worker.

Spiritual life

Before discussing the average Roman woman's role in religion, let us first consider the Vestal Virgins. Though they dedicated themselves for thirty years to virginity and tending the sacred flame (which represented the health and salvation of Rome), they were not under the power of any man, not bound by oaths other than their sacred one, and not subject to the limitations of the Vocanian Law of 169 B.C. which prevented women from testifying without swearing an oath. Vestals were women of property. At the beginning of their service, at the young age of six to ten years, they were given a dowry twice that of a rich matron because they had "married" the state for thirty years. They were required to attend certain religious festivals and were allowed to go to lavish dinners and to visit matrons if they were not on their eight-hour duty period. The Vestals were considered so trustworthy that statesmen would leave important documents and wills with them to guard. They were also emissaries of peace for the state or the imperial family. After an evil such as a plague or fire hit Rome, the Vestals were called upon to do propitiatory acts. There were only six Vestals at any one time, however, and thus they were not representative of the relationship of the average matron or free woman to Roman society or religion.

There were basically two types of Roman religions – *native cults* supported by the state, such as that of Vesta, and *imported cults* such as that of Isis or the Eleusinian mysteries.[5] The Romans, using their gifts for organization, had different native cults for different stages in a woman's life. Rome used these cults to promote socially desirable behavior. The goddess Fortuna Virginitis was patroness of young girls; Fortuna Primigenia was patroness of mothers and childbirth, as well as giver of virility and material success to men. There was the cult of Fortunata Muliebris for women married only once; and the cult of Venus, Changer of Hearts, dedicated to encourage women to marital fidelity. In contrast, Fortuna Virilis was a prostitutes' cult in which such women met in the men's baths to worship a god of sexual relations.

In his social reforms, the Emperor Augustus promoted the cults advocating chastity, childbirth, and strong familial bonds. Coupling this with Augustus' effort to legally force widows and divorcees to remarry, and the fine he placed on both males and females for remaining single past accepted ages, we can see how much Augustus desired to eliminate public and private situations where women were independent of men. His attempts to recapture the morality of "idealized" ancient Rome by legislation appear to have failed on the whole. However, Augustus could boast of having restored

23

or built eighty-two temples in an attempt to rectify the neglect of traditional religion in Rome.

It is important to realize that Augustus tried to assert the older views about male dominance through this building campaign. Festivals and cults which had formally been the exclusive domain of women were integrated, while male-only public rituals, such as the sacrifice to Mars for the well-being of the herds, were retained. Thus, women usually did not find new roles in the traditional cults.

As early as the second century B.C. these cults were dying, but Augustus' attempts to revive them were too little, too late. Eventually, the influx of imported oriental cults finally gave women new religious roles as they worshipped Isis, Serapis, Cybele, or Attis. Symbolic of how much the matrons welcomed these new cults is the fact that when the cult of the Idaean mother was introduced in 204 B.C. they went out of the city to welcome its arrival. When the Bacchanalia was introduced in 186 B.C. it was open to women only and the matrons became its priestesses. The inclusion of men into the cult led to scandal and to its suppression for a while, though it sprang up again in the later Republic. Gradually, these foreign gods won over most of the female population so that in the first century A.D. the author Petronius bemoaned the fact that Roman matrons no longer worshipped the traditional gods at all. Tacitus recorded legislation attempting to eliminate certain Egyptian and Jewish rites.

It was Isis above all the others which Roman men rightly feared. The reasons why this cult had such a powerful impact on Roman women are several. First, the only state cults allowing women even a limited role as priestesses were that of Vesta (six women) and that of Ceres, a goddess of procreation. Secondly, the cult of Isis, unlike any previous cult, was not for the benefit of the state, but to meet the religious and emotional needs of individuals. Isis promised healing, blessing, sympathy, and understanding for her devotees' sorrow and pain, for she herself had lost a son. Thus, she was a goddess of loving mercy with whom women could identify and to whom men could become intimately attached as a compassionate mother figure. She was all gods summed up into one personality and was said to have certain powers that usually only male deities possessed. Finally, unlike other cults the rituals of Isis were flexible and her temples were at once a haven for prostitutes and a sanctuary for women to spend the night dedicated to chastity. Thus, the cult of Isis had tremendous appeal because it was open to all, it ignored class barriers, and both men and women could hold high office.

Naturally, Isis most benefited lower-class members, for they held equal status with the upper-class members of the cult. From the extant inscriptions we know that at least one-third of Isis' devotees were women but this figure probably underestimates the number of females since, instead of being categorized, women were treated as equals with men. We read of at least six women priestesses in this cult including one of senatorial rank and one freed woman in Italy. We should not think that this cult affected only a small minority just because the temples of Isis were not allowed within Rome's walls until A.D. 38. On the contrary, there was a multitude of temples just outside the city wall long before the reign of Gaius Caligula. Five times during the Republic attempts were made to abolish this cult which honored only the individual and not the state. In 28 B.C., Octavius and later Tiberius made attempts to abolish Isis' cult, all to no avail. It is no coincidence that the rise of the cult of Isis in the later Republic period coincided with the increase in women's liberation in Rome. It is possible that these two trends fostered each other, and it was perhaps in reaction to this that Augustus undertook his ill-fated attempts at moral and religious reform.

Conclusions

Roman women had both more and less freedom than their counterparts in the Mediterranean world depending on which country and which aspect of woman's life one uses as a basis for comparison. It is certainly true that Roman women had more political power than women in Greece or Palestine because, though they could not sit on the throne or hold elected office, they could be the power behind such positions. The fact, however, that women could not hold such offices in Rome makes clear that politically upper-class or imperial Macedonian women had more freedom since they often did sit on the throne in the Hellenistic and Roman periods. Roman women do not compare favorably in political rights with women in Asia Minor who often held public offices.

Further, until the advent of the foreign cults in Rome, women there had fewer opportunities to be priestesses than women in Greece. On the other hand, educated women were more plentiful in Rome than elsewhere in the Mediterranean world. A Roman woman's right to property and freedom in marriage rivaled or surpassed all other Mediterranean women except native Egyptians. It is fair to say that Roman matrons had the opportunity to perform more than the functions of mother and wife, and this cannot be said of Greek citizen-women. Even a Roman freed woman was in a better position than many citizen-women in Athens. It is certainly to the credit of the Romans that they at least raised the question of the place of women in society.

As elsewhere in the Empire, there is no denying that Roman society operated within a definite patriarchal framework. That many Roman women were able to lead full, informed, and satisfying lives perhaps testifies to the fact that patriarchy need not always lead to misogyny. Rome offered more to women than Greece or Palestine, but Roman women had more disadvantages than some of their counterparts in Asia Minor and Macedonia until the advent of various foreign cults and certain Hellenistic and Egyptian ideas into the Eternal City.

PART II

JESUS AND WOMEN

4

TEACHINGS ON FAMILY AND SINGLE LIFE

Our first task will be to examine the attitude of Jesus toward women as reflected in His teaching.[1] This will entail a discussion of His views on parenthood, childhood, and the single state, and on marriage, divorce, and adultery. Through this investigation we can begin to evaluate the way Jesus thought the new demands of the Kingdom would affect women in their roles as mothers, daughters, wives, widows, harlots, and believers.

Parents – Mk 10.19, 7.9 – 13

You know the commandments: "Do not kill, Do not commit adultery, Do not steal, Do not bear false witness, Do not defraud, Honor your father and mother." (Mk 10.19)

And he said to them, "You have a fine way of rejecting the commandment of God, in order to keep your tradition! For Moses said, 'Honor your father and your mother'; and, 'He who speaks evil of father or mother, let him surely die'; but you say, 'If a man tells his father or his mother, What you would have gained from me is Corban' (that is, given to God) – then you no longer permit him to do anything for his father or mother, thus making void the word of God through your tradition which you hand on. And many such things you do." (Mk 7.9 – 13)

There has often been a feeling of uneasiness on the part of many people about Jesus' view of the family. Some have said that for Jesus the claims of the family of faith necessarily supplant any claims of the physical family on Him and His followers. Yet there are clear indications that Jesus not only accepted but also strengthened the physical family's bond in some respects.

The Gospels reveal two separate instances where Jesus reaffirmed

29

the teachings of Exod. 20.12, Lev. 19.3, and Deut. 5.16, thus indicating that honoring one's parents was an important part of His teaching. In Mk 10.19 the command to honor parents is counted as part of the cost of discipleship which is necessary in order to obtain a place in the Kingdom. Thus, Mk 10.19 and parallels indicate there was a place for the physical family and the promotion of filial piety within the teaching of Jesus. It is significant that Mark, followed by Matthew, places this affirmation of Mosaic teaching after two other passages in which the physical family is reaffirmed in different ways (10.2–9, 13–16). In the placement and presentation of this passage, Mark, Matthew and, to a lesser degree, Luke, make their own affirmation of these values.

Our second example is Mk 7.9–13 where we find a saying that has high claims to authenticity because of its conflict with Jewish attitudes of Jesus' day concerning the oral law, and because of the improbability that the Christian community would create a saying involving the matter of *corban*. Vincent Taylor says, "There can be no reasonable doubt that the words were spoken by Jesus and illustrate His attitude to the oral law."[2]

In Jesus' day it was possible to declare in a vow or oath using the technical term *corban* or *conam* that one's parents were forbidden to benefit from one's property because that property was dedicated to other purposes (perhaps to the Temple).[3] What originally had been intended as a means of setting aside property or even oneself for the purposes of God, became a means of preventing others from having a claim on one's person or property. Contemporary inscriptions and parallels from the Mishnah suggest that such a practice was well known in Jesus' day. Such a vow might be taken in a moment of anger, i.e. in the sense of wishing evil on one's parents. This may explain why Jesus makes reference to the commandment against cursing or speaking evil of one's parents.

Some rabbis taught that by means of a legal fiction or because of the honor due to one's parents, such a vow could be circumvented or annulled in some cases if the vower wished to do so. On the other hand, there is evidence from Jesus' time that in some instances a person could not repent of his oath even if it was taken in haste or anger because some rabbis believed that his life would be forfeit and he would stand in danger of the judgment of God against oath-breakers. Apparently, it was against this last opinion that Jesus was arguing. Jesus' point seems to be that any vow that makes void the word of God *must* be annulled. Because of their traditions, the rabbis had allowed the duty to fulfill any vow to take precedence over (and in effect nullify) the duty to honor one's parents.

In Mk 7.9 – 13 and parallels we find Jesus affirming the same Mosaic commandment in the midst of a pronouncement concerning the traditions of men and the commandments of God. Jesus, with more than a little anger and irony, charges His audience with "setting aside the commandments of God in order to keep your own traditions." In this instance, Jesus is attacking the misuse of the practice of making something *corban* to someone. First, Jesus reminds His listeners that Moses said one was to revere *both* father and mother. In addition, Jesus also reasserts the negative enjoinder of Moses: "The one cursing father or mother must be put to death." It is hard to imagine a more strongly worded way of enforcing the obligations of children to parents and, especially in this case, to dependent parents.

Thus, in Mk 7.9 – 13, we have a strong affirmation of the traditional family structure with special emphasis on the obligation of a child to provide for his aging or needy parents. This obligation is not to be overridden by any vows or oaths. Jesus, far from taking a less-stringent view of filial duties than His Jewish contemporaries, actually intensified the demands placed on a Jewish son or daughter by disallowing any interfering vows. In this He makes clear His desire that both mother and father be honored in word and deed.

Children – Mk 9.33 – 7, 10.13 – 16

And they came to Capernaum; and when he was in the house he asked them, "What were you discussing on the way?" (34) But they were silent; for on the way they had discussed with one another who was the greatest. (35) And he sat down and called the twelve; and he said to them, "If any one would be first, he must be last of all and servant of all." (36) And he took a child, and put him in the midst of them and taking him in his arms, he said to them, (37) "Whoever receives one such child in my name receives me; and whoever receives me, receives not me but him who sent me."

(Mk 9.33 – 7)

31

And they were bringing children to him, that he might touch them; and the disciples rebuked them. (14) But when Jesus saw it he was indignant, and said to them, "Let the children come to me, do not hinder them; for to such belongs the kingdom of God. (15) Truly, I say to you, whoever does not receive the kingdom of God like a child shall not enter it." (16) And he took them in his arms and blessed them, laying his hands upon them.

(Mk 10.13–16)

Considering the Gospel writers' selectivity, the very existence in the Synoptics of two separate incidents of a positive nature about children may intimate that the attitudes expressed in these passages were seen by the Gospel writers as characteristic of Jesus and His ministry. They are noteworthy because they stood in contrast to common attitudes of that era.

Even in the first century A.D. exposure of infants, especially girls, was known in Roman and Greek contexts. As A. Oepke points out though, there was a gradually improving attitude toward children in the Graeco-Roman world from the early period of the Republic to the latter days of the Empire.[4] It is true that children were valued more highly in Judaism than in first-century pagan cultures; nonetheless, even among Jews, sons were generally valued more highly than daughters. There is no evidence that children, either male or female, were considered religious models by the rabbis, for in early Judaism it was the wise and learned rabbi, not the child, who was set up as an example to disciples who wished to be great in the Kingdom. Further, no rabbi is known to have so closely identified himself and his teaching about the Kingdom with children as the Evangelists portray Jesus doing.

Mk 9.33–7 is set in the context of the disciples' dispute about who would be greatest in the Kingdom. At verse 36, Jesus puts a child in their midst. Mark and Luke make the child an object lesson with only a concluding summary (Mk 9.37, Lk. 9.48) which involves the rather remarkable assertion that whoever receives one child of this sort in Jesus' name, welcomes Him. The verb translated "receive" here often is used to refer to hospitality, the welcoming of a guest. "In my name" probably means "for my sake." It is not likely that Jesus is suggesting that the child is His representative though that is grammatically possible. Rather, Jesus is saying to the disciples who are His representatives, "receive a child such as this

32

for My sake." His disciples are to serve even children and in so doing they serve Jesus Himself. If Jesus had held certain of the negative opinions about children that existed in the Roman Empire, or if He had a low view of the family and its offspring, then He probably would not have identified Himself so closely with children.

Few scholars doubt the authenticity of Mk 10.13–16 and parallels, though possibly verse 15 was originally an independent saying and Matthew has presented his version at 18.3 rather than in this context. In Mark and Matthew we have a series of incidents intended to give Jesus' teaching on marriage, divorce, children, and possessions (Mk 10.1–12, 13–16, 17–31).

The narrative begins with parents and possibly older children bringing younger children to Jesus so that He might touch them. Perhaps reflecting the typical attitude that children were less mature and thus less important than adults, the Synoptics all say that the disciples rebuked those who were bringing children forward. Jesus reacts to the disciples' action with anger: "Allow the children to come to Me and do not hinder them for to these and those like them belongs the Kingdom of God." Though Alfred Plummer and others insist that the Greek text here refers not "to these children, not all children, but those who are childlike in character,"[5] it seems more likely that it refers to those children who come or are brought to Jesus as well as those adults who are "of this sort."

After this saying there follows in Mark and Luke (see Mt. 18.3) a word of Jesus: "Truly I say to you, unless you receive the Kingdom as a child, you shall not enter it." The point seems to be that the Kingdom of God involves or is made up of children and those like them, not that the Kingdom of God is like a child. In the context of Mk 10, the contrast between the ease with which children enter the Kingdom and the difficulty with which the rich enter is notable. In Mark (10.16), this passage closes with an action of Jesus which indicates an unmistakably clear acceptance and affirmation of children and of the intentions of the parents who brought them. If children are received openly by Jesus and if they have a place in the Kingdom, this may imply that giving birth to children and being a parent are seen as good things.[6]

Far from setting up the family of faith as an alternative to the physical family, Jesus uses the smallest member of the family as a model for members of the family of faith. The evidence of Jesus' positive attitude toward children, their place in the Kingdom, and how they might serve as models for disciples and be served by disciples seems to imply a positive estimation of a woman's role as child-bearer and mother (as well as a positive estimation of the father's role). While it might be objected that this material tells us only about Jesus' attitudes toward the helpless who are already born rather than about the bearing of children *per se* (and thus about women's roles), at the very least it would seem that Jesus would have refrained from such remarks about, and actions for, children if He had not wished to endorse the physical family with its parental and filial roles. These roles seem to have been affirmed by Jesus so long as they did not conflict with God's Kingdom priorities.

Widows – Mk 12.38–40, 12.41–4

And in his teaching he said, "Beware of the scribes, ... (40) who devour widows' houses and for a pretense make long prayers. They will receive the greater condemnation."   (Mk 12.38–40)

And he sat down opposite the treasury, and watched the multitude putting money into the treasury. Many rich people put in large sums. And a poor widow came, and put in two copper coins, which make a penny. And he called his disciples to him, and said to them, "Truly, I say to you, this poor widow has put in more than all those who are contributing to the treasury. For they all contributed out of their abundance; but she out of her poverty has put in everything she had, her whole living."   (Mk 12.41–4)

In regard to Mk 12.40 (see Lk. 20.47), there are no significant critical problems or reasons to doubt that this saying goes back to Jesus' actual conflicts with and denunciations of the scribes. It is possible, however, that this saying is not in its original setting but has been placed here together with a collection of similar sayings.

Scribes were the scholarly lawyers of Jesus' day and their chief function was to give expert advice and interpretation concerning matters of the law. They were not paid for their services but lived on free-will offerings, hospitality, and other subsidies. Except for the few scribes employed by the Temple priests, they were quite poor. Thus, Jesus is probably referring to the Temple scribes whose status allowed them to wear fine robes and attend large and expensive banquets.

In this context we can understand Jesus' warning to His disciples to beware of the scribes who devour the houses of widows. Most likely, this phrase connotes a sort of abuse of a widow's property. ''To devour a house'' is a technical phrase in extra-biblical Greek sources for bilking someone of their funds or property. How were the scribes doing this? The most common suggestion is that the scribes were taking advantage of the kindness and hospitality of well-to-do widows beyond all reasonable bounds. However, a more probable view holds that these scribes, as a trade, were legal managers of well-to-do widows' estates, and were taking more than their fair share of expenses for the task.[7]

This saying presents us with a picture of widows of some means being taken advantage of by unscrupulous scribes who were their legal estate managers. The widows' trusting nature is contrasted to the scribes' deceitful and avaricious practices. Jesus is stepping forward as a strong advocate of oppressed or abused widows.

The second passage of interest is Mk 12.41–4 (Lk. 21.1–4). The possibility that this story *told by* Jesus has become a story *about* Jesus cannot be ruled out. Jesus may well have used His own variation of a familiar parable to make His point about giving. For our purposes it is irrelevant whether this is a story once told by Jesus, or an actual incident in His life.

In the Marcan narrative Jesus is standing in the Temple where He could see the crowds streaming in to pay their private offerings to the Temple treasury. Particularly noticeable by their apparel and perhaps by the length of time they spent putting in their money were ''many rich ones who threw in much.'' Also noticeable by apparel was one poor widow wanting to make an offering to God out of devotion. Her free-will offering was two copper coins of the smallest denomination. In Mark's account, Jesus, by calling His disciples to Himself, is portrayed as wishing to use this woman as a model for His disciples. This narrative focuses *not* on the amount given, but on the attitude of self-sacrificial giving. In a startling statement, Jesus says, ''Truly, I say to you, this poor woman has put in more than all those who are contributing to the treasury.'' She gave ''her whole living,'' that is, her means of subsistence. Even more significantly, the reason why Jesus says she gave more than all others was that she gave out of her deficit, while the others gave out of their abundance. Her devotion and her self-sacrifice were complete. This is a clear model of devotion.

In these two sayings we note certain obvious contrasts. In Mk 12.40 (Lk. 20.47), there is a contrast between rich trusting widows and deceitful male scribes. In Mk 12.41–4 (Lk. 21.1–4), a poor widow is set over against the rich men. In addition, the devotion and self-sacrifice of the poor widow stands out against the dark background of the self-indulgence and false piety of the scribes and the easy and ostentatious giving of the rich. In the former case, Jesus defends a group of women; in the latter, one woman is His model of self-sacrificial giving. Jesus' special concern and admiration for women is perhaps nowhere more juxtaposed with His disgust over certain groups of privileged and supposedly pious men than here. A theme of reversal (the humble being exalted, the exalted being humbled) comes to the fore. Jesus' choice of the widow as a model reflects His view of how the advent of the Kingdom means just recognition of the truly godly, and just judgment of those who oppress the poor and disenfranchised (the widow being a prime example).

Marriage and adultery – Mt. 5.27–30, Jn 8.2–11

The sayings on marriage, adultery, and divorce fall into two categories: isolated sayings (Mt. 5.27–32, Lk. 16.18) and the controversy dialogues (Mt. 19.3–9, Mk 10.2–12). Both groups are essential to our understanding of Jesus' view of the family and women's roles. Along with our discussion of marriage and adultery (Mt. 5.27–30) we will also examine the story of the woman caught in adultery (Jn 8.2–11).

You have heard that it was said, "You shall not commit adultery." (28) But I say to you that every one who looks at a woman lustfully has already committed adultery with her in his heart. (29) If your right eye causes you to sin, pluck it out and throw it away; it is better that you lose one of your members than that your whole body be thrown into hell. (30) And if your right hand causes you to sin, cut it off and throw it away; it is better that you lose one of your members than that your whole body go into hell."

(Mt. 5.27–30)

This saying is located in the Sermon on the Mount and is presented in the familiar antithetical form: "You have heard that it was said ... but I say to you." The saying which precedes the divorce discussion deals with the related matter of sexual sin; therefore, we must see how it sets the stage and relates to the content of what follows.

Mt. 5.27 opens with, "You shall not commit adultery." The Greek word translated "commit adultery" was used most commonly in the specific sense of extra-marital intercourse by a married man or woman with someone betrothed or married who is not his or her legal spouse. However, this word can be used in a wider sense of various sorts of sexual misbehavior – feelings, thoughts or acts that involve sexual sin. It appears that the term is used in its narrower sexual sense of adultery in 5.27, 32, and in a somewhat wider sense in 5.28.

Traditionally, Mt. 5.28 has been translated, "Every one who looks at a woman lustfully has already committed adultery with her in his heart." K. Haacker rightly challenged this translation by suggesting, "has led her astray to adultery," since in early Judaism it was almost always the woman who was associated with the act and term adultery.[8] Possibly we should translate "Anyone who so looks on a woman that she shall become desirous has in his heart already committed adultery with her." If this is correct, then it is not the same idea that we find in rabbinic sources, where men are warned against looking at women (or women looking at them) lest they, *the men*, be led astray. Here we have the antithesis to such an idea, for what is being treated in our passage is not male weakness in the face of a temptress, but male aggression which leads a woman into sin. Thus, the responsibility for such sin is placed on the male, and consideration is given to the woman, often labeled the more suspected party in a male-oriented society. This saying is at one and the same time a reaffirmation of a man's leadership and responsibility for the community welfare, and an attempt to liberate women from a social stereotype.

Consistent with this stress on restraint of male aggression is the radical remedy Jesus proposes for those unable to control themselves: "If your right eye causes you to sin, pluck it out and throw it away; it is better that you lose one of your members than that your whole body be thrown into hell. And if your right hand causes you to sin, cut it off …'' (Mt. 5.29 – 30). While it is often assumed that this is Jesus' hyperbolic way of saying that we must sever ourselves from whatever causes us to sin, in this context it is possible that sexual sins are being alluded to in verses 29 – 30. This becomes more likely when we realize that loss of an eye was a well-known punishment for sexual misbehavior (such as voyeurism), and loss of a hand was a punishment for stealing another's property, even his wife. Derrett says, ''Thus, the whole passage … is speaking in terms of punishments actually known in Palestinian practice in order to throw light on the great difficulty of remaining effectively loyal to … the Kingdom of heaven.''[9] Jesus' words would have sounded more like a threat than a dramatic hyperbole to the male listeners He addressed.

Early in the morning he came again to the temple; all the people came to him, and he sat down and taught them. (3) The scribes and the Pharisees brought a woman who had been caught in adultery, and placing her in the midst (4) they said to him, ''Teacher, this woman has been caught in the act of adultery. (5) Now in the law Moses commanded us to stone such. What do you say about her?'' (6) This they said to test him, that they might have some charge to bring against him. Jesus bent down and wrote with his finger on the ground. (7) And as they continued to ask him, he stood up and said to them, ''Let him who is without sin among you be the first to throw a stone at her.'' (8) And once more he bent down and wrote with his finger on the ground. (9) But when they heard it, they went away, one by one, beginning with the eldest, and Jesus was left alone with the woman standing before him. (10) Jesus looked up and said to her, ''Woman, where are they? Has no one condemned you?'' (11) She said, ''No one, Lord.'' And Jesus said, ''Neither do I condemn you; go, and do not sin again.''
(Jn 8.2 – 11)

The teaching in Mt. 5.27 – 30 is similar to this story of the woman caught in adultery. Here, too, men's motives are questioned, and their failure to live up to their responsibilities is pointed out.

The story of the woman caught in adultery, while probably not part of the earliest and best text of the New Testament, is still included in most modern translations, albeit often in the margins. As H. J. Cadbury once pointed out, ''Its internal character, agreeing as it does with the Synoptic stories, bespeaks its genuineness as a tradition.''[10] It is plausible that because the story recorded ideas found elsewhere in the Gospel tradition and because it may have called into question the early Church's strict disciplinary measures when sexual sin was committed, it was not originally included in any Gospel. That the story represents the character and methods of Jesus as they are revealed elsewhere, favors the view that the portrayal here is an accurate description of Jesus' "typical" attitude in such cases even if it is not a description of one particular historical incident.

The setting for this encounter is the women's court in the Temple where Jesus is teaching the people. Suddenly, into this court come the scribes and Pharisees with a married woman caught *in the very act* of adultery. Thus, the Evangelist depicts a highly suspicious situation: Where is her partner in crime? Did the husband hire spies to trap his wife? Why had the husband not utilized the usual practice of the "ordeal of the bitter waters" if he had reason to suspect his wife of unfaithfulness? Finally, why, since it was a necessary prerequisite, had the witnesses not warned the woman if she was seen in the very act?

The scribes and Pharisees confront Jesus by saying that Moses prescribed stoning for such a woman, and by asking, "What then do you say?" Thus, Jesus is invited to set Himself against Moses, and perhaps openly against the Roman law since the Romans would not try an adulterous woman. But Jesus appears to avoid the issue, for He stoops down and draws with His finger on the earth. There are many possible interpretations of this act, but since the Gospel writer does not think it important enough to tell us what Jesus wrote, it is likely that the *gesture*, not the words, are important. The gesture implies that Jesus does not wish to be associated with the wickedness of this business and/or that He is as ashamed of *their* actions as of the woman's sin.

If it is true that only Mosaic law opposed adultery, and only the Roman law could pass the death sentence, then it seems that Jesus is caught in a trap. If He fails to pronounce judgment, the He will appear to reject Moses; if He pronounces judgment, then He will appear to usurp the Roman right to final judgment and execution. Jesus, however, does not refrain from judgment; rather, by implication He pronounces this woman guilty by saying, "If anyone of you is without sin, let him be the first to cast a stone at her." Jesus has good cause to suspect the motives of these men but He does not render invalid their judgment on the gravity of this woman's sin. He applies the principle, ''He who reproves others, must himself be above reproach in the case at issue.'' It is the motives of the witnesses and their own culpability, not the woman's lack of sin, which decides the matter here. The witnesses who must cast the first stone (Deut. 17.7), though technically qualified, are not morally qualified. Neither are the scribes or Pharisees qualified, for they are guilty of trying to use God's law to trap the one man in this crowd who *is* morally qualified to pass judgment.

Jesus effectively springs the trap that hovers over Himself and the woman by passing judgment in such a way that its execution is impossible. The Jewish leaders, who were supposed to be moral examples to the people, knew what Jesus was implying about them, and thus one by one they silently slipped away. The hunters have lost not only their game, but also their bait.

When the woman tells Jesus that no one has condemned her, Jesus says emphatically, ''Neither do I condemn you.'' Perhaps He rejects implicitly the whole procedure that the scribes and Pharisees were following as inherently discriminatory against women in such a sin-tainted setting. Jesus does not approve of a system wherein a man's lust is not taken as seriously as a woman's seduction. Jesus, by saying, ''do not sin again,'' does not pronounce this woman's sin forgiven since she has not repented; rather, He shows her the balance of mercy and justice calculated to lead one away from a sinful life to repentance and salvation. As in Mt. 5, we see a critique of men who fail to live up to their responsibility of being examples of virtue for the community, and we see a rejection of certain stereotypes in which women are treated as scapegoats responsible for social ills. This comports with the emphasis we find in some of the Synoptic material (notably Mt. 5.31–2, 19.3–9 [Mk 10.2–12], and Lk. 16.18).

Divorce – Mt. 5.31–2, 19.3–9 (Mk 10.2–12), Lk. 16.18

Although there is some overlap with the adultery material, we will at this point examine one isolated saying from the Sermon on the Mount and the controversy dialogue with the Pharisees in Matthew and its Marcan parallel. Finally, we will examine the short saying recorded in Lk. 16.18.

"It was also said, 'Whoever divorces his wife, let him give her a certificate of divorce.' (32) But I say to you that every one who divorces his wife, except on the ground of unchastity, makes her an adulteress; and whoever marries a divorced woman commits adultery."   (Mt. 5.31–2)

And Pharisees came up to him and tested him by asking, "Is it lawful to divorce one's wife for any cause?" (4) He answered, "Have you not read that he who made them from the beginning made them male and female, (5) and said, 'For this reason a man shall leave his father and mother and be joined to his wife, and the two shall become one flesh'? (6) So they are no longer two but one flesh. What therefore God has joined together, let not man put asunder." (7) They said to him, "Why then did Moses command one to give a certificate of divorce, and to put her away?" (8) He said to them, "For your hardness of heart Moses allowed you to divorce your wives, but from the beginning it was not so. (9) And I say to you: whoever divorces his wife, except for unchastity, and marries another, commits adultery."   (Mt. 19.3–9)

"Every one who divorces his wife and marries another commits adultery, and he who marries a woman divorced from her husband commits adultery."   (Lk. 16.18)

In Mt. 5.31–2, the broadening of the meaning of adultery in 5.28 and the antithetical form used in 5.27, 29, 30 naturally lead one to expect an intensification of Old Testament and Jewish teaching. Verse 32 continues the unique stress on man's responsibility by saying that it is the male who causes the woman to commit adultery if he divorces her and she remarries.[11] Further, the second husband commits adultery if he marries the divorced woman. In Mt. 19 we run into difficulties if we take 19.9 to involve a genuine exception because then 19.10, in terms of the logic the Evangelist is trying to convey in placing 19.1–9 and 10–12 together, makes no sense. Thus, simply talking in terms of Matthean logic, we meet problems if we too quickly assume that the exceptive clauses are serious qualifications of an absolute prohibition of divorce.[12]

In terms of historical probabilities, there is much to be said for the suggestion that the First Evangelist at Mt. 19 has more primitive material than the Second at Mk. 10. For one thing it is much more probable that the Pharisees would ask Jesus about the grounds of divorce than about the rectitude of divorce *per se*. Again, it is *a priori* more probable that the discussion would have proceeded as we find it in Mt. 19.3 – 9 than in Mk 10.2 – 12 since it seems likely that Jesus would have spoken of a Mosaic *permission* to divorce (Mt. 19.8) rather than a Mosaic *command* (Mk 10.3). The Matthean form of the debate makes perfect sense for it is the Pharisees who speak of Moses' command while Jesus counters that it was only a permission and quite logically He is able to appeal to a higher and prior principle found in God's creation plan (verses 4 – 6, 8b).

To sum up, in regard to the controversy dialogues, the Matthean form appears to be more primitive and authentic with the possible exception of the exceptive clauses. The Marcan discussion and particularly 10.12 appears to be a modification of Jesus' original teaching for a Hellenistic audience. The antithesis formula found in Mt. 5.31 – 2a may be original or at least modeled on the authentic contrast in Mt. 19.7 – 9. The saying found in Mt. 5.32b and Lk. 16.18b appears to be an isolated phrase and is probably quite primitive. Luke 16.18a is probably a saying found in the Q material and possibly more original than the form found in Mk 10.11.[13] We will now discuss the controversy dialogues and the isolated saying.

In Mt. 19.3 – 9 and Mk 10.2 – 12, Jesus is confronted by a group of rabbis who wish to ask Him a question about divorce in the hopes of trapping Him in His own words. The Matthean debate is centered on the grounds for divorce (the lawfulness being taken for granted), while the Marcan debate is centered on the lawfulness of divorce.

In Matthew the discussion begins with the Pharisees' question, "Is it lawful for a man to divorce his wife for any (and every) cause?" The Pharisees are asking about divorce, not separation, for the latter did not exist as a legal reality in first-century Judaism. Matthew and Mark differ as to how Jesus began to reply. The Matthean form (in which the Pharisees ask Him, "Why then did Moses command to give a bill of divorce and to divorce?") is probably the more original response to Jesus' first remarks on divorce. Jesus answers their question with, "Moses permitted you to divorce your wife because of your hard heartedness" (Mt. 19.7 – 8). The Mosaic permission referred to, Deut. 24.1 – 4, required a bill of divorce be given to make clear that the woman was no longer married, in order to protect her from further charges or abuse. Jesus intimates that Moses' provision was meant to limit a practice widespread at that time, but it was not meant to license divorce for any cause as some rabbis had deduced.

In the Matthean account, Jesus quotes two different texts in response to the Pharisees' initial question. The phrase "from the beginning" (19.4) prefaces the first text: "He made them male and female" (Gen. 1.27, 5.2). Then the text, citing Gen. 2.24, reads, "Because of this (fact) 'a man shall leave his mother and be joined to his wife, and the two shall become one flesh'." The implication is that the one-flesh union becomes more constitutive of a man and a woman's being than their uniqueness. Only two can become one, and when they do they are no longer two. From these texts Jesus deduces that a man and a woman are no longer two but one flesh. What then God has joined, human beings must not put asunder. Jesus argues that because of the nature of humanity's creation in two distinct but complementary genders (a divine act) and the nature of marriage created by God between male and female (a divine act), no third human party is allowed into this relationship. Anyone who seeks to divide those who share such a marriage and a one-flesh union attacks not only the marriage and the two people united in marriage, but also the unifier, God. Jesus has appealed to the intended creation order and the Creator, both of which undergird, not undermine, Mosaic law and its true intention even if it may seem to contradict a certain concession to sinfulness. Mosaic law was meant to be used as a tool to limit, not license, an existing evil.

In the Matthean account of this discussion, Jesus goes on to say that even though Moses permitted divorce, this was not God's original plan. Thus, despite what Moses had allowed, "I say to you, whoever divorces his wife except for *porneia* and marries another, commits adultery." As in Mt. 5.31–2, the words of Jesus have built up to a point where one naturally expects Jesus to contrast His teaching with that of other rabbis or even Moses. Certainly the "but I say to you" points in this direction. It thus appears unlikely that even the First Evangelist intended the exceptive clauses to be seen as real qualifications of Jesus' absolute prohibition of divorce in cases of legitimate marriages. If an incestuous relationship is in view, then the Evangelist may have introduced an exception that merely interprets Jesus' absolute prohibition for an exceptional situation or problem. I am thus suggesting that Jesus is referring to an incestuous relationship such as the infamous one of Jesus' day – the marriage of Herod Antipas to his relative and brother's wife Herodias.[14]

There is a unique feature about Mk 10.11–12 that deserves attention. Here we read, "And he said to them, 'Whoever divorces his wife and marries another, commits adultery against her; and if she divorces her husband and marries another, she commits adultery'."

Normally "commits adultery against (or with) her" is taken to mean commits adultery against the first wife. While this is grammatically possible, the Jews never spoke (although Mark could have done so) in terms of a man committing adultery against his own wife. Some have suggested that "with her" means with the second woman. This makes sense of the text because adultery by definition is committed by a married person with a third party. Further, this translation still means that the husband is labeled an adulterer, contrary to the common use of the word. It also implies there has been a crime against one's wife, but reveals that the crime itself was *with* a third party.

Mk 10.12 is said to be Mark's adaptation of Jesus' teaching on divorce to a Graeco-Roman setting. Despite its textual difficulties, there is no doubt that it is referring to the act of a woman. The woman either "separates from" or "divorces" her husband (probably the latter). Most scholars argue that this is a Marcan formulation and not a word of Jesus since it is assumed that Jewish women could not divorce men in first-century Palestine. Even though this is true in most cases, it is conceivable that Jesus could make such a remark either as a Semitic parallelism, meant to complete and balance the saying in Mk 10.11, or as a pronouncement to place women on equal terms with men even in hypothetical legal matters. The statement, however, need not have been hypothetical.

There is some evidence that even Jewish women in first-century Palestine could not only write out their own divorce bill, but also pronounce the divorce formula. Some Jewish women of high rank were able to divorce their husbands. Without doubt, most scholars will continue to see Mk 10.12 as Mark's own formulation meant to convey Jesus' basic teaching to a Hellenistic audience – and they may well be right. However, considering the remarks Jesus appears to have made elsewhere about Herodias (Lk. 13.31 – 2), and His commendation of John the Baptist, the possibility that Jesus Himself made an allusion to Herod's wicked wife by way of a general statement on women divorcing men is far from inconceivable and should be given more serious consideration than it has received in the past.

Finally, Lk. 16.18 is an absolute prohibition against divorce and remarriage. The onus for divorce and its consequences is placed on the man in both Mt. 5 and Lk. 16. While the First Evangelist speaks of the first man making his divorced wife an adulteress, and the second man who marries a divorced woman becoming an adulterer, Luke speaks of both the first husband as an adulterer (if he remarries), and the second man as the same if he marries the divorced woman. What is new in this teaching, besides making the man primarily responsible for sexual sin or divorce and its consequences, is the idea of a man committing adultery against his former wife by remarriage, or making his wife an adulteress by divorce. In all probability this new thrust, because of its originality, goes back to Jesus, who believed that the first one flesh union, as the basis of marriage, was indissoluble. Jesus opposed with vehemence both male aggression that led a woman astray (5.27 – 30), and the adultery that resulted from it.

The net effect of Jesus' views is that various stereotypes of women as temptresses are countered, and at the same time a woman is given greater security in marriage by making the man responsible for its continued maintenance and by prohibiting the man from using his power to cause its dissolution. Jesus thus reaffirms and also reforms the traditional family structure which resulted in giving women a more stable foundation in their traditional roles.

"Eunuchs," the single life – Mt. 19.10 – 12

The disciples said to him, "If such is the case of a man with his wife, it is not profitable to marry." (11) But he said to them, "Not all men can receive this saying, but only those to whom it is given. (12) For there are eunuchs who have been so from birth, and there are eunuchs who have been made eunuchs by men, and there are eunuchs who have made themselves eunuchs for the sake of the kingdom of heaven. He who is able to receive this, let him receive it."

The radical nature of this teaching probably supports the view that verse 12 is to be traced back to Jesus Himself. Furthermore, the first two categories of eunuchs mentioned reflect the common Jewish division between natural and man-made eunuchs. Thus, we probably have both a genuine teaching of Jesus on eunuchs and the actual reaction of His disciples to His divorce teaching – a reaction which reveals that they had typically male Jewish attitudes about these matters.

The First Evangelist records that the disciples' reaction to Jesus' marriage teaching is both amazement and dismay – an expected reaction from a group of Jewish men used to having the freedom of both polygamy and divorce. The verb "is profitable" perhaps indicates the common Jewish view of marriage as essentially a property transaction between the groom (including his father) and the bride's father in which both hoped to profit financially and through the birth of children. On the other hand, it may mean that the disciples were saying it is better not to marry in such a case because of the difficulties of remaining faithful to or keeping the loyalty of one's spouse.

The response, "Not all can accept (understand) this word but only those to whom it is given" follows. It seems that the Evangelist intends "this word" to refer to Jesus' previous teaching which implies that it is given only to some to follow His strict rules on marriage and divorce. But what of those to whom this word is *not* given? What other option is there to lifelong marital fidelity?

Jesus answers, "Some are born eunuchs from their mother's womb, and some are made eunuchs by other men, and some make themselves eunuchs for the sake of the kingdom." The eunuch was well known in various oriental cultures and often served in royal houses as a guardian of a king's concubines. Jesus' disciples would be familiar with such men through contacts with people from Syria, Asia Minor, or Northern Africa. But it is more likely they would have met or heard of the celibates of the Qumran community. The attitudes toward sexuality and celibacy reflected in such communities were not compatible with mainstream Jewish thinking since most rabbis found castrated men abhorrent and viewed non-castrated celibates as violators of God's commandment to procreate. Jesus' teaching on eunuchs was probably as shocking to the disciples as His instructions on marriage and divorce.

There are some difficulties in regard to the meaning of eunuch. An unmarried single man is never called a eunuch in classical literature; this appears first in Christian literature. The selection of the word eunuch is remarkable because for Jewish and Greek listeners it had a very negative connotation. Normally, a eunuch is one incapable or unfit for marriage through castration, deformity, etc. Clearly this is the subject in 19.12a, 12b. The Evangelist's audience would probably have understood the term literally in verse 12c as well. It is not likely, however, that Jesus or the Evangelist was advocating literal self-mutilation.

The structure of this saying on eunuchs from a Jewish perspective proceeds from least objectionable (eunuchs by nature) to more objectionable (man-made eunuchs whether by crime or as punishment for a crime), to most objectionable (self-made eunuchs). The saying builds to a climax, and the third group of eunuchs is marked out in a special way from the other two groups by the phrase, ''The one who is able to accept this.'' Jesus here implies that His words are addressed to those who have an option, unlike the first two types of eunuchs. J. Blinzler suggests we should translate Mt. 19.12: ''There are those who are born unfit for marriage from their mother's womb, there are those who are made unfit for marriage by men, and there are those who have made themselves unfit for marriage for the sake of the kingdom of heaven.''[15]

The key to understanding 19.12 is the phrase ''for the sake of the kingdom.'' According to J. Blenkinsopp, ''The motivation for accepting the celibate life ... was eschatological.''[16] Jesus' views of this subject and those of the Qumran community are similar in this respect. But the reason for renouncing marriage or family in Jesus' teaching has nothing to do with ritual purity or the idea that sexual relations made one impure (as the Qumranites taught). The word translated ''make oneself a eunuch'' is never used, here or elsewhere in the New Testament, to refer to a disciple's past, once-for-all decision to give up everything to follow Jesus. In our text it refers specifically either to the giving up of the right to marry for the sake of the Kingdom, or less probably to the giving up of one's family for the sake of the Kingdom. In short, it is the decision to follow Jesus that precipitates the renunciation of marriage and family, but the two decisions are not synonymous.

Jesus thus provides two alternatives for His disciples: some are given the gift to be joined by God as husband and wife and to live in exclusive monogamy to the glory of God; others are able to make themselves "eunuchs" (celibate) for the sake of the Kingdom because God has enabled them to do so. In neither option is obeying God's word or following Jesus absent. Jesus thus rejected the Jewish teaching that marriage and propagation were a divine imperative enjoined on all normal men (and all women, according to some rabbis). Possibly, it was Jesus' teaching on eunuchs for the Kingdom that allowed women to be present among the traveling company of disciples (Lk. 8.1–3), and to remain single and serve the community of faith. In any event, it is clear that Jesus' reasons for giving such teaching were because of His view of the radical claims of the Kingdom, not ascetical tendencies in His thoughts. That Jesus offers two equally valid callings, either to life-long marriage or to celibacy for the Kingdom, is in itself evidence that Jesus did not have negative views about human sexuality or sexual relations in marriage. Nor did He accept the connection of holiness and abstention from sexual relations. There is no hint here that being a "eunuch for the Kingdom" was a higher or more holy calling than life-long marriage.

Conclusions

We can find no negative teaching by Jesus on family life. On the contrary, He seems to uphold the importance of each family member and strengthens their position within the family structure. Parents are to be honored in word and deed; their children have an obligation to give respect and material support to their parents. Children are not to be hindered from coming close to Him. Jesus' positive attitudes toward children can only reflect a positive estimation of women in their role of child-bearer. Widows especially are to be treated with respect and one in particular is upheld as an example for His disciples to follow. All of this endorses the importance of the physical family. The effect of this teaching is to strengthen the traditional family structure.

Jesus' teaching on marriage and the single life strikes an intriguing balance between old and new. His views remain within a patriarchal framework, but male headship for Jesus entails extra responsibility, not extra liberty (Mt. 5.27 – 32), a view which could only strengthen a woman's stature and security within the family. In contrast to common Jewish teaching, Jesus does not warn men against the wiles of loose women, but against their own lust and aggression that leads women into sin. Both the responsibility and the onus for such sin is placed on the male, and consideration is given to the woman whose motives were often suspect. What is intriguing about this teaching is that it is not only a reaffirmation of men's leadership and responsibility for the community welfare, but also an attempt to liberate women from a social stereotype. Jesus does not approve of a system where a man's lust is not taken as seriously as a woman's seductive wiles. As in Mt. 5, we find in Jn 8.2 – 11 a critique of men who fail to live up to their responsibility of being paradigms of virtue for the community. The overall effect of Jesus' teaching on marriage and divorce is that the traditional family structure is not only reaffirmed but also strengthened through the intensification of the demands made on a husband's fidelity and the rejection of divorce outright. This teaching also gives women greater security in marriage. By appealing to the creation plan and the one-flesh union, Jesus equally rejects male and female promiscuity and freedom to divorce, thus requiring a standard of fidelity and life-long partnership that goes beyond much of the teaching on this subject. No other Jewish teacher spoke of a man committing adultery against his former wife by remarriage.

In light of the broad-based feeling in the Mediterranean in the first century and earlier about the duty of procreation, one must adequately explain why, in Jesus' community, singleness was seen as a viable option. It is not clear whether Jesus ever rejected the Jewish mandate that all, or at least all men, who are able must be fruitful and multiply, but clearly His teaching on ''eunuchs for the Kingdom'' and some of His more radical statements on the cost of discipleship reflect a new attitude toward the single person.

We have conjectured that it was Jesus' teaching on eunuchs that allowed some women to be present among Jesus' traveling company. It is also possible that the teaching in Mt. 19.10 – 12 provided the precedent for women in the Christian community to remain single and serve the community (Ac. 21.9). For both men and women, however, this teaching certainly allowed some believers to live and work in roles apart from those involved in the traditional family structure.

Lest the impression be given that Jesus wished to strengthen the traditional family structure as an end in itself, it must be affirmed that all His teaching on such subjects is conditioned by the demands of discipleship. The physical family must be seen in light of the context of the higher priorities of the family of faith. As we shall see, the basis of the new Kingdom community is not kinship ties, but association between disciples and Master, disciple and disciples (Mk 3.33 – 5). While some rabbis recognized that for men discipleship had higher claims than one's family, it is doubtful whether anyone before Jesus taught this principle to women (Lk. 10.38 – 42). That Jesus gave positive teaching on the physical family implies that He thought there was no necessary conflict between the demands of the family of faith and of the physical family so long as the latter was oriented to serve rather than to sever the former. All of this is most significant in its effects on women and their roles since it is clear that they are called to be disciples first and foremost, and their roles as wives or mothers then necessarily become subordinate, or at least oriented so as not to interfere with the demands of discipleship.

It is not clear whether Jesus thought that marital relations would cease in the age to come (Mk 12.18 – 27, Mt. 22.23 – 33, Lk. 20.27 – 40). Probably, He saw marrying and propagating as ceasing when the Kingdom was consummated, but this does not necessarily entail the dissolution of the marital bond in all respects. In any event, it is clear that Jesus rejected those views of the rabbis in which the age to come is envisioned as simply this age on a grander scale.

Jesus' sayings involving widows give us a picture of His concern for a particularly disadvantaged group. Jesus shows equal concern for the plight of widows with property as for those who were impoverished. His concern for widows is one important facet of His concern for the poor and disenfranchised (Mk 12.40, 41 – 4).

Jesus has a vision in which the creation order and the new demands

of the Kingdom are appealed to in order to reform common prejudices and misunderstandings in regard to God's will on marriage
and the single state. It is a vision that Paul seems to have imbibed
and implemented further some twenty years after the ministry
of Jesus.

5

WOMEN IN THE PARABLES AND JUDGMENT SAYINGS

Parables

Perhaps no form of Jesus' teaching has received closer scrutiny or more diverse treatment than His parables. The lack of uniformity, either in the means or in the results of parable interpretation, has not deterred scholars from trying to make sense of these likable vignettes which make up about one-third of Jesus' reported teaching. If, as A. M. Hunter suggests, the parables were "Jesus' justification of his mission to the last, the least, and the lost,"[1] then it is not at all surprising that women figure prominently in some of them.

The obstinate widow and the obdurate judge – Lk. 18.1–8

And he told them a parable, to the effect that they ought always to pray and not lose heart. He said, "In a certain city there was a judge who neither feared God nor regarded man; and there was a widow in that city who kept coming to him and saying, 'Vindicate me against my adversary.' For a while he refused; but afterward he said to himself, 'Though I neither fear God nor regard man, yet because this widow bothers me, I will vindicate her, or she will wear me out by her continual coming.'" And the Lord said, "Hear what the unrighteous judge says. And will not God vindicate his elect, who cry to him day and night? Will he delay long over them? I tell you, he will vindicate them speedily. Nevertheless, when the Son of man comes, will he find faith on earth?"

This parable, unique to the Third Gospel, gives us occasion to further explore Jesus' attitude toward widows. It is one of many parables in chapters 15–19, a section T. W. Manson has labeled The Gospel of the Outcast.[2]

The parable of the obstinate widow and the obdurate judge is the first of two passages in Lk. 18 which, according to the Evangelist,

52

deal with prayer. Luke's interest in male – female parallelism comes to the fore here in that 18.1 – 8 has an oppressed woman, and 9 – 14 a despised man (tax gatherer) as prayer models. This procedure betrays much about Luke's purpose in writing his Gospel, since we find this male – female parallelism throughout his work, not just in the paired parables. "Other than as a teaching device for repetition, there is no apparent reason for stating the same message twice except to choose examples that would make the message understandable to different groups – the female and male listeners."[3] What emerges is Luke's desire to show that women are equally objects of God's salvation and equally good illustrations of God's dealings with humanity.

Lk. 18.1 – 8 is important for our study first because Jesus' choice of a *woman* in need of help as an *example* for His disciples perhaps indicates Jesus' sympathy and concern for this particular group of people in a male-oriented society, and also because the aspect of this woman's behavior that Jesus focuses on (her perseverance or persistence) is a characteristic that in a patriarchal society was often seen as a negative attribute in a woman (see Prov. 19.13b). The parable should be seen as a struggle between the widow and the judge, for the widow's legal opponent plays no part in the story.

If Derrett is correct in holding that we are dealing with a case in an administrative, not religious, court, then probably the widow's opponent has preceded her to civil court in order to bribe the judge.[4] The judge, not being a righteous man, not caring about God's or man's opinion of him, was ruled only by self-interest and self-preservation. It is unlikely that the widow had anything to offer the judge, and so her case looked hopeless. Her only asset was her persistence; thus, she kept coming to him. She did not ask for vengeance, but vindication of her claims to her own belongings, or perhaps protection from her oppressor. The wicked judge resisted her continual pleading for some time, but he feared the woman's persistence might wear him out. To get rid of her, he gives her what she desires.

The case of the widow is like the case of the disciples. Thus, Jesus says, "Listen to what the unrighteous judge says." In contrast to the normal Jewish practice of praying at certain times of the day, the disciples are to cry out to God continually night and day. They are left alone in a world that oppresses and opposes them, but the attitude of God is not like that of the wicked judge. Jesus argues, if this wicked judge will vindicate this woman, how much more will the good God vindicate His own elect. Jesus indicates that the disciples' only hope of attaining certain vindication is by being persistent at all times, pleading for God's coming and the faith to be ready. For this task, which they have during the interim, they are given only the model of a destitute, resolute woman.[5]

The search for the lost coin – Lk. 15.8–10

Or what woman, having ten silver coins, if she loses one coin, does not light a lamp and sweep the house and seek diligently until she finds it? And when she has found it, she calls together her friends and neighbors, saying, "Rejoice with me, for I have found the coin which I had lost." Just so, I tell you, there is joy before the angels of God over one sinner who repents.

Though brief, Lk. 15.8–10 is an interesting example of a parable which involves a woman, since Jesus is drawing an analogy between the activity of a female and that of Himself or God. This parable intends to show *God's* love for and seeking of the lost (the coin), and His joy over their salvation. Thus, we should *not* see it as an analogy between a woman searching for a lost coin, and a person seeking the Kingdom (see Mt. 13.34–5).

Although it is true that we have *three* parables in Lk. 15, all of which have a similar point about God's redemptive activity and His joy over the repentance of the lost, probably the opening phrase "And he said" in 15.11 separates the story of the prodigal son from the two preceding parables. This is why Joachim Jeremias can call the parables of the lost sheep and the lost coin twin parables – they "play on the contrast between man and woman, and perhaps between rich and poor."[6] Indeed, they play on the contrast between the roles men and women assumed in Jesus' time. But this contrast is meant neither to disparage either role, nor to elevate one above the other as more important; rather, it illustrates in a pointed fashion that the activity of the man and the woman are equally admirable and important, and serve equally well as analogies to the activity of God in Jesus' ministry.

At the beginning we are told of a woman who had ten drachmas but lost one. Scholars suggest that the ten coins were the woman's dowry and may have been worn by her on her headdress. If so, she was poor and her diligent search for the coin is understandable. Luke may wish to contrast this poor woman with the preceding shepherd who, with his one hundred sheep, would have been financially comfortable. This woman would lose the equivalent of a day's wages if she did not find the coin; thus, she commences a thorough search of her dark, windowless, oriental home. She seeks carefully, leaving no corner uninspected until she finds the coin. The woman's reaction to her discovery was joy so great that she called her women friends and neighbors because she wished to share her joy, perhaps in a celebration.

To this point, Jesus has presented only His human analogy to the theological point He wishes to make. He concludes by making the point of comparison plain – ''there is rejoicing in the presence of the angels of God over one sinner who repents.'' Is Jesus intending to compare this woman's activities with those of God the Father or His own? While the last verse indicates that the rejoicing takes place in heaven, A.M. Hunter remarks, ''the three great parables of Luke 15 ... are all ripostes to scribes and Pharisees who had criticized Jesus for consorting with publicans and sinners.''[7] Thus, it is better not to distinguish the work of the Father and the Son here. God's redeeming plan, especially to ''the lost,'' was ultimately shown in the person and ministry of Jesus – the fruit of His labor causes joy in heaven.

Summing up what this parable has to say about women, we note that Jesus' choice of this housewife, possibly a widow, as a positive example shows that women (15.8–10) as well as men (15.1–7) and their work were considered by Jesus to be equally good points of analogy to describe the activity of the heavenly Father in finding the lost. She could have been cited for her carelessness. That Jesus chose to use each as an example in a positive manner indicates His desire to present even a fallible man (who loses his sheep) and a fallible woman (who loses her money) as equally good examples of God's activity. It also reflects a concern on Jesus' part to convey the Good News in terms with which women could identify.

The leaven and the dough — Mt. 13.33 (Lk. 13.20 – 1)

He told them another parable. "The kingdom of heaven is like leaven which a woman took and hid in three measures of flour, till it was all leavened."

The parable of the leaven follows that of the mustard seed in both Matthew and Luke, but not in Mark. These two parables draw analogies between the traditional roles of men and women, and the nature of the Kingdom. The former focuses on the outdoor labor of a man planting a seed; the latter depicts the indoor work of a woman putting leaven in dough. The presence of this male – female parallelism may favor the view that these two parables were originally told as twins. If such twins do convey the same message, then the reason for telling them would be related to the fact that a man is the focus in one, a woman in the other. This may imply that Jesus deliberately chose His illustrations to emphasize that the Good News was for men and women equally, and that their present roles and functions were equally good and positive points of analogy to His work.[8]

Beyond this only a few other remarks need to be made. First, it is a woman who puts the leaven in the dough, which is not unexpected considering that it was "woman's work" to make the bread. Since Jesus is drawing a positive analogy between a woman's work and His own crucial work of preaching (leavening the whole world with the leaven of the Gospel), this would seem to indicate that Jesus presupposed the worth of such "woman's work." Secondly, the leaven which this woman took is hidden in no less than 0.5 bushels of flour – which could probably feed one hundred people! This may be a case of comic exaggeration since normally no housewife would bake so much bread. Possibly, she is baking for a festive occasion of significant proportions. If Jesus is implying by the huge amount of dough that she is baking for a special offering or occasion, then reversal of expectations may be intended by mentioning the leaven and the woman, for it is the priest who bakes the unleavened cakes for special offerings. Thus, perhaps not only the dynamic action of the leaven, but also the amount of meal and who prepares it may tell us something of the nature, the participants and the results of God's future Kingdom. With this parable Jesus reassures His followers that however small and insignificant the Kingdom may appear now, God/Jesus/Kingdom, like the woman/leaven, will not cease working until the whole lump is permeated.

The wise and foolish virgins – Mt. 25.1–13

Then the kingdom of heaven shall be compared to ten maidens who took their lamps and went to meet the bridegroom. Five of them were foolish, and five were wise. For when the foolish took their lamps, they took no oil with them; but the wise took flasks of oil with their lamps. As the bridegroom was delayed, they all slumbered and slept. But at midnight there was a cry, "Behold, the bridegroom! Come out to meet him." Then all those maidens rose and trimmed their lamps. And the foolish said to the wise, "Give us some of your oil, for our lamps are going out." But the wise replied, "Perhaps there will not be enough for us and for you; go rather to the dealers and buy for yourselves." And while they went to buy, the bridegroom came, and those who were ready went in with him to the marriage feast; and the door was shut. Afterward the other maidens came also, saying, "Lord, Lord, open to us." But he replied, "Truly, I say to you, I do not know you." Watch therefore, for you know neither the day nor the hour.

If in Mt. 13.33 (Lk. 13.20–1) it is possible that a reference to a Kingdom celebration is *implicit*, then this celebration is *explicit* in Mt. 25.1–13. From the point of view of a study of women and their roles, Mt. 25.1–13 is somewhat unusual – it is the only teaching passage that says anything negative about women. There are negative remarks about Jesus' mother and family in Mk 3.21, 33–5, and there could be a negative element to Lk. 11.27–8. But this parable is singular in both its commendation of some women (the wise) and its condemnation of others (the foolish).

Mt. 25.1–13 may be a twin to the parable of the talents (25.14–30). If so, it involves the complementary male–female parallelism found in Luke, and it intimates the equality of male and female in regard both to God's blessings and banes, and to their ability to be included in or excluded from the Kingdom. In comparing the parable of the talents to the parable of the virgins, W. D. Ridley says, "There, judgment comes to the slothful; here to those women who are not prepared. There the question is one of the outer life; here of the inner life ... There of action; here of insight."[9] Thus, we see the Evangelist drawing on the common roles, joys, and anxieties of Jewish women in order to make a point to Jesus' followers about the eschatological coming of the Bridegroom.

Young maidens or virgins actually played a crucial part in the Jewish nuptial celebration. They were always given the role of torch-bearers in the torch-light procession to the groom's own house, and in the nocturnal torch-light celebration dance held outside that house. Considering their important role and their knowledge that the bridegroom might come at any time, their negligence is truly inexcusable. Jesus likens their exciting role in the wedding to that of the joyous role of the saints meeting and celebrating with the Bridegroom in the Kingdom.

The message of preparation is emphasized because the women were the bearers of torches that burned for only about fifteen minutes at a time, and thus it was incumbent upon them to bring extra oil because no one knew when the bridegroom would arrive. They were to wait in full preparation at the bride's house until that time. There is no criticism of the fact that these women fell asleep, for that was true of both the wise and the foolish virgins. But one group slept the sleep of those prepared to leave at a moment's notice no matter how long the wait; the other group did not. The main criticism is that the foolish virgins failed to come prepared with enough oil. This meant that the foolish virgins had to go for more oil, and thus they arrived at the groom's house too late to perform the role expected of them as is indicated by the fact that all the others are inside at the feast and the door is closed.[10] Obedience through proper preparation and fulfilling one's appointed role is necessary if one is to enter the feast.

Finally, this feast is not pictured as an all-male feast, but one at which both men and women, bridegroom, bride, and bridesmaids attend. This is not in conflict with what we know of Jewish meals of celebration such as a wedding or Passover feast. Nevertheless, the presence of men and women at this feast could symbolize the equal position men and women have and will have in the Kingdom which Jesus brings. Jesus used the foolish virgins as negative examples, and the wise virgins as positive examples for His disciples. The latter's wise preparedness is to be emulated if one wishes to partake in the marital feast when the Bridegroom returns.

Female imagery in the judgment sayings

Our survey of Jesus' attitudes toward women and their roles as reflected in His teaching would not be complete without an examination of how women or female imagery figure in His sayings about the Last Judgment and the judgment on Jerusalem. What is significant about these "last days" teachings is that they reflect the same male – female parallelism, and the same equality of man and woman as objects of God's salvation and judgment that we have found elsewhere in Jesus' teaching.

The Queen of the South – Mt. 12.42 (Lk. 11.31)

The queen of the South will arise at the judgment with this generation and condemn it; for she came from the ends of the earth to hear the wisdom of Solomon, and behold, something greater than Solomon is here.

As we have seen in the parable of the wise and foolish virgins, Jesus did not hesitate to use women as both positive and negative examples of God's dealing with humanity. In the course of explaining the sign of Jonah (Mt. 12.38 – 41), Jesus uses both the men of Nineveh and the Queen of the South to emphasize His point.

The Queen of the South clearly is the Queen of Sheba of Old Testament fame. She came to Solomon "to test him with difficult questions" (1 Kgs. 10.1, 2 Chr. 9.1). Since Jesus was being tested, His choice of the Queen of the South and Solomon was most apt for this occasion. Because of the way Jesus presents His reply, His listeners, as part of this generation, are in the end the ones being weighed in the balance: "The Queen of the South will rise at the judgment with the men of this generation and condemn them." She will appear in court on Judgment Day as a key witness for the prosecution against this generation. More importantly, her witness will *not* be thrown out of that final court as it probably would be in early Judaism since one woman's word against that of many men would have carried little if any weight in the first century. Rather, it will be accepted as a decisive testimony condemning this generation. Even a Gentile woman compares favorably with Jesus' audience, for she recognized the favor of God in Solomon's wise words and ways; yet, this generation cannot understand the greater

59

wisdom which Jesus reveals about the inbreaking Kingdom. Here again is an illustration of a repeated Gospel motif – a woman (in this case, undesirable and foreign) being praised as exemplary in the presence of those who ought to be the examples, the Jews.

The final separation – Lk. 17.34–5 (Mt. 24.40–2)

I tell you, in that night there will be two in one bed; one will be taken and the other left. There will be two women grinding together; one will be taken and the other left. (Lk. 17.34–5)

Then two men will be in the field; one is taken and one is left. Two women will be grinding at the mill; one is taken and one is left. Watch therefore, for you do not know on what day your Lord is coming. (Mt. 24.40–2)

Luke and Matthew's discussion of the final separation is probably taken from Q material and provides evidence that the Gospel tradition is concerned to show how eschatological events affect both men and women. Matthew's examples involve two in a field and two at a handmill, while Luke has two in a bed and two at (or with) a handmill.

Jesus' reference to women grinding is merely a descriptive statement drawing on the common roles women assumed in His own day – it should not be taken as some sort of announcement of what their roles will be in "that day." This is true of many of Jesus' statements about the roles men and women assume. His concern is more with *which* Master one serves, not *how*. Jesus' reference may, however, tell us that He thought some division of labor between male and female was natural and acceptable both in His own day and in the future. It may be significant that Jesus did not argue *against* or refrain from using examples that relied on the traditional division of labor.

Though both Matthew and Luke describe their examples in terms of the genderless "two," Luke is probably portraying one pair of men and one pair of women. Using complementary parallelism, Luke wishes to make clear that men and women are equal in honor and grace, dishonor and disgrace, as half of each example reveals.[11] The point of these examples is that both men and women are accountable before God as responsible human beings, and there will come a day when a person will either be taken into God's presence or left behind to face the wrath to come.[12]

Jesus weeps over Jerusalem – Mt. 23.37–9 (Lk. 13.34–5)

O Jerusalem, Jerusalem, killing the prophets and stoning those who are sent to you! How often would I have gathered your children together (just) as a hen gathers her brood under her wings, and you would not! Behold, your house is forsaken and desolate. For I tell you, you will not see me again, until you say, "Blessed is he who comes in the name of the Lord."

A judgment saying of a very different sort is to be found in Mt. 23.37–9 (Lk. 13.34–5), and it is relevant for our discussion because it involves the "Mother of Jerusalem" imagery. In this passage, the role of Jesus is conceived of in terms of feminine, albeit female animal, imagery. The expression "just as" or "in the manner which" in both Matthew and Luke, makes clear that Jesus is speaking of a comparison of functions, not natures. He would have gathered in Jerusalem's children in the same manner as the mother bird gathers in her brood under her wings.

When Jesus says, "Jerusalem, Jerusalem, you who kill the prophets and stone those sent to you, how often I have longed to gather your children together (just) as a hen gathers her chicks under her wings, but you were not willing," we are reminded of the lament of God over His wayward children in Hosea or, since female imagery is used here, Rachel weeping for her lost children. It should not be overlooked that Jesus takes on a role normally performed by a Jewish woman of publicly and "prophetically" mourning for Jerusalem. Also, Jesus chooses here one of the most proverbially gender distinctive roles a woman or female animal takes when he describes His desires in terms of a mother's care and protection, which may tell us something of how He felt about a loving mother's role. This saying gives strong incidental evidence of Jesus' appreciation of a mother's role. Otherwise He would not have used this imagery to make a positive point about His own desires and role.

The daughters of Jerusalem – Lk. 23.27–31

And there followed him a great multitude of the people, and of women who bewailed and lamented him. But Jesus turning to them said, "Daughters of Jerusalem, do not weep for me, but weep for yourselves and for your children. For behold, the days are coming when they will say, 'Blessed are the barren, and the wombs that never bore, and the breasts that never gave suck!' Then they will begin to say to the mountains, 'Fall on us'; and to the hills, 'Cover us.' For if they do this when the wood is green, what will happen when it is dry?"

Jesus, who had lamented and wept over the fate of Jerusalem, now reaches the point on His own *via dolorosa* where the "daughters of Jerusalem" lament for Him.[13] In this uniquely Lukan passage we are told He was followed by "a great multitude of the people and women who mourned and wailed for him." These two groups are seen by Luke as distinct entities. It is the women alone who are said to be mourning and wailing, and it is to them that Jesus addresses His comments. It was not uncommon for Jews to mourn prior to a death, especially if they were relatives of the one mourned, or if he was a famous person whose death would mean a great loss. But we know of no instance where *professional* mourners were called upon to perform their task in advance. These women were probably inhabitants of Jerusalem who were sympathetic to Jesus and grieved at His present plight. Their act was a spontaneous show of their feelings, but it was also a dangerous one for the Jews did not permit such public crying and wailing for a criminal.

Jesus addresses them as a group that will share the destiny of Jersualem. In view of what will happen to their homes and families in the year A.D. 70, He suggests that they should weep for themselves and for their own children, not for Him. Jesus (perhaps drawing on Is. 54.1–2), says to these women, "Behold, the time will come when you will say 'Blessed are the barren women, the wombs that never bore, and the breasts that never nursed!'" He is not saying that barrenness or childlessness is in itself a blessing, only that in "that day" one's blessings become one's burdens, and thus those without children are better off. Jesus knew well that for these daughters of Jerusalem their children were their greatest delight, and thus His address to them is dramatic and appropriate. The loss of their

62

children will lead them to ultimate despair, to cry out for a speedy death. "They will say to the mountains, 'fall on us', and to the hills, 'cover us'."

Jesus leaves these women, who represent the heart of the old Israel, with a question – If an innocent man cannot escape the Judgment, what will happen to guilty Israel? Even in the waning minutes of His earthly ministry, Jesus shows His concern for women by identifying with their plight, for they too must face suffering and judgment as He does now.

Conclusions

An indirect source of information about Jesus' attitude toward women may be found in His parables and the eschatological sayings. For instance, in the parable of the obstinate widow and the obdurate judge (Lk. 18.1 – 8) we see not only a concern for a widow, but also a desire to an even indigent (even annoying) woman as a model for the behavior of the disciples. We noted the elements of reversal of expectations or roles involved in such sayings. In addition, while Luke stresses male – female parallelism more than the other Evangelists, there are good reasons for thinking that Jesus Himself deliberately indulged in pairing sayings with a similar message – one directed to females, and the other to males. In this manner, both Jesus and especially Luke indicate their desire to see women as equally worthy to be examples, equally objects of God's grace, and equally an accepted part of their audiences.

There are also parables and sayings where Jesus likens God's or even His own redemptive activities to the everyday activities of women (Lk. 15.8 – 10) and even a mother hen (Mt. 23.37 – 9/Lk. 13.34 – 5). The parables of the lost coin and the leaven (Lk. 15.8 – 10, Mt. 13.33/Lk. 13.20 – 1) show that Jesus took care to express His Kingdom message so that women would be able to identify with it immediately. The parable of the wise and foolish virgins uses women as both positive and negative examples for Jesus' disciples, and there is perhaps a hint of a woman's right to participate in the Messianic banquet when the Bridegroom returns for His own.

If women are envisioned equally with men as objects of God's grace and participants in the community of Jesus and the coming

Kingdom, then it is also true that such sayings as Lk. 17.34 – 5 reveal that women are equally objects of God's judgment. Mt. 12.42 and parallels indicate Jesus' readiness to refer even to a Gentile woman as a valid witness against men on the Day of Judgment, and His willingness to stress how God's ways are often the opposite of what men expect. What Jew would expect to be told that a Gentile queen would stand as a witness against his generation?

Jesus weeps for Jerusalem (Mt. 23.37 – 9) and counsels the "daughters of Jersualem" to weep also for themselves (Lk. 23.27 – 31). That Jesus would stop on His way to Calvary to speak to the "daughters of Jerusalem" shows how He could identify with a woman's plight in the midst of His own.

Jesus' teaching relating to women and their roles is sometimes radical, sometimes reformational, and usually controversial in its original setting. Even when Luke wrote his Gospel, it is likely that the very reason he felt a need to stress male – female parallelism and Jesus' positive statements about women was that his own audience had strong reservations about some of Jesus' views on the subject. The case for women being seen as equal objects of God's grace and equal examples for disciples, as well as being disciples, had still to be argued when Luke wrote his Gospel. All of this teaching prepares us for an examination of Jesus' actions, and His manner of relating to harlots, widows, small girls, foreign women, mothers, and women made unclean through illness or incapacitated through injury.

6

STORIES OF HELP AND HEALING

Considerable space is devoted in the Gospels to Jesus' interactions with women from all walks of life. In some instances, a healing of a woman is involved, in others, Jesus helps certain women by revealing their sins, forgiving their sins, or healing their relatives. After a review of seven passages dealing with specific women in the Gospels, we can evaluate Jesus' attitude toward women as reflected in His actions.

The Lucan anointing – Lk. 7.36–50

One of the Pharisees asked him to eat with him, and he went into the Pharisee's house, and took his place at table. And behold, a woman of the city, who was a sinner, when she learned that he was at table in the Pharisee's house, brought an alabaster flask of ointment, and standing behind him at his feet, weeping, she began to wet his feet with her tears, and wiped them with the hair of her head, and kissed his feet, and anointed them with the ointment. Now when the Pharisee who had invited him saw it, he said to himself, "If this man were a prophet, he would have known who and what sort of woman this is who is touching him, for she is a sinner." And Jesus answering said to him, "Simon, I have something to say to you." And he answered, "What is it, Teacher?" "A certain creditor had two debtors; one owed five hundred *denarii*, and the other fifty. When they could not pay, he forgave them both. Now which of them will love him more?" Simon answered, "The one, I suppose, to whom he forgave more." And he said to him, "You have judged rightly." Then turning toward the woman he said to Simon, "Do you see this woman? I entered your house, you gave me no water for my feet, but she has wet my feet with her tears and wiped them with her hair. You gave me no kiss, but from the time I came in she has not ceased to kiss my feet. You did not anoint my head with oil, but she has anointed my feet with ointment. Therefore I tell you,

65

her sins, which are many, are forgiven, for she loved much; but he who is forgiven little, loves little." And he said to her, "Your sins are forgiven." Then those who were at table with him began to say among themselves, "Who is this, who even forgives sins?" And he said to the woman, "Your faith has saved you; go in peace."

In the Gospels there are two stories about Jesus being anointed by women. While it is possible that Luke has radically revised the Marcan anointing story (14.3–9) and added a parable to suit his purposes, a more probable view is that there are two different traditions about Jesus being anointed by a woman which may have interacted with one another in their language and details at the stage of oral transmission. This would not be surprising since the two stories have certain similarities. Lk. 7.36–47, 49 was probably an original unit which Luke derived from his special source (making certain editorial changes, see verses 48, 50), and then presented in a special way in order to illustrate the scandal of Jesus' love for sinners (Lk. 7.34) and to show how they reacted to His offer of forgiveness and healing.

Simon the Pharisee, perhaps in order to discover for himself what kind of man Jesus was, invited Him to a banquet in His honor. After Jesus arrived, an unnamed woman entered the house to perform a deed of loving devotion. This is no ordinary woman coming into the house but "a woman who was a sinner in the city," most likely a prostitute. Considering the openness of Jewish homes and the feeling of Judaism that one should help the poor and hungry, it was not uncommon for a poor person to come into a house during a banquet to beg or grab something to eat. Thus, Simon is not surprised that the woman comes in, but he is shocked at what she does. The woman is carrying an alabaster container of good perfume, much the same as that found in the Matthean and Marcan anointings. By mentioning the perfume at this point, Luke intimates that it is the woman's intention to anoint Jesus.

If common banqueting customs were being followed, then the woman is probably visible to Simon but not to Jesus as she enters. Perhaps Jesus follows the progress of events in Simon's shocked face. Jesus' body is reclining on the couch with His bare feet turned away from the table and His left elbow on the table itself. It is not until Jesus later turns toward the woman that He clearly sees her. Thus, this woman is standing or kneeling behind Jesus' couch near His feet. Whether the woman had previously met Jesus is uncertain, but the presentation of her unsolicited act of anointing and her emotional outburst makes it inconceivable that she had not at least heard of Jesus' message of forgiveness. Her act is one of loving devotion and possibly gratitude, for she sees in Jesus *acceptance*, not rejection, despite her past life of sin. Just as her tears speak of remorse over sin, so too Jesus' silence speaks of His acceptance of her gift and, more importantly, of this woman herself. She is overcome and weeps on Jesus' feet. In the midst of emotion, she quickly wipes Jesus' feet with her loose hair, a clear violation of Jewish customs of propriety.

Simon's reaction is typical and legally correct. This woman has defiled Jesus. Simon is portrayed as expecting Jesus, as both a teacher and a prophet, to know what sort of person this woman is. That Jesus passes over the woman's act in silence proves to Simon's satisfaction that He is not a prophet. The use of the term teacher is intended to show that Simon has some respect for Jesus, and enough interest to invite Him to a banquet; however, he has not performed for Jesus the special works of kindness (washing the feet, kiss of greeting, anointing with oil) which a gracious host should do for a special guest. This was *so much* a part of the system of hospitality Jesus was used to in His day, that He missed it when it was omitted. By contrast, the woman's deed was one of exceptional humility and love, for it was not common in Judaism to kiss someone's feet. Kissing the feet is usually the act of someone, such as a criminal, who has just been freed or whose debt was remitted, and in some sense this was the condition of this woman. That the anointing was on the feet means that the woman is assuming a servant's position.

The example of two debtors is given in order to lead Simon to see the woman as He sees her. When Jesus asks, "Who will be more grateful to the money lender?" Simon, not wishing to be trapped in his own words, responds, "I suppose that one to whom he forgave more" or "I suppose that it will be the one to whom more has been remitted." Jesus affirms that he has judged properly. In order to apply His illustration, Jesus turns to the woman clinging to His feet and speaks to Simon. Jesus explains that Simon has failed to perform three expressions of hospitality and contrasts them to the three deeds performed by the woman. Simon did not wash Jesus' feet but she washed them with her tears; Simon did not give Jesus a kiss of greeting, yet she has kissed His feet; Simon did not anoint Jesus' head, yet she has humbly anointed His feet. I. H. Marshall says, "Not only is Jesus willing to accept the touch of a sinful woman, but he even suggests that her action is more welcome to him than that of his host."[1] Here we see a clear example of reversal – a sinful woman is praised at the expense of and by comparison to a "good" Jewish man. Jesus has violated, or perhaps transcended, the letter of the law of clean and unclean in the presence of a Pharisee. He has implied that Simon, by not receiving Him with more graciousness, does not bear the same grateful and loving heart toward Him that the woman does.

Finally, Jesus says in effect, "I can say with confidence that her sins are forgiven because her love evidences it." Gratitude is the *proof, not the ground*, of forgiveness. Thus, Jesus demonstrates that He is indeed a prophet for He has discerned the thoughts of Simon's heart and knows the condition of the woman. In fact, even more is at stake here because Jesus' listeners would understand Him to mean that her sins had been forgiven *by Him*, which from their point of view was blasphemy – only God can forgive sins.

In conclusion, Jesus has taken the part of a woman who was the object of scorn. He thus proclaims a Kingdom where the unclean are cleansed by forgiveness through faith. The breaking down of the barrier of clean and unclean and of social ostracism by forgiveness opened the door for a return of such women to a more normal life and perhaps even a place in His community. This is one reason why women often showed their gratitude and devotion to Jesus; they were finally treated by Him as fellow creatures of God without special restrictions.

The woman at the well – Jn 4.7–42

There came a woman of Samaria to draw water. Jesus said to her, "Give me a drink." For his disciples had gone away into the city to buy food. The Samaritan woman said to him, "How is it that you, a Jew, ask a drink of me, a woman of Samaria?" For Jews have no dealings with Samaritans. Jesus answered her, "If you knew the gift of God, and who it is that is saying to you, 'Give me a drink,' you would have asked him, and he would have given you living water.'' The woman said to him, ''Sir, you have nothing to draw with, and the well is deep; where do you get that living water? Are you greater than our father Jacob, who gave us the well, and drank from it himself, and his sons, and his cattle?'' Jesus said to her, ''Every one who drinks of the water that I shall give him will never thirst; the water that I shall give him will become in him a spring of water welling up to eternal life.'' The woman said to him, ''Sir, give me this water, that I may not thirst, nor come here to draw.'' Jesus said to her, ''Go, call your husband, and come here.'' The woman answered him, ''I have no husband.'' Jesus said to her, ''You are right in saying, 'I have no husband'; for you have had five husbands, and he whom you now have is not your husband; this you said truly.'' The woman said to him, ''Sir, I perceive that you are a prophet. Our fathers worshipped on this mountain; and you say that in Jerusalem is the place where men ought to worship.'' Jesus said to her, ''Woman, believe me, the hour is coming when neither on this mountain nor in Jerusalem will you worship the Father. You worship what you do not know; we worship what we know, for salvation is from the Jews. But the hour is coming, and now is, when the true worshippers will worship the Father in spirit and truth, for such the Father seeks to worship him. God is spirit, and those who worship him must worship in spirit and truth.'' The woman said to him, ''I know that Messiah is coming (he who is called Christ); when he comes, he will show us all things.'' Jesus said to her, ''I who speak to you am he.'' Just then his disciples came. They marveled that he was talking with a woman, but none said, ''What do you wish?'' or , ''Why are you talking with her?'' So the woman left her water jar, and went away into the city, and said to the people, ''Come, see a man who told me all that I ever did. Can this be the Christ?'' They went out of the city and were coming to him. Meanwhile the disciples besought him, saying, ''Rabbi eat.'' But he said to them, ''I have food to eat of which you do not know.'' So the disciples said to one another, ''Has any one brought him food?'' Jesus said to them, ''My food is to do the will of him who sent me, and to accomplish his work. Do you not say, 'There are yet four months, then comes the harvest?' I tell you, lift up your eyes, and see how the fields are already white for harvest. He who reaps receives wages, and gathers fruit for eternal life, so that sower and reaper may rejoice together. For here the saying holds true, 'One sows and another reaps.' I sent you to reap that for which you did not labor; others have labored, and you have entered into their labor.'' Many Samaritans from that city believed in him because of the woman's testimony, ''He told me all that I ever did.'' So when the Samaritans came to him, they asked him to stay with them; and he stayed there two days. And many more believed because of his word. They said to the woman, "It is no longer because of your words that we believe, for we have heard for ourselves, and we know that this is indeed the Savior of the world."

In Jn 4.7 – 42, the author of the Fourth Gospel proceeds to develop his portrait of Jesus by presenting Him in a new and perhaps surprising setting. In Jn 2, Jesus changes water into wine while interacting with a woman; in Jn 4, Jesus persuades another woman to exchange natural water for living water. Perhaps there is also a contrast between Nicodemus of Jn 3, a teacher and representative of orthodox Judaism who fails to understand Jesus, and the common Samaritan woman of Jn 4 who gains some insight into Jesus' true character.

The story of the Samaritan woman at Jacob's well (4.7 – 42) deals with the process of coming to faith, but in it faith is a response to Jesus' word, not to any sign.[2] Finally, Jesus Himself, who has been shown to be the fulfillment of Old Testament and Jewish expectation, makes clear here that though salvation is of the Jews, it is for all who believe and receive it. Various factors indicate that we are dealing with an actual occurrence. The story betrays a considerable knowledge of Samaritan beliefs, local color, geographical factors, and Jewish – Samaritan relationships that would seem to point us in the direction of an historical account. Also, the dialogue between Jesus and the woman seems very fitting for the occasion. It is quite believable that the woman would have understood Jesus' claims against the background of the Samaritan expectation of the Taheb – their term for the coming Messianic figure. Thus, it is not implausible that we are dealing with an historical event.

The first major point of this story begins with Jesus' request for a drink of water from a woman who is rightly surprised at this for two reasons: Jesus is both a Jew and a man. John makes an editorial comment to explain why she was surprised, "Jews do not have dealings (or share common cups) with Samaritans." The Samaritan woman is in a somewhat similar position to that of Martha in Lk. 10.38 – 42. She supposes that she is the hostess and it is Jesus who needs something; however, it is Jesus who has something to bestow – living water. Thinking on an earthly plane, she believes Jesus is referring to running water, rather than standing water, and thinks she might be saved repeated trips to the well. Her Samaritan pride rises to the surface in this discussion when she asks if Jesus is saying He can give better water than Father Jacob, "who gave us the well." Jesus responds in the affirmative by saying that His water satisfies forever.

Unlike many of the other people whom Jesus encounters in His ministry, the Samaritan woman wins the reader's admiration because of her openness to the revealing word of Jesus even when she does not understand. Her attitude is one of inquiry, not rejection, and it is this that makes her a suitable subject for faith.[3]

In the second enlightening point of this story, Jesus commands the woman to go and call "her husband." The Evangelist indicates that Jesus, through His supernatural insight, knows this woman's life and wishes to bring her sins out into the open so that they may be forgiven. The woman's response is deliberately evasive – "I don't have a husband." Jesus' rejoinder probably means that the woman has had five legal husbands (all now deceased or divorced from her) and she is now living with a man who is not her legal husband. In the context of Judaism it was not the custom to have more than three marriages in a lifetime – legally, any number might be admissible, but morally more than three would be suspect. If this woman was living with a man other than her husband, she would be ritually unclean, yet Jesus shows no signs of maintaining the distinctions of clean and unclean. He asks for a drink and continues to pursue His discussion so that she may believe, thus violating the well-known Jewish warning against speaking to a woman (especially a known harlot) in public.

The third crucial factor in this interchange comes to light as the discussion turns to the matter of worship. The woman changes the subject from her own personal life to the old debate of whether Mount Gerizim or Jerusalem was the proper place to worship. If Jesus says Jerusalem, then as a Samaritan she will reject the possibility that Jesus is the Messiah. The Samaritans did not expect a Davidic Messiah, but rather a *Taheb* which means either "the one who returns" (Moses come back to life) or "the one who restores" (a prophet like Moses). For the Samaritans, Moses was the *only* prophet and thus only of him or the expected one could it be said, "I see that

you are a prophet.'' The first-century historian Josephus tells us that
the Samaritans had expectations of the *Taheb* returning even during
Jesus' day.

Rejecting her either/or, Jesus says that the crucial issue is not the
place but the *manner* in which God is worshipped – in spirit and truth.
This phrase means true or proper worship as God would have it.
The Samaritans may worship the right God but ''you worship what
you do not know.'' Perhaps it is this statement that leads the woman
to assert, ''I know that Messiah is coming ... he will explain all things
to us.'' Again she understands the nature of the *Taheb* who will be
a revealer, not a deliverer. Jesus adds, ''The hour is coming and
now is'' when the worship of God will depend neither on where one
is nor who one is. Salvation may be from the Jews, but it is for all
those who will worship God in spirit and truth. Thus, Jesus does
not exclude this woman from those who may offer such worship.
There is no hint of separation of male and female, and no hint of
other special restrictions on women, as would apply in the Temple
worship in Jerusalem.

After the woman has expressed her belief about the Coming One,
Jesus says, ''I am he, the one speaking to you.'' Probably this means
that Jesus is claiming to be the Messiah. With this statement the
Evangelist brings the first dialogue to a dramatic close, just as the
disciples return from town. They are amazed that He would speak
with this strange woman, but they are circumspect enough not to
ask questions.

The Evangelist then summarizes the woman's witness as follows:
''Come see a man who told me everything I have done. Could he
perhaps be the Messiah?'' Her remark is perhaps hyperbolic and
tentative, but it implies hope and expectation. Her witness, which
appears to speak openly of her own notoriety, induces the towns-
people to leave the village and go in the direction of Jesus and the well.

While this traveling scene develops in the background, Jesus has
His second dialogue, this time with the disciples. They offer food
to Him, but Jesus remarks that He has a source of nourishment
unknown to them, namely, bringing this woman to faith and to the
point of sharing that faith (a particular example of doing the will of
God). The disciples, like the woman, misunderstand Jesus' remark
by thinking merely on the physical level.

Jesus next speaks metaphorically about teaching and witnessing and the fruit it bears when it leads people to faith in Him. They are exhorted, "Open your eyes and look at the fields! They are ripe for harvest." Jesus clearly distinguishes between the reapers, i.e. the disciples, and the sowers, i.e. Jesus and the Samaritan woman. Jesus has sown the Word in her and she, in turn, has sown the Word in the other Samaritans. The disciples must now see the fruit of the evangelistic work of Jesus and the woman.

The Evangelist makes clear that this woman's witness was fruitful – "But from the town many of the Samaritans believed in him because of the word of the woman's testimony." This should be compared to Jesus' prayer – "I pray also for those who will believe in me through their word." This woman is presented as one of Jesus' witnesses, through whom others are led to Him.

John 4 reveals that Jesus rejected various sorts of prohibitions that would have separated Him from those He came to seek and to save, such as the rabbinic warning against talking with women in public places, especially women who were known sinners. While the Evangelist is concerned to make the legal point that Jesus was willing to share a common cup with a Samaritan, incidentally this text serves to reinforce what we found in Lk. 7.36–50, that Jesus did not accept the Levitical distinctions between clean and unclean persons. Further, the discussion in Jn 4 suggests that Jesus rejected the distinctions that separated Jewish and Samaritan worshippers and perhaps those imposed in the Jerusalem cult that separated men and women. This is implicit in His affirmation of worship ("neither on this mountain, nor in Jerusalem, but in spirit and truth") and the fact that He could make such statements to a Samaritan woman. It may be that *some* of this portrayal of Jesus is more of a "typical" picture than an actual picture of what took place on this occasion, but the Evangelist would still be conveying that these attitudes were characteristic of the historical Jesus.

In summary, Jesus and the woman had discussed a more universal source of life and basis of worship. The witness of Jesus and this sinful Samaritan woman bore fruit in Samaria and led to the confession and acknowledgement of the presence of the universal Savior. "The hour is coming and now is" when even women, even Samaritan women, even sinful Samaritan women, may be both members and messengers of this King and His Kingdom.

The Syrophoenician woman – Mk 7.24 – 30 (Mt. 15.21 – 8)

And from there he arose and went away to the region of Tyre and Sidon. And he entered a house, and would not have any one know it; yet he could not be hid. But immediately a woman, whose little daughter was possessed by an unclean spirit, heard of him, and came and fell down at his feet. Now the woman was a Greek, a Syrophoenician by birth. And she begged him to cast the demon out of her daughter. And he said to her "Let the children first be fed, for it is not right to take the children's bread and throw it to the dogs." But she answered him, "Yes, Lord; yet even the dogs under the table eat the children's crumbs." And he said to her, "For this saying you may go your way; the demon has left your daughter." And she went home, and found the child lying in bed, and the demon gone.

This unusual story presents one of the so-called "hard sayings" of Jesus. It is most unlikely that the Church would have created this conversation, given the flow of Gentiles into the community and a growing devotion to Christ. R. A. Harrisville states, "If the Evangelist were to yield to the temptation to reconcile his narrative with the current situation, it would certainly have been in this instance. The fact that he did not attests to his having kept faith with the tradition."[4]

Mark stresses the woman's political and national identity, a Greek born in the region of Syrian Phoenicia, while Matthew may be referring to her religious affiliation by calling her a Canaanite. Characteristically, Mark says that *immediately* after the woman heard Jesus was in the area, she implores Him to exorcize an unclean spirit from her daughter and falls at His feet in a gesture of supplication. After her request, the Marcan narrative proceeds directly to the saying of Jesus about the children and their food, while Matthew relates a three-part response by Jesus.

And behold, a Canaanite woman from that region came out and cried ... But he did not answer her a word. And his disciples came and begged him, saying, "Send her away, for she is crying after us." He answered, "I was sent only to the lost sheep of the house of Israel." But she came and knelt before him, saying, "Lord, help me." And he answered, "It is not fair to take the children's bread and throw it to the dogs." She said, "Yes, Lord, yet even the dogs eat the crumbs that fall from their masters' table." Then Jesus answered her, "O woman, great is your faith! Be it done for you as you desire." And her daughter was healed instantly.

First, when the woman says, "Have mercy on me Lord, Son of David," and then asks for exorcism, Jesus says nothing. Matthew appears to cast Jesus in an uncharacteristically unresponsive role. Possibly we are meant to think that this woman was trying to curry favor with Jesus by using the title Son of David. Yet, it was precisely because He was the Son of David that she had no claim on Him. The silence of Jesus is perhaps a means of testing the woman's faith, or His disciples' character by giving them time to react to the situation. Their response is best translated, "Send her away because she is crying after us."

Jesus' second response is directed *primarily* to the disciples, "I was sent only to the lost sheep of Israel." It seems very cold of Jesus given the plight of a woman in need. But she is not put off and pleads again, "Lord, help me."

The third or "hard" saying of Jesus is found in both Matthew and Mark: "It is not good to take the food of the children and throw it to the dogs." No matter how one interprets the word translated as dog or puppy, it is an insult, especially when spoken by a Jew to a Gentile. Perhaps she hears something in Jesus' tone of voice that indicates there is still hope because she is not to be put off but enters into the spirit of the test by accepting Jesus' judgment on her. In the end, the woman achieves her desire, not so much by a witty remark, as by a faith that goes on imploring even though it recognizes that it has no claim on the Master. She is similar to the persistent woman of Lk. 18.1 – 8.

With regard to Jesus' views of women, we may deduce the following. Jesus' willingness to talk with and help this foreign woman is proof of His rejection of certain Jewish teachings concerning discourse with women and the uncleanness of Gentiles. In Mark, the woman's trust is indicated by the fact that she believes Jesus when He says her daughter is healed and leaves in full confidence. Matthew makes explicit what is implicit in Mark, "O woman, great is your faith." Only one other in the Synoptic tradition is praised in these

terms, again a non-Jew (Mt. 8.5–13/Lk. 7.1–10). This woman
serves as an example to the Evangelists' audiences. In Matthew her
great faith contrasts with the disciples' great annoyance at her
persistent pleading. How surprised Matthew's audience must have
been to hear this Gentile woman's faith called great, when a
characteristic description of Jesus' own disciples in that Gospel is
that they have little faith! Both in Jesus' words and deeds, and in
the editorial activity of the Gospel writers, the theme of reversal of
expectations brought about by the Gospel is emphasized.

Peter's mother-in-law – Mk 1.29–31 (Mt. 8.14–15, Lk. 4.38–9)

And immediately he left the synagogue, and entered the house of Simon
and Andrew, with James and John. Now Simon's mother-in-law lay sick
with a fever, and immediately they told him of her. And he came and took
her by the hand and lifted her up, and the fever left her; and she served them.

Jesus' ministry to diseased women is the subject of several passages
in the Synoptic tradition. In each instance we are given further
evidence of His outright rejection of various taboos inhibiting His
ability to heal those in need. In Mk 1.29–31 and parallels, we see
Jesus' willingness to heal a diseased woman even on the Sabbath.
That this healing is paired with that of a man (Mk 1.21–8, Lk.
4.31–7) may be the Gospel writer's way of saying that Jesus was
willing to perform such an act on the Sabbath for both men and
women.

It is in the context of the Sabbath that Jesus performs His first
two miracles, as presented in Mark: the healing of the man with the
unclean spirit in the synagogue, and the healing of Simon's mother-
in-law in her home. Mark says that after Jesus preached and healed
in the synagogue, He immediately left and entered a house where
Simon Peter's mother-in-law lay sick with a fever. Mark and Luke
tell us that some of those in the house speak to Jesus about her,
probably asking Him to do something about her illness. Jesus'
response is quick and dramatic. Mark, in contrast to Matthew and
Luke, does not merely say that the woman arises and serves but that
Jesus *raises* her up, a phrase which may point to the Resurrection.
Luke, stressing Jesus' confrontation with the effects of Satan as seen

here in sickness, states that Jesus rebukes the fever while standing over her. In Mark there is the hint of Jesus' Resurrection power; in Luke the power of the King and His Kingdom over Satan; and in Matthew the awesomeness of Jesus' person in that He can heal by a mere touch.

Though there were precedents for rabbis taking the hand of another man and miraculously healing him, there are no examples of rabbis doing so for a woman, and certainly not on the Sabbath when the act could wait until after sundown.[5] Indeed, a man could be suspected of evil desires if he touched *any* woman other than his wife. At the very least Jesus could be accused of contracting uncleanness and violating the Sabbath laws against working. Jesus, however, was willing to be denounced so that this woman might be healed.

Note that there is no delay in her recovery – Jesus' healing is complete not only in driving out the sickness but also in restoring her wholeness. Having been freed from servitude to disease, she is now free to serve others. However, even her service could also be a violation of the Sabbath restrictions against working. Perhaps she realized that if Jesus was free to heal her on the Sabbath, then she was also free to serve and help others even on the Sabbath. In this act, she shows a new freedom and courage similar to that of Mary and Martha in Jn 12, the women in Lk. 8.1 – 3, or the sinful woman in Lk. 7.36 – 50, all of whom took upon themselves the role of servant in gratitude to Jesus. It is striking that these women all respond in ways that were conventional, and serve in capacities that were traditional for women or, in Mk 1.31, perhaps even "beneath" the traditional roles for women who were not servants.

Much can be learned from this short story. Just as Jesus dismissed the idea that the touch of a sinful woman or non-Jewish woman was defiling, so too He rejected the idea that the touch of a sick woman was defiling. If we accept that this story occurred at the beginning of Jesus' ministry, then we see that even from the first Jesus showed His concern for women and His willingness to violate the common view of the Sabbath and the standing rules about the uncleanness of a sick person in order to help them.

Finally, Marshall is probably right in saying that the use of the verb "to serve" is not meant to indicate that this is the only appropriate form of Christian service for women – "it simply indicates the normal domestic arrangement."[6] Nonetheless, Jesus accepts such service, which in many homes would probably be done only by a servant, not the matron of the house. This may also indicate Jesus' rejection of the prevailing ideas about what was and was not appropriate work for woman. We will say more about this when we discuss Lk. 10.38–42.

Healing a cripple on the Sabbath – Lk. 13.10–17

Now he was teaching in one of the synagogues on the sabbath. And there was a woman who had had a spirit of infirmity for eighteen years; she was bent over and could not fully straighten herself. And when Jesus saw her, he called her and said to her, "Woman, you are freed from your infirmity." And he laid his hands upon her, and immediately she was made straight, and she praised God. But the ruler of the synagogue, indignant because Jesus had healed on the sabbath, said to the people, "There are six days on which work ought to be done; come on those days and be healed, and not on the sabbath day." Then the Lord answered him, "You hypocrites! Does not each of you on the sabbath untie his ox or his ass from the manger, and lead it away to water it? And ought not this woman, a daughter of Abraham whom Satan bound for eighteen years, be loosed from this bond on the sabbath day?" And when he said this, all his adversaries were put to shame; and all the people rejoiced at all the glorious things that were done by him.

Lk. 13.10–17 illustrates what precedes and prepares for what follows. The unfruitful fig tree (13.6–9), just like the unfruitful approach to the Sabbath (13.10–17), must be cut down and fruitful attitudes which bring glory to God must be planted, just like the healthy growing tree in 13.19. Once again Jesus is presented as rejecting certain Jewish teachings about the Sabbath. Not the absence of work, but the presence of a creative and healing peace is the essence of the Sabbath. David Daube notes here a three-part structure that is used elsewhere in the Gospels – revolutionary action, protest, and silencing of the protesters.[7] Thus, Lk. 13.10–17 is carefully placed in relation to its context and carefully presented in its content.

The story opens with Jesus teaching in one of the synagogues on the Sabbath. A bent-over woman who has been sick for eighteen years enters the synagogue. Apparently her disease did not make her unclean. There is no indication that she came to be healed, but probably she wished to slip in unnoticed for often it was assumed by first-century Jews that long sickness meant great sin.[8]

Upon seeing her, Jesus interrupts His teaching to say, "Woman, you are released from your sickness." He not only heals her, but also lays hands upon her whereupon she stands upright. Now she truly has a reason to praise God on this Sabbath and she does so then and there. No doubt the congregation would be stunned at this striking miracle but the ruler of the synagogue is not at a loss for words. Though he is angry with Jesus for healing on the Sabbath, he directs his comments to the crowd. His objection is not to *where* the miracle took place, but *when*: "It is necessary to work six days, but we should not on the Sabbath." In his mind, healing was a violation of the prohibition against work on the Sabbath. Apparently, the objection is made on the basis of the Jewish idea that such acts of healing should not be performed on the Sabbath unless life was in danger. The woman who had suffered eighteen years could clearly wait one more day.

Jesus' reply shows that the coming of the Kingdom will not wait. He sees the hypocrisy in the ruler's remark and condemns all who agree with him. He argues from the lesser to the greater: if one can help a donkey then surely one can help a human being. The synagogue ruler appealed to the importance of the Jewish interpretations of the laws of Moses, but Jesus appealed to the *original purpose* of the Sabbath. Ellis says, "From the beginning the Sabbath was prophetic of the consecration of creation to its good and proper end … This will be accomplished by the deliverance of God's creation from Satan's power."[9] In Jesus' thinking the Sabbath was the perfect day to present an example of God's perfect will for His creatures.

The phrase "daughter of Abraham" had been applied to Israel as a whole but never before to an individual. Brennan contends, "By giving this woman this rarely-used title, Christ echoes the phrase 'son of Abraham' and in doing so asserts that this woman is a child of Abraham, a member of the people of God, and should be treated as such, instead of being valued less than a mere pack animal. The woman, then, is not only healed but restored to her true dignity."[10]

Notice the specific contrast between the label ''hypocrite'' that Jesus places on the synagogue ruler and the title ''daughter of Abraham'' He bestows on the woman. Again we see a woman not only being used as a positive example as she praises God, and even given a positive title, but also being defended at the expense of the males in the synagogue who object to Jesus' actions. By using the title, Jesus implies that she is as worthy of His concern and healing as any Jewish man and has as full a claim to her religious heritage as anyone else. She is an example of the oppressed set free (Lk. 4.18 – 19). The Sabbath is to be a day of release from the effects of the fallen order, and Jesus was willing to go to great lengths to help her, even with the threat of outright rejection by religious leaders.

Jairus and the Jewess – Mk 5.21 – 43 (Mt. 9.18 – 26, Lk. 8.40 – 56)

And when Jesus had crossed again in the boat to the other side, a great crowd gathered about him; and he was beside the sea. Then came one of the rulers of the synagogue, Jairus by name; and seeing him, he fell at his feet, and besought him saying, ''My little daughter is at the point of death. Come and lay your hands on her, so that she may be made well, and live.'' And he went with him. And a great crowd followed him and thronged about him. And there was a woman who had had a flow of blood for twelve years, and who had suffered much under many physicians, and had spent all that she had, and was no better but rather grew worse. She had heard the reports about Jesus, and came up behind him in the crowd and touched his garment. For she said, ''If I touch even his garments, I shall be made well.'' And immediately the hemorrhage ceased; and she felt in her body that she was healed of her disease. And Jesus, perceiving in himself that power had gone forth from him, immediately turned about in the crowd, and said, ''Who touched my garments?'' And his disciples said to him, ''You see the crowd pressing around you, and yet you say, 'Who touched me?' '' And he looked around to see who had done it. But the woman, knowing what had been done to her, came in fear and trembling and fell down before him, and told him the whole truth. And he said to her, ''Daughter, your faith has made you well; go in peace, and be healed of your disease.'' While he was still speaking, there came from the ruler's house some who said, ''Your daughter is dead. Why trouble the Teacher any further?'' But ignoring what they said, Jesus said to the ruler of the synagogue, ''Do not fear, only believe.'' And he allowed no one to follow him except Peter and James and

John the brother of James. When they came to the house of the ruler of the synagogue, he saw a tumult, and people weeping and wailing loudly. And when he had entered, he said to them, "Why do you make a tumult and weep? The child is not dead but sleeping." And they laughed at him. But he put them all outside, and took the child's father and mother and those who were with him, and went in where the child was. Taking her by the hand he said to her, "Talitha cumi"; which means, "Little girl, I say to you, arise." And immediately the girl got up and walked (she was twelve years of age), and they were immediately overcome with amazement. And he strictly charged them that no one should know this, and told them to give her something to eat.

Mk 5.21 – 43 (and parallels) has been submitted to great scrutiny in regard to its historical worth. Nonetheless, a reasonable case can be made that Mark is drawing on Peter's stories and thus there is a solid core of historical material in this narrative. If so, while we must examine the differences in the three Synoptic accounts, we may accept the nucleus of the story as revealing something of Jesus' views of women.

The story of Jairus and the woman with the twelve-year flow of blood builds from the healing of one person to the raising of another, and there is an interesting contrast between the elicited witness of the woman and the command to silence of Jairus' family and the three disciples. This story illustrates the progress of the Gospel reaching those at the bottom of the Jewish social ladder (the impoverished unclean woman) and those at the top (Jairus and his family).

Matthew opens the story with Jesus being approached by a synagogue leader named Jairus who, because of his desperate need, forgets his pride and position and falls at Jesus' feet begging for help for his daughter. This need not imply worship or special reverence, but rather respect and a sense of urgency which the First Evangelist has made more explicit than his Marcan source. The condition of the girl is described in three different ways by the Synoptic accounts, but they all probably mean that the girl is dying or at the point of death. Jesus is requested to lay hands on the young girl in order to heal her.

As Jesus sets off to Jairus' home, the crowd presses in and nearly suffocates Him. In the midst of this crowd, a woman with a twelve-year flow of blood, in hopes of a cure, touches Jesus' upper garment. Miraculously, her flow of blood immediately dries up. One must ask whether she showed little or great, weak or strong, pure or magic-tainted faith. Undoubtedly, there was an element of superstition in her belief that she might be cured by touching the Healer's garment, nevertheless, she did have faith enough to believe that Jesus might help her. Perhaps it was because of her ritual uncleanness or natural modesty that she tried to fade into the crowds again. She risked being restrained or cast out, yet she approached Jesus in faith.

Instantly, Jesus knew He had been touched in faith and thus He asks, ''Who touched my clothes?'' (Mark and Luke only). Jesus probably asks this question in order to educate and elevate the faith of the woman above just a belief in a magical power in Jesus and His garments. He wants the unclean woman to bear witness to the crowd of her faith and cure through Jesus. He wishes to make an example of her, in the good sense of the word. Luke, with his special emphasis on the liberation and witness of women, says ''In the presence of all the people she told why she had touched him and how she had been instantly healed.'' Matthew, as he did in the case of the Syrophoenician woman, makes this woman an explicit example of faith when he presents only these words of Jesus as a climax: ''Woman your faith has saved you.'' Though the woman trembled when she was found out, perhaps fearing Jesus' censure, Jesus reacts in a way she never expected. Not only was this woman no longer to be avoided, but now she was presented as a living example of faith for all to emulate. By contrast, the disciples are shown to have little faith in Jesus and little understanding of why Jesus would ask who touched Him in such a mob. As was the case with the Samaritan woman and the Syrophoenician woman, Jesus' words mean more than His disciples' interpretation leads them to believe.

At this point in the Marcan and Lucan accounts messengers arrive to report to Jairus, ''Your daughter is dead ... Why bother the teacher any more?'' Jesus overhears these messengers and, to prevent Jairus from despairing, interjects ''fear not, only believe.'' When Jesus arrives at the house He allows only Peter, James, and John to enter with Him. These three serve as witnesses to the miracle and, as representatives of the disciples, receive this privilege perhaps in preparation for their leadership role and their commissioning to perform similar acts. Already present in the house were mourners, some of whom may have been members of the family. The scornful or mocking response to Jesus' statement, ''the child is not dead but sleeping,'' may indicate the bitter rejoinder of grieving relatives who would view such a remark as flippant. The meaning of Jesus' remark has been debated, but the mourners clearly interpret it to mean that Jesus thought the girl was still alive. Mark is not using the word ''sleeping'' as a metaphor for death, since He is not saying, ''Yes, she is dead, but death is like a sleep.'' The explanation probably lies in who Jesus is, the Lord of life, and what He is about to do, raise the girl. The girl is dead and her death is not merely like a sleep; in His presence it *is* sleep rather than death. It is not an end, but an interim condition from which she returns healthy and hungry.

In order to perform the miracle, Jesus casts out all those in the house except the three disciples and the parents. Perhaps it is significant that Jesus treats the mother as equally worthy with the father and the Apostles of witnessing this act. As in the case of Peter's mother-in-law, Jesus takes the girl by the hand and Mark and Luke record that He adds the command, ''Girl, I say to you arise.'' To further a return to normality, Jesus commands a renewal of attention to the girl's physical needs. This was not magic but the power and word of God harnessed in the service of a young girl and of her family.

If one still has doubts about Jesus' attitude toward the clean/ unclean distinctions accepted in Judaism, an examination of this story should remove any uncertainties. Bearing in mind Jesus' operative principle that ''it is only what comes out of a person's heart that defiles him'' (Mk 7.15, 21), we have clear evidence that Jesus treats neither the touch of the woman with the twelve-year blood flow, nor the contact of a dead girl as defiling. Neither woman is viewed as unclean or as a source of uncleanness by Jesus, but rather is treated as a person in need of help.

Though not elucidated in our text, the implications of Jesus' views are important to this study. If a woman with a blood flow is not defiled or defiling, then the Jewish reason for not requiring a woman to fulfil all of the Law's positive commandments, and not permitting her to be counted on for all the periodic feasts and functions of the faith is by implication rejected by Jesus' deeds in the first of these two stories. Thus, the way is paved for women to participate more fully in Jesus' own community. In both stories, faith is a key commodity which the healed woman is as capable of possessing as Jairus. Since this is also the commodity which is the basis of association in Jesus' community, the woman and perhaps Jairus, become examples to the Gospel writers' audiences. Certainly, the healed woman is made an example by Jesus when He calls her to center stage and speaks of her faith. In Mark's presentation of the event, the woman appears in a more favorable light than the exasperated disciples. The Jairus story is also significant in that it shows Jesus' desire to reunite a physical family despite the great obstacle of death. Here is further evidence that the family of faith and the physical family were not mutually exclusive alternatives in Jesus' mind. Indeed, it appears that Jairus' faith is in part the basis of the reunion of his physical family. While an ordinary rabbi might have treated the loss of a daughter as less significant than the loss of a son, when one compares this story to that of the raising of the widow of Nain's son, Jesus exhibits an equal concern over the loss of either son or daughter.

The widow of Nain – Lk. 7.11 – 17

Soon afterward he went to a city called Nain, and his disciples and a great crowd went with him. As he drew near to the gate of the city, behold, a man who had died was being carried out, the only son of his mother, and she was a widow; and a large crowd from the city was with her. And when the Lord saw her, he had compassion on her and said to her, ''Do not weep.'' And he came and touched the bier, and the bearers stood still. And he said, ''Young man, I say to you, arise.'' And the dead man sat up, and began to speak. And he gave him to his mother. Fear seized them all; and they glorified God, saying, ''A great prophet has arisen among us!'' and ''God has visited his people!'' And this report concerning him spread through the whole of Judea and all the surrounding country.

Lk. 7.11 – 17, beyond all doubt, is a story about the raising of the dead. Perhaps it is significant that every example in the Gospels of Jesus performing such a miracle involves women either as the object of the miracle (Mk 5.21 – 43 and parallels) or as those for whom the miracle is performed (Lk. 7.11 – 17, John 11). Luke, with his interest in pairing male and female stories of similar content and intent, presents the healing of the centurion's servant (7.1 – 10) followed by the text at hand. Lk. 7.11 – 17 reflects Luke's general theme of the ministry of Jesus to women, and his special interest in the way the Gospel aided such disenfranchised groups as widows and the poor.

Luke sets the scene by indicating that Jesus went to Nain with His disciples and a huge crowd. As they were entering the city gate a funeral procession was leaving. Luke indicates that this was the saddest sort of funeral by saying, "Behold, a dead person was being carried out – the only son of his mother, and she was a widow." The mother was left alone and her family line was cut off. Luke says that Jesus felt compassion for this woman in her pitiful state and decided to perform an act solely on her behalf, that is, an act of mercy which did not involve forgiveness or faith.

Jesus is so certain of the outcome of His actions that He first tells the widow, who would be walking in front of the bier, "Don't cry." Next, He violates Jewish practice by stopping the funeral procession and touching the coffin, an act which causes those carrying it to stand still. Jesus needs only to speak to raise the young man, and thus addresses him not as a body or soul, but as a person: "Young man, I say to you, get up." The dead young man sits up, begins to speak, and is given back to his mother. The crowd was "filled with fear/awe and praised God." They interpreted this raising as an act of God visiting His people through a great prophet.

Our story succinctly illustrates Jesus' concern for women, particularly widows. The raising is a deed of compassion – faith is not a prerequisite, though the deed does engender the praise of Jesus as a great prophet of God. The act was also a practical one since it provided the woman with a means of support as well as a source of joy. It demonstrates Jesus' continual rejection of certain Old Testament and Jewish distinctions of clean/unclean, and certain Sabbath rules which prevented Him from helping women and others in need, that is, those with whom He especially chose to associate (Lk. 4.18 – 19, 24 – 7, 5.30 – 2, etc.). Luke views this miracle as a demonstration of the inbreaking of the Lord's favor, and indicates both by his introduction (verse 11) and his conclusion (verse 17) that it did not go unnoticed or unreported. In a sense, the

Evangelist himself, by including this story, made certain that such would be the case.

Conclusions

Our study of Jesus' interactions with women has brought to light several fundamental principles which seem to have guided Him in His dealings with the opposite sex. Jesus' outright rejection of Jewish ideas of sin and sickness leading to ritual impurity or defilement allowed Him to relate to many women He might not have reached otherwise. We have suggested also that Jesus' implicit rejection of the idea that a blood flow in a woman caused her to be defiled or to be a source of defilement removed the Jewish basis for excluding women from synagogue worship and periodic feasts and functions of the faith. This was perhaps one of the factors which paved the way for women to travel with Jesus and to be full-time followers of their Master without special restrictions (Lk. 8.1 – 3).

Jesus' rejection of certain Jewish Sabbath restrictions also allowed Him to serve and to accept service at the hands of grateful women when normally such activities were forbidden (Mk 1.29 – 31 and parallels). In Jn 4.7 – 42 and Mk 7.24 – 30 and parallels, we see clear examples of Jesus' willingness to relate openly to women who were not fully Jewish or, in the case of the Syrophoenician woman, perhaps not Jewish at all. This nullified numerous Jewish warnings about foreign or Samaritan women, as well as the familiar prohibitions against talking with women, especially sinful women, in public, and opened the door for a more normal and natural basis for relationship. While it is true that Jesus' earthly ministry was directed to the lost sheep of Israel, He did not reject other lost sheep who encountered or sought Him, and perhaps this set a precedent for the acceptance of non-Jewish women in the early days of the Gentile mission. It seems likely that one reason why Luke gives special prominence to women in his Gospel is to explain the influx of women into the Christian community of which he was a part and later wrote about in his book of Acts.

We noted a certain pattern in the Gospels of presenting women as examples of faith, and in one case of witness (Jn 4), often at the expense of either good male Jews or even Jesus' male disciples.

Stories of help and healing

We suggested that this pattern of reversal, while certainly owing something to the Gospel writers, nonetheless is to be traced back to Jesus Himself as one example of His teaching that the last and least shall be the first to be liberated as the Kingdom breaks into history with His ministry. We also detected a certain tendency on the part of the first three Evangelists to pair male – female healing stories, perhaps to stress Jesus' equal concern for men and women. This tendency, though less obvious than the male – female pairings of the parables, may reflect the purposes of each Evangelist, since there is at least one example in each Synoptic Gospel of a male – female pair not found in the other two Gospels.

Throughout the passages we have examined, Jesus' concern for women as persons, rather than as sources of potential temptation or defilement, is obvious. It is significant that Jesus was willing to perform extraordinary miracles, and to violate the Jewish Sabbath regulations even in the presence of rabbis and in the synagogue, in order to help women. Jesus did not pass over a woman's sins, indeed, by bringing some women to confession and pronouncing their sins forgiven He revealed His desire to heal the whole person and His recognition that women were as capable of as many sins as men.

All of this reveals Jesus' attitude that women were God's creatures, even daughters of Abraham, and thus as worthy as men to receive the benefits of God's love and salvation. If even a Samaritan woman, in contrast to His male disciples, could bear witness for Jesus and bring Him "true food," who could dispute a woman's right to a place among His followers? On this note, we turn to an examination of those women most often mentioned in the Gospels as associates of Jesus – His mother Mary, His friends Mary and Martha, and His female traveling companions.

87

7

WOMEN IN THE MINISTRY OF JESUS

There were several distinct groups of women who interacted with Jesus during His ministry (we will exclude here the birth and Resurrection narratives). After a study of the mother of Jesus, we will investigate Jesus' relationship to Mary and Martha, and those women who traveled with Jesus and played a crucial role in the events surrounding His death. By examining the status and role of these women in Jesus' earthly ministry, we will perhaps discover the background for and explanation of the new roles women assumed in the primitive Christian community.

Mother Mary, Jesus' disciple

The credal phrase, "Born of the Virgin Mary," rightly emphasizes that Mary's importance in the New Testament is due to her relationship to her Son. We must recognize that Mary is not mentioned in the Gospels as a result of any independent interest in her as a person, but because of the important role she played in Jesus' life.

The Wedding Feast at Cana – Jn 2.1–12

On the third day there was a marriage at Cana in Galilee, and the mother of Jesus was there; (2) Jesus also was invited to the marriage, with his disciples. (3) When the wine gave out, the mother of Jesus said to him, "They have no wine." (4) And Jesus said to her, "O Woman, what have you to do with me? My hour has not yet come." (5) His mother said to the servants, "Do whatever he tells you." (6) Now six stone jars were standing there, for the Jewish rites of purification, each holding twenty or thirty gallons. (7) Jesus said to them, "Fill the jars with water." And they filled them up to the brim. (8) He said to them, "Now draw some out, and take it to the steward of the feast.'' So they took it. (9) When the steward of the feast tasted the water now become wine, and did not know where it came from (though the servants who had drawn the water knew), the steward of the feast called the bridegroom (10) and said to him, ''Every man serves the good wine first; and when men have drunk freely, then the poor wine; but you have kept the good wine until now.'' (11) This, the first of his signs, Jesus did at Cana in Galilee, and manifested his glory; and his disciples believed in him. (12) After this he went down to Capernaum, with his mother and his brothers and his disciples; and there they stayed for a few days.

Jn 2, in its present form, has been written by someone who was conscious of Old Testament miracles and the ancient Hellenistic miracle stories. The amount of wine produced, for instance, may be a touch to show that Jesus was greater than Bacchus who reputedly also changed water into wine. Nevertheless, the retouching has not been done with a heavy hand, and it is possible to produce a pre-Gospel form of this narrative. For instance, it is plausible that the direct quotations of Jesus and Mary (Jn 2.3–4a, 5) have real historical value, especially since verse 4a (''O Woman, what have you to do with me?'') is not likely to be a product of the Evangelist's imagination and cannot stand alone as an isolated saying. In regard to the rest of the story, the arguments against its historicity are not conclusive.

In the Fourth Gospel, the miracle of Cana and the episode with the mother of Jesus and the beloved disciple beneath the cross (19.25–7) frame the public ministry of Jesus, and one expects to find a certain development and continuity between the two episodes. The phrase ''the mother of Jesus'' is almost a technical term in John; the Evangelist never calls Mary by her own name. This phrase is an honorable title for a woman who has borne a son; however, it implies no veneration of Mary's person, but focuses on her role. The Fourth Evangelist is usually very explicit in his use of names with the exception of two people – the mother of Jesus and the beloved disciple.

The dialogue between Jesus and Mary is at the heart of both Jn 2 and 19 – both include the address, ''Woman,'' and both involve Jesus doing something to help Mary. One should note the significant positioning of the mother of Jesus at the inception and climax of

Jesus' ministry (and only in these two places). Our discussion of Jn 2.1 – 12 must focus on the central dialogue in verses 3 – 5 and especially verse 4.

One's view of Mary's role here will be determined to a great extent by how one translates verse 4. The vocative "Woman" is a term of respect or affection. It is the normal way Jesus addresses women that He either does not know well, or must address in a formal manner. There are, however, no known uses of this word in either Hebrew or Greek by a son addressing his mother. It is likely that while it is not intended to carry a derogatory connotation toward Mary's motherhood, "Woman" is Jesus' way of placing His relationship to Mary on a different basis, that is, He is disengaging from her parental authority. *If* "Woman" is the Evangelist's own addition to the narrative, then it is one way that he has softened the blow of Jesus' remark.

The most probable explanation of verse 4a is that Jesus is disengaging from Mary in her role of parent in authority over Him and not from her concern for the problem at the wedding feast. He sees in her statement, "They have no wine," an implied imperative, "Do something." He does not reject the need, but the authority of the one expressing it, for she has failed to understand her Son's mission and His primary allegiance to the spiritual family. Jesus' heavenly Father, not His earthly mother, must determine when His hour is to come and what He is to do until then.

By "My hour has not yet come," the Evangelist implies that in that hour Jesus will have an obligation to fulfil to Mary and then she will have a claim on Him (see Jn 19.25 – 7). In the Fourth Gospel it is not until the word comes from the cross that the mother of Jesus is ushered officially into the spiritual family of Jesus (those who do have a claim on Him). For now He must be about His Father's work (Lk. 2.49). They will be reunited as a spiritual family when His hour comes; however, at Cana she is not placed among the group that has faith in and travels with Jesus as disciples. Jn 2.5, if it is an original part of this story, may imply that historically Mary had some faith and knowledge of Jesus' compassionate nature, and perhaps of His miracle-working power, but her powers to intercede for others with Him are not stressed here.

So far as its historical worth is concerned, this dialogue reveals both that Jesus disengaged from Mary in her role as mother and that Mary, unlike Jesus' brothers, was apparently not without some faith in Jesus long before the post-Easter community was formed. In the schema of Johannine theology, Jesus' disengagement from Mary is related to the theme of Jesus' "hour" and thus the scene at the cross is prepared for and the blow of disengagement is softened. The point seems to be that Mary must work out the tensions between the physical and spiritual family as a woman, for the Evangelist indicates that it is as "woman," not as Jesus' mother, that she enters the community of faith.

Mary in the Synoptics – Mk 3.19b – 21, 31 – 5 (Mt. 12.46 – 50/ Lk. 8.19 – 21), and Mk 6.1 – 6 (Mt. 13.53 – 8/Lk. 4.16 – 30)

Then he went home; (20) and the crowd came together again, so that they could not even eat. (21) And when his family heard it, they went out to seize him, for [those from among his] people were saying, "He is beside himself."
(Mk 3.19b – 21)
And his mother and his brothers came; and standing outside they sent to him and called him. (32) And a crowd was sitting about him; and they said to him, "Your mother and your brothers are outside, asking for you." (33) And he replied, "Who are my mother and my brothers?" (34) And looking around on those who sat about him, he said, "Here are my mother and my brothers! (35) Whoever does the will of God is my brother, and sister, and mother."
(Mk 3.31 – 5)

There is very little information on Mary in the Synoptic Gospels apart from the birth narratives of Matthew and Luke. Before the Passion narratives there is only Mk 3.19b – 21, 31 – 5, (Mt. 12.46 – 50/Lk. 8.19 – 21) and Mk 6.1 – 6 and parallels. Both are passing remarks, and thus we see that the Evangelists are not compelled either by controversy or personal interest to develop a fuller picture of Mary. Probably this reflects the fact that Mary was not a prominent influence in Jesus' earthly ministry. What references we do have refer also to Jesus' brothers and sisters, and therefore we will deal with the question of whether or not these are Mary's children.

Mark 3.19b – 21 is set in the context of Jesus' exorcisms (7 – 12) and the Beelzebub controversy (22 – 30). The references to Jesus'

91

family seem to serve as a frame for His teaching on Satan as well as a setting for Jesus' word about His true relatives. Mark has combined two (or three) originally separate narratives into an effective unit with three accusations and three answers. Of the material in 3.20–1, Taylor says, "The narrative is based on the best historical tradition. No one has the hardihood to suggest that it is a creation of the [Christian] community, for without the warrant of fact no early narrator would have alleged that the family at Nazareth thought that Jesus was beside Himself and went out to restrain him."[1] A similar judgment should be pronounced on 3.31–5 even if it should prove to be at one time a narrative independent of 3.20–1, for the contrast between Jesus' physical and spiritual family is not likely to be a creation of the post-Easter community.

Mark probably intended the phrase "those from among his people" to be explained in verse 31 ("his mother and his brothers"), since he uses "those *around* him" to refer to the disciples. It is interesting that recent Catholic scholars agree with this interpretation, but either do not see this entire group as the subject of the verb "they said" in verse 21, or say that the subject is indefinite. This is unlikely because when one has a plural subject in the immediate context, it is natural for it to be related to this plural verb.

The purpose of the family's action is made clear in the Marcan account: Mary and the brothers have gone to seize Him because they thought He was "beside himself" or not in control of His situation. At the least, verses 20–1 indicate that Mary and Jesus' brothers misunderstood His mission and ministry at this point. Further, the way Jesus contrasts His physical and spiritual family in verses 31–5 implies that the former group is not the same as the latter. Jesus' disciples are sitting and surrounding Him while His physical family stands outside the crowd. It is of the *disciples* that Jesus says, "Behold my mother, brothers, sisters." The point is that there are some among those sitting who are, or are more nearly, His spiritual kin at this point than His family outside. In its Marcan context, this contrast would have little force if Jesus' family did not share the opinion expressed by those who were saying "he is beside himself." Thus, in the first two Gospels someone other than Mary is identified, at least hypothetically, by Jesus as His spiritual mother.

Neither the Matthean nor the Lucan parallels are as strong in tone as Mark. Neither includes Mk 3.21 and thus Jesus' family is spared at this point. The door is left open, however, for Jesus' physical family to join His spiritual family, even in Mark – "Whoever does the will of God" will belong to His spiritual family (Mk 3.35, Mt. 12.50, Lk. 8.21). Mark did not want his readers to identify with the relatives of Jesus since they misunderstood His mission. Thus, his plan in this passage is to reveal the nature of true kinship.

Mk 3.20 – 1 also indicates that whether or not Mary led the efforts to seize Jesus, at the very least her faith was not strong enough to resist her own protective instinct or the determination of the others. There may be reflected a concern for Jesus' person by His family, but it is due to a serious misunderstanding of what He was doing, and leads them to think that He is not properly caring for Himself.

In Mk 3.31 – 5 and parallels, Jesus does not agree to His family's request for an audience, but whether or not He knew their intention is unclear from the text. The pronouncement which closes this story, even in its Marcan form, leaves the door open for the inclusion of His physical family within the family of faith at some future time if they will relate to Him on the basis of faith as His disciples.

He went away from there and came to his own country; and his disciples followed him. (2) And on the sabbath he began to teach in the synagogue; and many who heard him were astonished, saying, "Where did this man get all this? What is the wisdom given to him? What mighty works are wrought by his hands! (3) Is not this the carpenter, the son of Mary and brother of James and Joses and Judas and Simon, and are not his sisters here with us?" And they took offense at him. (4) And Jesus said to them, "A prophet is not without honor, except in his own country, and among his own kin, and in his own house." (5) And he could do no mighty work there, except that he laid his hands upon a few sick people and healed them. (6) And he marveled because of their unbelief. And he went about among the villages teaching.   (Mk 6.1 – 6)

Mk 6.1 – 6 (Mt. 13.53 – 8; see also Lk. 4.16 – 30) is another text which requires close scrutiny as we examine the Gospel tradition about Mary. It is hard to imagine the early Church inventing, for example, the reference to Jesus' relatives in verse 4 (which was insulting to some who later came to be prominent in the Church), and the designation of Jesus as "son of Mary." The Marcan form of the tradition then probably preserves material of real historical value.

In Mk 6.1 – 6, the family of Jesus is not present; however, they are mentioned first by Jesus' listeners and then by Jesus Himself. What connects this passage with Mk 3.21, 31 – 5 and parallels is the idea that physical relationships or knowledge of Jesus' physical relations proves to be a stumbling block to seeing Jesus as He truly is. There is also a connection in that Jesus places His relatives and His own household once again in a category other than that of believer or disciple.

Mk 6.3 and its parallel in Mt. 13.55 – 6 are of prime concern. The original form of the saying is likely to be found in Mark's version and reads, ''The carpenter, the son of Mary.'' This reading is best for the following reasons. First, calling Jesus a carpenter would not be seen as demeaning to a Jewish or early Christian audience familiar with the Jews' high estimation of manual labor, while it might be to a later Hellenistic or Roman audience. Thus, this reading could be the earlier form of the two. Secondly, the reference to Jesus as ''son of Mary'' may reflect a setting of controversy and an insult would be implied by this phrase. Thus, the First Evangelist may have changed this phrase because of its negative connotations. Thirdly, if the phrase ''son of Mary'' is original to Mark, then it reveals one of the reasons why Jesus' wise words were not received. How could a child of undistinguished or dubious origins be able to interpret the Torah accurately? It is Mark alone who records that Jesus placed His own family in the group with those who stumbled over His apparently ordinary or mysterious origins. It is difficult to believe that Mark would record such statements if they had no basis in fact, especially with the Church's tendency to revere the family of Jesus after His death.

Mk 6.3 and Mt. 13.55 are the only references in the Gospels where Jesus' brothers are mentioned by name. Traditionally, there have been three main views concerning the relation of these brothers and sisters to Jesus, to which have been added various modifications. The Helvidian view says that they were Jesus' actual brothers, being the children of Mary and Joseph after Jesus' birth. The view most widely held in the Western Church is that of St Jerome, first put forth in a treatise against Helvidius in A.D. 382. He asserts that the Lord's brethren are cousins, being the children of Mary's sister. The third view, proposed by Epiphanius in A.D. 376 – 7, holds that the brothers

94

of Jesus were children of Joseph by a previous marriage. This latter view drew on certain statements in earlier apocryphal Christian documents but was fully presented first by Epiphanius himself. All were formulated in their more or less final states between A.D. 375 and 385. In this book we will support the Helvidian view. As Taylor says, "It may also be fairly argued ... that the expressions used in Lk. ii.7 and Mt. i.25 would have been avoided by writers who believed in the perpetual virginity of Mary."[2]

How does accepting the Helvidian view affect our understanding of Mary and her role? It reveals her as a normal Jewish mother who saw her blessedness primarily in bearing children and in raising them properly. It also reveals that she was perhaps subject to the unbeliefs or misunderstandings about Jesus that her other children held. Mk 3.21, 31–5 reveals both her natural concern for and her misunderstanding of Jesus. Mark, and to a lesser degree Matthew and Luke, portray Mary during the ministry as an example of how kinship ties can hinder proper understanding of Jesus as Messiah. They also show that Mary was fully human and struggled with the difficulties of placing her spiritual allegiance to Jesus over her motherly love for Him and her other sons and daughters. In this she may be seen as a point of contact for other married women in the Gospel writers' audiences.

Mary at the cross – Jn 19.25 – 7

But standing by the cross of Jesus were his mother, and his mother's sister, Mary the wife of Clopas, and Mary Magdalene. (26) When Jesus saw his mother, and the disciple whom he loved standing near, he said to his mother, "Woman, behold, your son!" (27) Then he said to the disciple, "Behold, your mother!" And from that hour the disciple took her to his own home.

We have here a scene of which there is no trace in the Synoptic material. If Luke had known the story, he probably would have used it, for Acts 1.14 shows that he had some interest in whether or not Jesus' mother became a member of Jesus' community. Again, the scene with women standing *near* the cross seems to flatly contradict the Synoptic account and some have argued that the location is historically improbable. Then, too, the historicity of this incident is in part bound up with the question of whether or not the beloved disciple was an historical figure. Finally, the list of women differs from those found in the Synoptics, both in its names and in its position, and it is of particular importance that only the Fourth Evangelist includes Jesus' mother in the list.

These historical problems are basically solved *if*: (1) verse 25 is a traditional list to which the Evangelist added a narrative found in his sources; (2) originally the narrative in verses 26–7 was about Jesus providing ongoing care for His mother – a motif probably based on historical fact; (3) the Evangelist has transformed his material into a powerful statement about men and women as disciples at the foot of the cross and has used it as a vehicle to affirm the historical truth that at some point (not necessarily at the cross) Mary became a full-fledged disciple of her Son. There will be no attempt here to claim historical value for more than the substratum which the Evangelist used in writing his narrative, i.e. Mary's presence at the cross and in the Church, and Jesus' provision for Mary.

The story of Mary witnessing her Son's crucifixion should probably be seen as the climactic episode of the Passion narrative. Drawing on elements presented in Jn 2.1–12 (mother of Jesus, woman, the hour, physical family, disciples), the Evangelist presents the resolution of the tension or division between Jesus' physical family and His spiritual family in the context of Jesus' "hour." In Jn 19.25 we read of Jesus' mother standing near the cross with three other women. In the Johannine schema here is the point at which Jesus could not reject His mother's claims. His "hour" had come, and so too had hers in a different sense.

From among these four women, the Evangelist shows Jesus singling out His mother and addressing her as at Cana – "Woman." This time, however, the intention is not disengagement, but rather engagement or unification. The Evangelist wishes to show that Mary is accepted officially into Jesus' spiritual family, yet she is still addressed as "Woman," the same address used in Jn 2.1–12. Where is the point of similarity in these two narratives that warrants such an address? One would have expected the Evangelist to portray Jesus as using a more intimate term to address His mother in her anguish and sorrow. Perhaps the Evangelist is indicating the following: Jesus resolves for Mary the tension between her roles as mother and disciple of Jesus. He is in control of this scene, and He alone speaks and calls His mother "Woman" precisely because He does not wish to renew the filial bond, but rather to confirm her in her relationship to Him as disciple. As she loses Jesus both in a physical and spiritual sense, she gains a new family, the beloved disciple being her first "son" in the faith. She does not cease to be a mother; however, at Jesus' hour she becomes a mother of a different sort and joins with the family of faith.

Mary learns that she is to be a mother as a disciple, not a mother and also a disciple. Discipleship must be the larger context in which her role as mother is delimited and defined. Mary responds in silence and submission. She obeys the word of the Lord and goes with the beloved disciple. In so doing she is the model woman – a testimony to a woman's new freedom in faith and also to a woman's traditional roles of serving under the authority and headship of man. She is now under the charge of her new "son." This is reflected in the fact that, though John is first commended to her, she does not take charge but rather is received into the charge of the beloved disciple.

It is not without reason that Jesus calls her "Woman." She must enter the family of faith in full recognition of who she is as a sexual being. She will not lose that sexuality for some spirituality in the community of belief. Rather, she will assume both her old role of motherhood and her new roles as witness, prophetess, and proclaimer of God's word in relationship to believers. She will orientate her physical nature so as to engender and further the growth of Jesus' true kindred. In this, she is like the many other women who followed Jesus, being liberated by God's word, and serving Jesus and the Twelve in their traditional roles. This is the Evangelist's theological message. Perhaps Stauffer is closer to the historical truth in this matter when he suggests that Mary needed someone to provide for her after Jesus' death: "Jesus knew this. And a crucified man had the right to make testamentary dispositions even from the cross. Now Jesus took advantage of this right, and, using the formal language of Jewish family law, he placed his mother under the protection of John: 'Woman, behold your son!' And to the disciple: 'Behold your mother!'"[3]

In Jn 19.25 – 7, the Church is re-established in unity. Jesus unites His own family with the family of faith and gives them a home which is the home of the one faithful disciple. The "into his own" (home) in Jn 19.26 – 7 represents the Church gathered, in contrast to Jn 16.32, where the disciples are forewarned they will be scattered due to the events leading up to Jesus' death.

The Evangelist intends the scene to be balanced between attention given to the beloved disciple and attention given to Jesus' mother. Both are addressed and both receive a commission. While Mary's importance stands out here (she is addressed first and her future is considered at the end of verse 17), and it may be significant that the beloved disciple is only referred to as a son of Mary (while Mary is addressed as "Woman" and referred to as mother of this disciple), throughout this scene only the beloved disciple is called "the disciple" and it is he who takes charge of Jesus' mother at the close of this scene. It should be emphasized that this disciple's faith and his role as representative disciple antedate Mary's role as spiritual mother. Thus, Mary is not depicted here as the mother of the Church, but as a spiritual mother to and in the Church. Raymond Brown says, "Initially, it is significant that the scene brings together two figures for whom John never gives us personal names. That may mean that the significance of both figures lay in their respective roles."[4] It also means that the Evangelist's focus is on these two persons as models or types. Not Mary alone, but both Mary and the beloved disciple are in a sense a foreshadowing of the Church, standing beneath the cross of their Lord.

It is to be noted that Mary and the beloved disciple are depicted as representative male and female disciples. Jesus does not refer to them as "sister" and "brother." This is a scene about the new equality of male and female beneath the cross of Jesus, but the way that equality is expressed is by the woman resuming her role as mother with new significance, and the disciple becoming a son. In this scene then, the tension between physical family and the family of faith is resolved as Mary is included in the fold. Further, the tension between traditional roles and the role of disciple is resolved as the representative disciple becomes a son again, and Mary a mother. The Fourth Evangelist's vision of male – female equality in the Christian community entails an incorporation of physical family roles in light of the priorities of the family of faith. Thus, the new community is served rather than severed by traditional roles and relationships.

...rself, that is, responding to the word in faith by placing

...e case of Jesus' relation to His mother Mary, we again ...ganizing of traditional priorities in light of Kingdom ...ts. Martha's service is not denigrated but it does not come ...must reorientate one's lifestyle according to what Jesus ..."good portion." It is this universal priority of faith and ...h faith that gives women a new and equal place under the ...nant. This is the radical nature of the Gospel and why it ...ally affected women's status especially in first-century ... Luke portrays Mary as a disciple sitting and learning at ...of her Master, and as such she serves as a model for his ...e. The appeals to a woman's traditional role, here voiced ...tha, do not prevail against the fact that women (like men) ...ed to be hearers and obeyers of Jesus' word first.

A confession and a proclamation – Jn 11.1–44

...certain man was ill, Lazarus of Bethany, the village of Mary and ...er Martha. It was Mary who anointed the Lord with ointment and ...his feet with her hair, whose brother Lazarus was ill. So the sisters ... him, saying, "Lord, he whom you love is ill." But when Jesus heard ...aid, "This illness is not unto death; it is for the glory of God, so that ...n of God may be glorified by means of it." Now Jesus loved Martha ...er sister and Lazarus. So when he heard that he was ill, he stayed two ...longer in the place where he was. Then after this he said to the disciples, ...t us go into Judea again." … Now when Jesus came, he found that ...arus had already been in the tomb four days. Bethany was near ...salem, about two miles off, and many of the Jews had come to Martha ... Mary to console them concerning their brother. When Martha heard ...t Jesus was coming, she went and met him, while Mary sat in the house. ...artha said to Jesus, "Lord, if you had been here, my brother would not ...ve died. And even now I know that whatever you ask from God, God ...ll give you." Jesus said to her, "Your brother will rise again." Martha ...id to him, "I know that he will rise again in the resurrection at the last ...ay." Jesus said to her, "I am the resurrection and the life; he who believes ...n me, though he die, yet shall he live, and whoever lives and believes in ...e shall never die. Do you believe this?" She said to him, "Yes, Lord; ...I believe that you are the Christ, the Son of God, he who is coming into ...the world." When she had said this, she went and called her sister Mary,

The mother of Jesus is seen as the typical female disciple who struggles with the relationship of her physical and spiritual roles. She is depicted as a spiritual mother to and in the Church, though not as Mother Church that gives birth to spiritual children, since the beloved disciple's faith antedates Mary's role as spiritual mother. If this assessment of Mary as a symbol of "woman" in her new relationship to the community of faith is correct, then it appears to be part of the plan of the Fourth Evangelist to show that in Christ the dignity of woman is restored and her place of equality affirmed. Especially significant is that Jesus' mother typifies the traditional role of mother and that she is the symbol of woman in her new roles as spiritual mother and disciple. The Evangelist is indicating that her two types of roles, once confused, are now fused under the cross of Jesus, in service of His community, typified by the beloved disciple.

Having achieved the reconciliation of the physical family and the family of faith, of male and female, the Evangelist intimates that Jesus has accomplished the work the Father had given him (Jn 19.28). The Fourth Evangelist saw in the material he drew upon a great deal more than Jesus' act of filial piety. He saw in it an example of male and female standing as equals (though with different roles) beneath the cross of Christ.

Mary and Martha

Though it is doubtful that they traveled with Jesus, Mary and Martha may have been the most important and prominent women in Jesus' life after His own mother. The Gospels give us three accounts of how these women figured in Jesus' life – Lk. 10.38–42, Jn 11.1–44 and Jn 12.1–11.

Hosts or guests? – Lk. 10.38–42

Now as they went on their way, he entered a village; and a woman named Martha received him into her house. And she had a sister called Mary, who sat at the Lord's feet and listened to his teaching. But Martha was distracted with much serving; and she went to him and said, "Lord, do you not care that my sister has left me to serve alone? Tell her then to help me.'' But the Lord answered her, ''Martha, Martha, you are anxious and troubled about many things; one thing is needful. Mary has chosen the good portion, which shall not be taken away from her.''

This unique Synoptic passage on Mary and Martha raises the question whether this scene is an ''ideal'' or whether it contains good, historical tradition. The characterization of Mary and Martha is neither highly embellished nor detailed, rather it involves a simple contrast in activities and attitudes.[5] Secondly, in view of the uniqueness both of Mary's activity and of Jesus' attitude about it when compared to Jewish attitudes about women disciples and their proper role in the home and later attitudes in the Church about a woman's place and role in the Christian community and family (e.g. 1 Tim. 2.9–15), it is most unlikely that this scene is an ''ideal'' construction. Thus, this story has a sound basis in historical fact, even though Luke has presented the narrative in his own language and style.

Martha appears to be the older sister and the mistress of the house, for she ''opens her home to him.'' It is she who takes charge of preparing for the guest and she feels she has a right to her sister's assistance. Though this story focuses on Martha and what she must learn about ''the one thing necessary,'' Mary appears to know already, for she ''was listening to his word.'' Contrary to what some commentators have asserted, Mary is not sitting at her Master's feet at the table; here the meal is clearly yet to come. The use of the phrase ''to sit at the feet of'' is significant since evidence shows this is a technical formula meaning ''to be a disciple of.'' If so, then Luke is intimating that Mary is a disciple and as such her behavior is to be emulated. Though we previously mentioned that women could attend synagogue, learn, and even be learned if their husbands or masters were rabbis, for a rabbi to come into a woman's house and teach her specifically is unknown. Further, being alone with two women who were not one's relatives was considered questionable behavior by the rabbis. Thus, not only the role Mary assumes, but also the teaching task Jesus performs is in contrast to what was expected of a Jewish man and woman.

While Mary is taking on the not so traditional role of disciple,

Martha is engaged in what providing hospitality for her women were not allowed to se there were no servants to perfor behavior is atypical and reflect Jesus, even if it meant assuming because she resents not receivin envies Mary's ''portion,'' is ''dis Rather than quietly serving withou by accusing Jesus of not caring, a neglecting her when she needed h

Jesus does not respond as Ma however, are neither an attempt t hospitality, nor an attempt to attack rather, Jesus defends Mary's right to is the crucial thing for those who wish clear that for women as well as men, o proper disciple; only in that context can address to Martha shows a recognition tha ''many things.'' Such things as even on must be seen as of lesser importance, inde ordinate category, to the responsibility of being Jesus' disciple.

Unfortunately, the rest of Jesus' response of this story, is clouded with large textual no less than six possibilities for the text of Lk. the short reading translated ''but one thing is has the edge on the basis of manuscript sup Luke's story. It is one thing (''the good portio ing and learning, that He is defending. It is n trasting the active to the contemplative life; ra of contrasting the importance of listening to word of God to anything else. We are dealing priorities and only one thing can come first a necessary.

Jesus did not come to be served, but to serve. He Mary and Martha are the guests. Mary has just rece portion'' and this is something that the Evangelist in

saying quietly, "The Teacher is here and is calling for you." And when she heard it, she rose quickly and went to him. Now Jesus had not yet come to the village, but was still in the place where Martha had met him. When the Jews who were with her in the house, consoling her, saw Mary rise quickly and go out, they followed her, supposing that she was going to the tomb to weep there. Then Mary, when she came where Jesus was and saw him, fell at his feet, saying to him, "Lord, if you had been here, my brother would not have died." When Jesus saw her weeping, and the Jews who came with her also weeping, he was deeply moved in spirit and troubled; and he said, "Where have you laid him?" They said to him, "Lord, come and see." Jesus wept. So the Jews said, "See how he loved him!" But some of them said, "Could not he who opened the eyes of the blind man have kept this man from dying?" Then Jesus, deeply moved again, came to the tomb; it was a cave, and a stone lay upon it. Jesus said, "Take away the stone." Martha, the sister of the dead man, said to him, "Lord, by this time there will be an odor, for he has been dead four days." Jesus said to her, "Did I not tell you that if you would believe you would see the glory of God?" So they took away the stone. And Jesus lifted up his eyes and said, "Father, I thank thee that thou hast heard me. I know that thou hearest me always, but I have said this on account of the people standing by, that they may believe that thou didst send me." When he had said this, he cried with a loud voice, "Lazarus, come out." The dead man came out, his hands and feet bound with bandages, and his face wrapped with a cloth. Jesus said to them, "Unbind him, and let him go."

Few would dispute the fact that the story of the raising of Lazarus raises more problems than almost any other miracle recorded in the Gospels for the student of history. It is not possible to adequately deal with all the difficulties this narrative poses; thus, only a few points will be made. First, John probably had a source of information about Mary (and Martha?) other than the Synoptics. Secondly, it is believable that even if the other Gospel writers knew of the narrative, they could have chosen to omit it and include another raising story since theirs are, after all, a selective presentation of Gospel events. Thirdly, there are certain features in the story that point toward its basic authenticity. For instance, the characterization of Martha and in some respects Mary comports with Lk. 10, while probably being independent of the Lucan material. Further, Martha's faith in Jesus is not a full-blown Christian faith, but "her faith in his power is faith in the power of his prayer."[6] Finally, Martha's statement in verse 24 simply expresses a common Jewish idea about resurrection; there is nothing particularly Christian about it. Perhaps with Raymond Brown we may conclude: "From the contents of the Johannine account then, there is no conclusive reason for assuming that the skeleton of the story does not stem from early tradition about Jesus."[7] Thus, it seems reasonable to assign the characterization of Mary and Martha, the idea that Martha made a rudimentary confession of a Jewish belief in resurrection and in Jesus as Messiah, the self-proclamation of Jesus as a life-giving source, and the general encounter of Jesus with the grieving sisters to a real situation in the life of Jesus. And that is all of the historical substance of this narrative that concerns us here. Comments on the rest of the narrative will only involve discussing the Evangelist's own views and theology.

Jn 11.1–44 is the longest continuous narrative in the Fourth Gospel apart from the Passion narrative. In the Johannine schema of things it is the climactic and most miraculous episode in the series of signs he presents. In many ways this story parallels the first sign in Jn 2 and serves to bring together and reemphasize some of John's chief themes. The message Mary and Martha send in 11.3 is similar to the open-ended suggestion of Jesus' mother in 2.3. Further, Martha's remark in 11.22 about "whatever you ask" resembles Mary's statement in 2.5. In both scenes, the hope is implied that Jesus will act despite the seeming impossibility of the situations. It is fitting that verse 40 mentions glory, for this also relates back to the Cana miracle (2.11) and forward to the climax of this Gospel.

In this story, as in Jn 2 and Jn 7, Jesus can only act as the Father wills, not at the request of His mother, sisters, brothers, or friends. This causes the delay in Jesus going to Bethany. It is this fact that explains why He seems to reject mother Mary's request and the plea of Mary and Martha, and then in fact responds as if He had not rejected their suggestion. As the best is saved for last in Jn 2, so in the Gospel as a whole the best miracle is saved for last. In Jn 2, Jesus comes and brings new life and joy to the celebration of the union of two lives; in John 11 He brings new life and reunion to a family He dearly loved. Finally, both narratives involve women whom the Evangelist portrays as being in the process of learning Jesus' true nature and becoming His true disciples. For Mary and Martha and mother Mary there is perhaps knowledge of and belief in Jesus and

His miracle-working power, but in both cases this knowledge and faith is insufficient. They do not realize that Jesus is able to bring life because He is the Resurrection and the Life.

Realizing that Lazarus is the object and Jesus the subject of this story, it is interesting to note that Mary and Martha play a more prominent part than their brother. The factors in this narrative important to this study are not the emotions Mary and Martha express, but the way the Evangelist portrays these women, the confession of faith by Martha, and Jesus' proclamation to Martha.

The character portrayals of Mary and Martha in Jn 11 are on the whole true to the portrayals we saw earlier in Lk. 10.38 – 42. Both women are devoted to Jesus and are close friends whom He loved and visited on more than one occasion. *Martha* appears to be the elder sister and the hostess of the home. She is clearly the more out-going, thus it is she who goes out to meet Jesus first. Martha's outspokenness, which gives us more knowledge of her than we have of Mary, makes her appear to have less faith and understanding. The Evangelist portrays *Mary* as a woman of great devotion. She is always at her Master's feet whether to revere (11.32) or to anoint (12.3). In 11.2 Mary is described as ''the one who anointed the Lord with perfume and wiped his feet with her hair.'' This act reminds John's audience of Mary, thus the story in 12.1 – 8 must be based on well-known tradition.

The statement that Jesus loved Martha, Mary, and Lazarus is perhaps more significant than it first appears. Note that the order of the names (two women, then Lazarus) is unusual. Perhaps these women were closer to Jesus than Lazarus was, or were more prominent than Lazarus in the eyes of the Evangelists. It is pointed out frequently that Lazarus is the only male in the Fourth Gospel who is named as the object of Jesus' love (11.3, 5), but what is overlooked is that Martha and Mary are the only women so mentioned by name. It seems the Evangelist is implying that these women and Lazarus were disciples of Jesus; and that there were women prominent among the disciples even during Jesus' earthly ministry.

The Evangelist portrays Martha as one who sincerely believes Jesus and has faith in His power, for she says, ''I know even now God will give you whatever you ask'' (verse 22). This does not imply that she believes Jesus can or will raise her brother since her confession of faith does not go beyond the orthodox Pharisaic view of resurrection on the last day, and since her later comment (11.39) makes probable she still does not expect Jesus to raise Lazarus. Brown's summary about Martha's faith seems accurate:

Throughout the incident involving Martha we see that she believes in Jesus but inadequately. In vs 27 she addresses him with lofty titles, probably the same titles used in early Christian professions of faith; yet 39 shows that she does not as yet believe in his power to give life. She regards Jesus as an intermediary who is heard by God (22), but she does not understand that he is life itself (25).[8]

What is the Evangelist trying to convey by having Martha confess, "I believe that you are the Christ, the Son of God, the one coming into the world" (11.27)? Note its similarity to the confession of Peter (especially as found in Mt. 16.16). Perhaps it can be said that Martha's confession is the most adequate to this point in the Fourth Gospel. Certainly, it is more adequate than the Samaritan woman's hopeful question (4.29), or her affirmation that the Messiah will come into the world (compare 4.25 to 11.27). Ironically, Martha's confession is also a fuller and perhaps more satisfactory statement than the Petrine confession in Jn 6.68 – 9. It is possible that the Evangelist has constructed his Gospel so that alongside the crescendo of the miraculous, we have a crescendo of confessions. If so, Martha's confession takes on new importance because of its place in the climactic episode of the series of signs.

Perhaps a further indication of the importance of Martha is that she receives a revelation from Jesus about Himself that prompts the confession in 11.27. By giving his audience a story in which a woman is the recipient of one of Jesus' most profound and direct statements about Himself, and in which a woman makes a heartfelt and accurate response to Jesus' declaration, the Fourth Evangelist intimates that women have a right to be taught even the mysteries of the faith, and that they are capable of responding in faith with an accurate confession. In short, they are capable of being fully fledged disciples of Jesus.

In this story, the portrait of Mary is not favorable. In her audience with Jesus she makes the same initial remarks as Martha (11.21, 32), though probably this is not so much a complaint as a statement of loss and grief. She makes no confession, and her wailing in Jesus' presence suggests an attitude of hopelessness and lack of trust in Him. This must be balanced against the hint in 11.3 that both Mary and Martha had enough faith to believe that only Jesus could deal with their drastic situation.

In conclusion we have in Jn 11 not an idealized portrait of two women disciples, but one that indicates women are capable of faith and an accurate confession, and are worthy recipients of the teaching of Jesus about Himself. Martha's confession (11.27), even if only a rudimentary expression of certain conventional expectations coupled with a belief that Jesus was the one who had been sent to fulfil those expectations, is noteworthy. In its present form the confession rivals and resembles the great Petrine confession (Mt. 16.16 and parallels). By placing it on Martha's lips, the Evangelist makes his own statement about the ability of women to be exemplary Christians. It is also true that the Evangelist portrays Martha as having her bad moments when she so misunderstands Jesus and His intentions that she questions His reasons for having the stone rolled away. Finally, Mary is presented as one who has given herself over wrongly to an all-consuming sorrow even in Jesus' presence, though she too has faith, and the Evangelist indicates (11.2) that she will yet honor Jesus by anointing Him (12.1–8).

Another anointing – Mk 14.3–9 (Mt. 26.6–13, Jn 12.1–8)

And while he was at Bethany in the house of Simon the leper, as he sat at table, a woman came with an alabaster flask of ointment of pure nard, very costly, and she broke the flask and poured it over his head. But there were some who said to themselves indignantly, "Why was the ointment thus wasted? For this ointment might have been sold for more than three hundred *denarii*, and given to the poor." And they reproached her. But Jesus said, "Let her alone; why do you trouble her? She has done a beautiful thing to me. For you always have the poor with you, and whenever you will, you can do good to them; but you will not always have me. She has done what she could; she has anointed my body beforehand for burying. And truly, I say to you, wherever the gospel is preached in the whole world, what she has done will be told in memory of her."

This book endorses the view that the Lucan anointing story (7.36 – 50) is not the same as that found in Mk 14.3 – 9 and parallels, and we are justified in treating the latter as a separate story. It seems clear that Mk 14.3 – 9 rests on good tradition. The placing of this episode before the triumphal entry in John seems historically more likely than Mark's position, which may be located next to the Lord's Supper narrative for theological reasons. Probably the account in the Fourth Gospel is independent of the one in the Synoptics because there seems to be no compelling reason why the Fourth Evangelist would have altered the Marcan account if he knew of it. This leads to the suggestion that the two Gospels are reporting, independently of each other, two different versions of one sequence of events.

What then are we to make of the personal references unique to the Johannine account (Mary, Martha, Lazarus, Judas)? If the Fourth Gospel's account is independent of the Synoptics, it is perhaps likely that the names are original, for Jn 11.2 seems to indicate that the association of Mary with the anointing was already known to his audience (and thus went back to tradition that preceded the Fourth Gospel). In the Canonical Gospel tradition there is no definite trend to add names at the later stages of the tradition, the reverse was just as common. Thus, it would appear that the Fourth Evangelist presents, in most regards, a form of this anointing story that is closer to the original than Mark's generalized account.

The characterization of Martha and Mary in Jn 12 comports well with the Lucan portrayal. There is one noticeable difference, however, between the portrayal of Martha in Lk. 10 and Jn 12. In Jn 12 there are no complaints by Martha and no hint of a rebuke to Martha – she serves quietly. Thus, we may see the process of liberation and Christian service expressed in Martha's life for she is performing the functions a free servant or slave would perform at an all male feast. She apparently violates certain rules of Jewish practice in order to take on the role of servant and show love to her Master for what He has done for her and her family. Liberty in Christ is not only freedom from customs which restrict love, but also freedom to take a lower place, to humble oneself to serve.

Mary also may be taking on the role of servant when she anoints Jesus. There were many reasons for anointing in a Jewish context. As Lk. 7.46 implies, anointing with oil was not of the same order or purpose as anointing with perfume, especially fragrant and expensive perfume. The latter was reserved either for burial rites, or for cosmetic or romantic purposes in small quantities. What Mary poured on Jesus' feet is not oil, but perfume, nard being a well-known Eastern ointment with a potent fragrance. The Fourth Evangelist, perhaps with deliberate exaggeration to indicate that this is an act of complete devotion, says Mary used about a pound of nard, a very large amount considering the perfume's worth. It is not true that anointing of the feet is unknown in antiquity. Athenaeus tells us of a man having a female slave smear his feet with perfume. Though it may not be common practice, cases can be cited where the rabbis allowed a person to anoint their own feet, and in some places women could anoint rabbis. Thus, the possibility that Mary anointed Jesus' feet, especially if this was originally intended as an act of humble devotion, should not be dismissed.

A plausible explanation of Mary's act of wiping Jesus' feet with her hair might be found in the custom of wiping one's hands on the head or hair of a servant if the hands had excess oil or water on them at dinnertime. Mary could have used her hair to wipe off the excess perfume as she had seen servants do in the past. In a Jewish context, however, for a woman to let down her hair in the presence of unrelated men was scandalous. It is easy to see why Mark would change the anointing of the feet to an anointing of the head to emphasize Jesus' royal nature and role. It is not easy to explain the change to the feet if the anointing of the head was original.

In all three narratives the motive of the woman (unnamed in the Synoptics) appears to be devotional. In all three Gospels, Jesus interprets the act in relation to His burial. In Matthew and Mark it is evident that the act is seen as a prophetic anointing for Jesus' burial, thus she may be assuming the role normally performed by a prophet. In Mark and Matthew the act is described as a beautiful deed – which may indicate to the Evangelists' audiences that such extravagant devotion should be seen as an example for all disciples.

Jesus' response to the objection that Mary's extravagant act has wasted about a year's wages of a day-laborer is problematic in the Fourth Gospel. In Mark it seems clear that the sense is "Leave her alone." The correct translation of the Johannine verse seems to be "Let her alone; let her keep it." As C. K. Barrett has pointed out, it is most unlikely that John means "to retain" the ointment since the whole house is filled with the smell and Judas is indignant at the extravagance. Thus, it seems probable that "let her keep it" means "Let her observe it [the rite] now as though it were [i.e. with a view to] the day of my burial preparation."[9] The Fourth Evangelist then in essence is saying the same as the First and Second. If this translation is correct, then the implication is that Jesus prophetically sees that Mary will not have an opportunity to prepare Him for burial later, and thus she is allowed to have the opportunity now.

The first two Evangelists close their presentation of the anointing with the remark, "Truly I say to you, wherever the Gospel is preached throughout the world, what she has done will also be told in memory of her." This saying sets up this woman as an example for all time. The Fourth Evangelist gives evidence in 11.2 that those words were coming true already when he describes Mary as the one who anointed Jesus.

Women who followed Jesus

On the road with women disciples – Lk 8.1–3

Soon afterward he went on through cities and villages, preaching and bringing the good news of the kingdom of God. And the twelve were with him, and also some women who had been healed of evil spirits and infirmities: Mary, called Magdalene, from whom seven demons had gone out, and Joanna, the wife of Chuza, Herod's steward, and Susanna, and many others, who provided for them out of their means.

Lk. 8.1–3 is near the middle of a series of stories that make special reference to women. The list of women could be traditional and does not appear to be derived from Mark's list (15.40). Possibly, Luke himself has added the names of Joanna and/or Susanna as a result of personal knowledge or from a well-informed Palestinian source. There is little reason to question the authenticity of the information that women traveled with and served Jesus and the disciples since this conduct was unheard of and considered scandalous in Jewish circles. It is unlikely to have been invented by a Christian community which contained converted Jews and which did not wish to appear morally suspect to a Mediterranean world that was already sexually and morally indulgent.

Lk. 8.1 – 3 stands in contrast to its historical context in early Judaism in other regards as well. We know women were allowed to hear the word of God in the synagogue but they were never disciples of a rabbi unless their husband or master was a rabbi willing to teach them. Though a woman might be taught certain negative precepts of the Law out of necessity, this did not mean they would be taught the meaning of Torah. Yet it was apparently an intended part of Jesus' ministry for women to benefit from His teaching (Lk. 10.38 – 42) and healing.

While Jesus rejects much of Jewish teaching on women's ''flightiness,'' inferior nature, and monthly ritual uncleanness, this does not mean he abrogated all sexual, social, or creation order distinctions recognized under the old covenant. Indeed, it seems rather clear that He affirmed the headship and authority of the man when He chose Twelve men from among His disciples to be leaders of the community. Jesus broke with Jewish tradition in having women disciples and traveling companions, and there is no reason why He could not have continued this revolutionary trend by choosing some women to be among the Twelve. It appears then that male headship as a pattern of leadership, if refined and redefined according to the dictates of discipleship and Jesus' example, was acceptable to Him. Jesus' choice of Twelve men to be His special companions and to receive special teaching, and the fact that He recommissioned these men after the Resurrection to be leaders of His community is inexplicable on the supposition that Jesus was a ''feminist,'' i.e. one who rejects a patriarchal framework outright. Such a person would have felt it necessary to include at least one woman among the Twelve.

The first woman mentioned, Mary Magdalene, is the best known among these women, possibly because her healing was the most dramatic, i.e. seven demons indicates an extraordinary situation. She, and apparently the others mentioned, were living proof of the Gospel's power. Mary of Magdala is commonly placed first when listed with other women (Mt. 27.56, 61, 28.1, Mk 15.40, 47, 16.1, Lk. 24.10). She is undoubtedly important, and Luke wishes to mention her so her special devotion and witness in the Resurrection narrative (Lk. 24) will be seen as the proclamation of someone who has long been one of Jesus' disciples. Similarly, Joanna is a long-standing disciple, present with Mary at the tomb and the upper room, and thereafter bearing witness. She is very unlike Mary of Magdala who came from a small town and was undoubtedly avoided by many until Jesus healed her. Joanna is the wife of Chuza who managed Herod's estate. Thus, she was a woman of some means and prominence. What is especially note-worthy about her presence among Jesus' followers is that apparently she had left her home and family to become a follower and traveling companion of Jesus. Here Luke gives evidence of how the Gospel breaks down class and economic divisions, as well as social barriers, and reconciles men and women from all walks of life into one community. The third woman, Susanna, though perhaps known to Luke's audience, is unknown to us and is not mentioned elsewhere in the Gospel.

Luke intends for us to understand that these three women were only the most prominent among many other women that followed Jesus. Luke indicates that Jesus' actions on behalf of these women freed them to serve both Him and the disciples ''from out of their own means.'' Though it was uncommon or unknown for women to be traveling disciples of a rabbi, it was not uncommon for women to support rabbis and their disciples out of their own money, property, or foodstuffs. What is unique about the actions of Jesus' women followers is that the traditional roles of hospitality and service are seen by them as a way to serve not only the physical family but also the family of faith. Being Jesus' disciples did not lead these women to abandon their traditional roles in regard to preparing food, serving, etc. Rather, it gave these roles new significance and importance, for now they could be used to serve the Master and the family of faith. The transformation of these women involved not only assuming new discipleship roles, but also resuming their traditional roles for a new purpose.

Women at the cross – Mk 15.40 – 1 (Mt. 27.55 – 6, Lk. 23.49, Jn 19.25)

There were also women looking on from afar, among whom were Mary Magdalene, and Mary the mother of James the younger and of Joses, and

Salome, who, when he was in Galilee, followed him, and ministered to him; and also many other women who came up with him to Jerusalem.

(Mk 15.40 – 1)

There were also many women there, looking on from afar, who had followed Jesus from Galilee, ministering to him; among whom were Mary Magdalene, and Mary the mother of James and Joseph, and the mother of the sons of Zebedee.   (Mt. 27.55 – 6)

And all his acquaintances and the women who had followed him from Galilee stood at a distance and saw these things.   (Lk. 23.49)

But standing by the cross of Jesus were his mother, and his mother's sister, Mary the wife of Clopas, and Mary Magdalene.   (Jn 19.25)

To this point we have noted several trends or patterns in our examination of women. One of these involved a reversal of male – female roles or a reversal of expectations. Another pattern found almost exclusively in Luke and John involves presenting narratives so that certain women are revealed as being or becoming disciples (Jesus' mother, Martha and Mary, the women of Lk. 8.1 – 3). Perhaps the most surprising reversal was that Jesus' women friends and traveling companions, not the Twelve or even the Three, became the primary witnesses to the final events in Jesus' earthly career – the events surrounding His death.

The Passion narrative was one of the first pieces of tradition to become fixed in the course of transmission. Accordingly, few would doubt that the reporting by the Evangelists of the betrayal, failure, or desertion of Jesus' trained male leadership, the Twelve, during the crucial events of the last days of Jesus' ministry is historically accurate. It is not something that the post-Easter community was likely to invent. Thus, we will take it as an historical given that there was at least one disciple who betrayed Jesus (Judas), that there was one who denied him (Peter), and that the general desertion described in Mk 14.50 took place during those crucial events.

Apart from the beloved disciple, who represents the model male disciple (Jn 19.26 – 7), not one of Jesus' male followers performs any good acts during the events immediately prior to or during the Crucifixion. It is striking that the Evangelists portray various

113

non-disciples, both Jews and Gentiles, as assisting or in part accepting Jesus (Mk 15.21 and parallels, 15.42 – 7 and parallels, 15.39 and parallels; Lk. 23.40 – 3). Some of this material may be editorial, but it is not likely that all of it is, and it is the general pattern we are concerned with here – abandonment by the Twelve, help or devotion expressed by others (the women or non-disciples).

Even more striking is the fact that this pattern of doubt and desertion among the Twelve persisted even after the reports of Jesus' Resurrection reached them. Even in Luke, who is fond of male – female parallelism, we have a picture of the failure and disintegration of the trained male leadership during the crisis. The first have become last or even lost; and it speaks well for their faithfulness to history that the Evangelists, especially Luke, have not omitted or glossed over this fact. But what of the last and least among the believers? We will now examine Mk 15.40 – 1 and parallels.

In the Synoptics, the brief paragraph about women at the cross follows the proclamation of the centurion about Jesus. In John, it follows the story of the soldiers dividing Jesus' garments. Apparently, the women were not limited in number to those listed in Mark's account. Luke mentions in addition to the women ''all his acquaintances.'' Since it appears Luke is following Mark at this point, this phrase may be his attempt to create a male group of witnesses to parallel the females. Probably he means us to think of Jesus' friends in Jerusalem or His relatives. One would expect Luke to use the term ''the Apostles'' or ''the Twelve'' (now ''Eleven'') if he meant them.

In Mark, we have the following women listed: Mary Magdalene, Mary the mother of James the Little and Joses, and Salome; in Matthew: Mary Magdalene, Mary the mother of James and Joseph, and the mother of the sons of Zebedee. In Luke, we have no specific list; however, the Third Evangelist may have intended us to recall the list of those whom Jesus helped or healed in Lk. 8.1 – 3, or planned for the reader to find out their names in 24.10. The former is perhaps more probable since he says these women at the cross are those who followed Jesus from Galilee. In John, we appear to have four women listed: Jesus' mother, the sister of Jesus' mother, Mary of Clopas, and Mary of Magdala.

Even though the First Evangelist is almost certainly following Mark, it is not certain whether he has omitted Salome's name and replaced it with another, or if he identified Salome as the mother of the Zebedees. Again, while Mary of Clopas may be the mother of James and Joseph, it may also be that these are two different people and to simply assume their identity is excessively harmonistic. This is especially so if Mark is correct that there were "many other women" present. Luke, if he means us to refer back to 8.1 – 3 has the additional names of Joanna and Susanna. If he means us to refer to 24.10, then he probably adds but one name, Joanna, who was perhaps important to Luke as one of his sources of information. It is striking that all four Gospels agree in listing Mary of Magdala and it appears that Mk 15.40, Mt. 27.56, Lk. 24.10 share at least two names in common. The Fourth Evangelist has special reason to list Jesus' mother, and it is strange that she is omitted in the Synoptics if she was actually present. Nevertheless, we have argued previously that the reference to her in Jn 19.25 may well be historical, especially if Jn 19.27b is, and since some explanation must be given for her presence in the Church (see Acts 1.14). In any event, the mention of various women by name indicates their importance in the eyes of the Evangelists and early Church and argues strongly for the view that historically at least some of these women (Mary Magdalene and another Mary, not Jesus' mother) must have played a crucial role in the Passion and Resurrection events.

The Synoptic lists are arranged perhaps in order of importance or familiarity both in relation to the Gospel writer and to his audience. In every instance in the Gospels where women followers of Jesus are mentioned, Mary Magdalene's name is placed first (except in Jn 19.25 where there is a special interest in Jesus' mother). Mary Magdalene's first place was not only because of her loyalty to Jesus or notable service, but also (and perhaps primarily) because of her witness about the risen Lord. These particular lists of those at the Crucifixion may be more like that in 1 Cor. 15.5 – 8 than is sometimes thought. They may be lists of those who saw and witnessed about the risen Lord. Each of the Synoptic accounts refers to the fact that they witnessed the Crucifixion, and the First Evangelist and Mark refer to the women's service specifically to Jesus (see Mk 15.41, Mt. 27.55) a fact noted earlier in Lk. 8.3 (though there the Twelve are also among those served), and thus not repeated by Luke here. In addition, all three accounts speak of these women as followers of Jesus.

115

David Flusser notes an intentional contrast in the Marcan account between those who represent the Christian community and those who reject Jesus: "all the 'non-Christian' Jews are enemies of Jesus, and as followers there are only the Christian women from Galilee (and the centurion)."[10] Thus, Mark wishes to show that except for His women followers, Jesus died amidst a host of enemies. Mark distinguishes between those women who followed Jesus when He was in Galilee, and "many other women" who came up with Jesus into Jerusalem. The long-standing women followers of Jesus are probably referred to in the former category. It may be that the latter was simply a group of women who came up with Jesus into Jerusalem (but see Acts 13.31). Alternatively, these may be Jesus' women followers from Judea. The discipleship status of the named women is indicated by Mark in three ways: they are said (1) to be witnesses of the most crucial events in Jesus' life; (2) to have served Jesus (note this is said only of the women in Mk 15.40 – 1a), and (3) to have followed Him. The reason why Mark does not use the word disciple of any of these women may be because usually he reserves this word for the official witnesses or inner circle of Jesus, i.e. the Twelve. We conclude that Mark intends to show that the named women are disciples of long standing, even while Jesus was *in* Galilee. Thus, they are prepared to be reliable witnesses to the events beginning with the Crucifixion.

In Luke we note that "they watched" is feminine and has the women as its antecedent, in which case there is a stress on women as witnesses. Further, it is the women alone of whom it is said "they followed with him" in Lk. 23.49. W. Bauer says that "follow" here has the connotation of being a disciple.[11] While this verb's other uses in the Gospels do not appear to have theological overtones (Mk 5.37, 14.51), and as the simple form of this verb is usually used of following as a disciple, the conjunction here of "following" and "witnessing" probably indicates that Luke is intending "they followed with him" to have theological overtones. Further, if we compare this "from Galilee" phrase to Acts 1.21 – 2 (see Jn 15.26 – 7), then it may be that "from Galilee" in itself is intended to accredit and authenticate the witness of the women to the empty tomb and the message about the risen Lord in Matthew and Luke. If they followed Jesus "from Galilee," then they were in a position to remember His words and appearance so that they could relate what they were hearing and seeing *now* to what they had known *before*.

In Matthew as in Mark we have three verbs, at least two of which refer to what disciples do or ought to do – "watch" Him ("look on"), "serve" Him, and "follow" Him. The First Evangelist is unambiguous in that he asserts that these women followed Jesus serving Him (Mk 15.40 – 1), perhaps implying that there was a history and a personal relationship behind this grateful service. Thus, some women in the Synoptics are depicted as faithful disciples of long standing who are being prepared to bear witness to the things they began to see and take part in at this time.

In the Fourth Gospel we noted that the beloved disciple and Mary are representative male and female disciples at the cross. Mary is portrayed as one who witnessed Jesus' death and was ushered into the community of faith, thus becoming a full-fledged disciple. The portrait, though perhaps in many regards an "ideal" one, nonetheless indicates that all four Evangelists were concerned to portray the women as disciples who had prior contacts with Jesus. That the women followers (save Jesus' mother) are specifically named and the men are basically anonymous (or go unmentioned) may be the Gospel writers' testimony to who had the more crucial roles and parts in the events of the last days of Jesus' earthly life.

Conclusions

In the first section, our main concern was with Jesus' attitude toward Mary, and only secondarily with how the Evangelists portray her in relation to Jesus. We seem to have a rather unanimous testimony to the fact that Jesus' first allegiance was to the family of faith and to doing His heavenly Father's will, not the will of His earthly mother. It is worth noting that Mary appears to be the only woman in the Gospels whom Jesus clearly distanced Himself from when she made requests of Him during His ministry. This does not necessarily indicate any antipathy of Jesus toward His mother as a woman or as a mother *per se*, but a rejection of her authority over Him when that authority was being exercised in a way that interfered with the principles and priorities of Jesus' mission.

In regard to the Evangelists' specific portrayal of Mary in her relationship to Jesus, Mark indicates only her misunderstanding of Jesus' mission. Matthew generally follows Mark, though he seems to soften the picture somewhat. Still, the portrait is not exemplary. Luke is more positive, at least in the birth narratives, and he also mutes the negative criticisms of Jesus' family. In John, Mary appears to have some sort of faith in Jesus. Mary is presented as the representative female disciple at the foot of the cross and the Fourth Evangelist indicates she gained a place among Jesus' disciples. What is particularly striking is that all four Gospels indicate both that Jesus' mother failed at some point to completely understand or honor her Son, and that Jesus distanced Himself from her in the process of distinguishing His physical family from His spiritual one. The overall impression left by the material in the Gospels about Mary is that no Evangelist made a concerted effort to give Mary more significance than she actually had in the ministry of Jesus; that no Evangelist attempted to paint a purely idealized portrait of her; and that no Evangelist attempted to portray a strictly Christian picture of Jesus' mother.

In the second section on Mary and Martha, we first learn that Jesus was willing to teach women, as a rabbi would teach his students, and it seems He was not afraid to do this in private. Secondly, from the Johannine material we may deduce that Jesus felt free to have close friendship ties with women who were not related to Him. Finally, though Jesus was willing to accept hospitality and service from women, He makes clear that hearing and heeding God's word was the "one thing necessary" in this life, the first task for all who would seek to please God.

Turning to the secondary matter of the Evangelists' portrayal of these women, we noted a striking correspondence between the Lucan and Johannine pictures. Mary is portrayed as a disciple who had a right to learn from Jesus, and to honor Him in an extravagant way by anointing Him. However, the Fourth Evangelist shows that she too was capable of misunderstanding Jesus' abilities. She is shown to be obedient and very devoted to Jesus. Martha appears to be the head of the household, yet she often takes on the role of servant. Her activities could correspond to those that deacons would perform for the Church community, thus giving precedence for deaconesses. She makes an important statement about the nature of Jesus, and

118

in turn receives one of the most dramatic revelations of Jesus' nature.

Here we see two women who have the new freedom to be taught as disciples, along with the freedom to take up the role of a servant. Having their priorities straight, they can become full-fledged disciples. Though they apparently did not travel with Jesus, this did not make them any less His disciples or "followers."

There were women, however, who took the unprecedented step of leaving their home and family in order to travel with Jesus. Despite the scandalous nature of their act, they stayed with Jesus and served Him out of their means. Their traditional roles are affirmed, yet their access to the teaching of Jesus makes the situation most unusual. Most importantly, they did not desert Him at the cross, but became witnesses to the Crucifixion. That women could be valid witnesses in the eyes of the Evangelists is in itself unprecedented.

In this chapter we have examined Gospel stories which depict women who are, or are in the process of becoming, Jesus' disciples. We have seen that this involved a woman who was a member of Jesus' physical family (His mother Mary), women who were His friends but did not travel with Him (Mary and Martha), and those women who followed Jesus in Galilee and to Jerusalem (Mary Magdalene and others). That Jesus taught women and allowed them to follow Him reveals how very different He was from other rabbis in His treatment of women. Probably, it is this precedent that explains why the Gospel writers, especially Luke and the Fourth Evangelist, include a considerable amount of material revealing women's new freedom and equality in the presence of Jesus and in the midst of His community. Jn 19.25 – 7 also reveals the new equality of male and female disciples beneath the cross of Jesus. His mother is not idealized in the Gospels, however, for at least three of the Evangelists reveal that she had some lack of understanding of her Son and the nature of His mission (Mk 3.21, 31 – 4, and parallels, Jn 2.1 – 12, and Lk. 2.50). Mary and Martha are also depicted as women in the process of becoming disciples. Lk. 10.38 – 42 portrays Mary as having a right to learn from and become a disciple of Jesus. Indeed, this story makes clear that even for women, learning from Jesus takes precedence over a woman's role of preparing a meal and her responsibility of providing for a guest. While in Luke it is only Martha who appears to misunderstand the nature and priorities of discipleship, in John we see that both Mary and Martha do not understand fully Jesus and the extent of His power (Jn 11). Nonetheless, the Fourth Evangelist also depicts Martha as making the least inadequate confession of Jesus in his Gospel (11.27), and Mary is presented as one who properly honors Jesus and perhaps unknowingly performs a prophetic burial rite for Him (12.1 – 8).

From Lk. 8.1 – 3 through the Passion narratives we followed the portrayal of the women who traveled with Jesus. These women are remembered chiefly for the crucial role they played during the time of Jesus' death and burial, and the ensuing events, a time when all the male disciples (with one possible exception) fled and abandoned Jesus. Thus, not only Jesus' teaching and actions, but also the relationships He was involved in and the events surrounding His death and burial, led to the acceptance of women as valid witnesses and genuine disciples of Jesus.

PART III

PAUL AND WOMEN

8

WOMEN AND THE PHYSICAL FAMILY

When discussing the Pauline epistles it is crucial to emphasize that we are dealing with *letters*, not gospels or documents such as the Acts of the Apostles. The letters of Paul are usually written to meet certain needs or to answer certain questions. Since almost all of Paul's letters were written in *response* to a communication, they represent only a portion of a larger dialogue, are not complete in themselves, and often require us to reconstruct the questions being raised or the pleas being urged that prompted his letters of reply.

There are gains and losses in dealing with letters instead of other New Testament literature. On the one hand, Paul's letters reveal the *views* of their author on certain subjects which means we can concentrate on Paul's views of women to a degree that is not possible when dealing with the Gospels. On the other hand, in order to evaluate women and their roles in Paul's communities, we often need to read between the lines to understand the historical situation which prompted Paul's letter writing. Through the framework of his letters we can only glimpse the life and problems of the primitive Christian church. What someone says to correct an error cannot be taken as a full or definitive statement of their views on a particular subject.

When Paul writes, he is attempting to further the Gospel of Jesus Christ in whatever way the situation demands. Thus, in the heat of a debate, Paul may use hyperbolic language to correct a problem or to emphasize his point (e.g. Gal. 5.12). It also means that Paul often tries to be diplomatic in order to achieve his ends (e.g. 1 Cor. 6.12–13, 9.9–12). Further, one must not make too much of what Paul does *not* say, since the agenda of his letters is usually set by the needs and problems of his audience. Finally, a context of controversy leads Paul to stress certain points, not because they are of greater

123

importance but because he must correct an imbalance in the thinking of his audience.

Misunderstandings are the result of not taking the above points into consideration when examining the letters of Paul. Therefore, in the following passages we will pay close attention to the immediate context and carefully compare each passage to the rest of the Pauline corpus if possible. In this way we hope to go beyond the narrow classification of Paul as either chauvinist or feminist.

Marriage, divorce, and the single life – 1 Cor. 7

Was Paul an ascetic who merely tolerated marriage in the Christian community because of the weakness of the flesh? Was he a disillusioned bachelor or widower who begrudged others a happy marital experience? Could he be called a champion of normal family relationships? Was his attitude toward human sexuality healthy? The large difference of opinion on these questions reflects the difficulties in assessing the material of 1 Cor. 7 and Eph. 5.

First, note the general structure and recurring patterns in 1 Cor. 7. It is evident that Paul's main interest is to answer questions raised by the Corinthians about marriage and related matters. Verses 1 and 25 begin with the phrase "Now concerning" which initiates a new section and possibly a new topic about which the Corinthians had written. However, in the middle of the chapter (verses 17–24) we have an unusual paragraph on circumcision and slavery. How can we explain its inclusion here?

F. Scott Bartchy argues that while the Corinthians are the cause of Paul's discussion of male–female relations, once Paul begins his response his mind proceeds along a certain pattern found elsewhere in the Pauline corpus (see Gal. 3.28, 1 Cor. 12.13, Col. 3.11).[1] This pattern involves three basic differences in Corinthian society – sexual (male–female), social (master–slave), and ethnic (Jew–Greek). Thus, it is not surprising that Paul digresses in verses 17–24 to discuss the major social and ethnic differences in the Corinthian congregation. By structuring his response in this way, Paul emphasizes that because they have been united into the one body of Christ, God's call and demands have come to the Corinthians regardless of the sexual, social, or ethnic category in which they find themselves. This means that each person must evaluate his or her differences in light of the priorities of the Christian faith. Thus, "In 1 Cor. 7 Paul answers questions about marriage, virginity and celibacy on the basis of his understanding of the meaning of 'no male and female in Christ'."[2]

Further proof that Paul is structuring 1 Cor. 7 in light of the equality of male and female in Christ is found in the large amount of male – female parallelism in this chapter (verses 2, 3, 4, 10 – 11, 12 – 13, 14 – 16, 28, 33 – 4). It is also important to note the verses where Paul addresses the males and females together (5, 7, and possibly 8, 17, 28b, 32, 35). As we shall see, at various points Paul differs with both Jewish and Greek ideas in assigning women equal rights and responsibilities with men in their relationships. Bartchy has also shown that there is a very deliberate and logical structure to Paul's arguments as he discusses various cases and possibilities in 1 Cor. 7. The general pattern is that of laying down a general principle (or reacting to one), qualifying it by an exception, and then giving reasons for the principle or exceptions to it. Sometimes the reasons and exceptions exchange places in the order, or alternate if more than one reason or exception is given. It is also true that in one or two cases the general principle is implied rather than stated. Still, the overall structure is evident and reflects an attempt to deal with the subjects at issue in a thorough and systematic fashion.

Finally, we should point out certain repeated motifs. The principle stated in verse 17 which advises against changing one's status or situation (unless it conflicts with being a good and faithful Christian or interferes with the peace to which God has called Christians) is also present in verses 8, 20, 24, 26, and 40. Closely related to this theme are the reasons given for this advice, reasons which seem to be interrelated and may have eschatological overtones (verses 26a, 29, 31b). Paul also stresses freedom of choice or freedom from any concern but pleasing the Lord (verses 5, 7, 9, 15, 22, 32, 35, 36, 38, 39). Paul expresses his wish that all be as he is, i.e. unmarried (verses 7, 8, 37b, 38, 40). This wish distinguishes Paul from most of his contemporaries in general and sets him at odds with his rabbinic background in particular. Keeping these factors in mind we can now make a careful study.

Paul and women

1 Cor. 7.1 – 9

Now concerning the matters about which you wrote. It is good for a man
not to touch a woman. (2) But because of the temptation to immorality,
each man should have his own wife and each woman her own husband.
(3) The husband should give to his wife her conjugal rights, and likewise
the wife to her husband. (4) For the wife does not rule over her own body,
but the husband does; likewise the husband does not rule over his own body,
but the wife does. (5) Do not refuse one another except perhaps by agreement for a season, that you may devote yourselves to prayer, but then come
together again, lest Satan tempt you through lack of self-control. (6) I say
this by way of concession, not of command. (7) I wish that all were as I
myself am. But each has his own special gift from God, one of one kind
and one of another. (8) To the unmarried and the widows I say that it is
well for them to remain single as I do. (9) But if they cannot exercise self-
control, they should marry. For it is better to marry than to be aflame with
passion.

1 Cor. 7.1 immediately brings out the difficulty of distinguishing
the positions of Paul and the Corinthians. What are we to make of
''It is good for a man not to touch a woman.''? Is this Paul's view,
the Corinthians' view, or both? Three possibilities emerge: (1) Paul
is quoting a statement of the Corinthians without approval and
intends to refute it; (2) Paul is quoting the Corinthians and/or his
own previous teaching with full approval; (3) Paul is quoting the
Corinthians and/or his own previous teaching with limited approval
(yes, but) and intends to qualify the statement because of an earlier
misinterpretation. Elsewhere in 1 Cor. it appears that Paul quotes
a Corinthian slogan and perhaps in an attempt to be diplomatic, he
agrees with the remark within certain carefully defined limits (6.12)
rather than rejecting the remark outright. Probably the ''but'' in
verse 2 is a strong qualification for what follows – yes, BUT. Thus,
it seems that option three is the most likely, whether this phrase first
originated with Paul or with the Corinthians. There were contexts
where Paul did agree with sexual abstinence, but not as a regular
practice between husband and wife.

Paul's dilemma here is two-fold. First, it is apparent from chapters
5 – 7 that there were both libertines and ascetics in Corinth. If Paul
agreed or disagreed with the statement in 1 Cor. 7.1, then he would
be siding with one or the other group, neither of which he agreed

126

with in full. Secondly, Paul did wish to advocate the single life but without disparaging the married state. Thus, he must stand between the libertines and the ascetics in Corinth. Perhaps this is why Paul is careful to qualify his statements and give reasons for his views.

In verse 2, Paul gives *one* reason, that of sexual immorality (*porneia*), to explain why the position stated in verse 1 cannot be applicable to all cases and people. This is the most relevant and forceful reason he could give in light of what was happening in Corinth, and in light of what the ascetic mentality would fear the most. Because *porneia* is in the plural here, we should render verse 2: "Because of cases of sexual sin (immorality), each (man) should have his own wife, and each (woman) should have her own husband." It is perhaps significant that Paul says, "each should have" which implies that Paul thought marriage should be the normal state for both men and women in the Christian community. Also note Paul's use of possessive adjectives here indicating that exclusive monogamy is required of Christians. Paul sees marital intercourse as an obligation, not an option, for both partners, which militates against the view that Paul is advocating "spiritual marriage" in verses 36 – 8.

Both partners not only have obligations but also rights in sexual matters, for neither husband nor wife has authority over his or her own body – it is under the authority and power of the mate. This is, in part, what it means to belong to each other. Therefore, Paul exhorts "do not deprive one another." This is not the advice an ascetic would give, and it was probably not accepted easily by the ascetics in Corinth. Paul allows for abstention within marriage only for a specific and limited period of time, only for the sake of devoting oneself to prayer, and only by mutual consent of the partners. Paul knows that too long an abstention by a couple having regular marital relations may lead either or both of them into temptation and possible sin. Notable by its absence is any reference to intercourse being solely or even primarily for the purpose of procreation. Rather, Paul implies that intercourse is necessary as a part of the duty of self-giving each partner has to the other.

Paul concedes a married couple's right to abstain for prayer, but he emphasizes that it is only a concession and not a command, thus forestalling the ascetics from using his words to order others to abstain. In verse 7 Paul diplomatically strives to identify with the ascetics in a limited way, perhaps in an attempt to exercise authority and guidance over them. Paul says that he desires everyone to be like himself, by which he probably means unmarried (verse 8). Paul knows, however, that to be unmarried *and* to act in a Christian manner requires one to remain continent. He also realizes that to remain continent is a "gift" from God, that each has his own "gift," and that not everyone's "gift" is to be continent. Thus, Paul cannot give a general command that all Christians remain unmarried; never-theless, he expresses his desire and goes on to emphasize that because of certain factors he thinks it is preferable for a Christian to be unmarried (verses 8, 27, 38, 40).

Paul now turns to address "the unmarried/widowers or formerly married and the widows," two different but probably related groups. In favor of the idea that the formerly married are in view here is the fact that in Koine or common Greek the word in question can mean widower (or at least someone who has had a marital partner whether widowed, separated, or divorced). Coupling this with the fact that Paul was probably a widower makes his identification with these two groups quite natural. Further, because Paul does not go on to say anything in particular solely to widows, it seems unlikely that he is singling them out of a general group of the unmarried here. Thus, we translate, "To the widowers/or formerly married and widows I say it is good for them if they remain/unmarried, as I am."

The alternative to self-control is marriage – "for it is better to marry than to burn [be aflame with passion]" (verse 9). How are we to understand "to burn?" It is usually translated to mean human passions which seems the most likely reference in view of the verb in this verse which refers to self-control. Further, 7.2a and possibly the difficult 7.36 would seem to support the traditional translation of this verse.

1 Cor. 7.10–16

To the married I give charge, not I but the Lord, that the wife should not separate from her husband (11) (but if she does, let her remain single or else be reconciled to her husband) – and that the husband should not divorce his wife. (12) To the rest I say, not the Lord, that if any brother has a wife who is an unbeliever, and she consents to live with him, he should not divorce her. (13) If any woman has a husband who is an unbeliever, and he consents to live with her, she should not divorce him. (14) For the unbelieving husband is consecrated through his wife, and the unbelieving wife is consecrated through her husband. Otherwise your children would be unclean, but as it is they are holy. (15) But if the unbelieving partner desires to separate, let it be so; in such a case the brother or sister is not bound. For God has called us to peace. (16) Wife, how do you know whether you will save your husband? Husband, how do you know whether you will save your wife?

In verses 8, 10, and 12 Paul addresses three different groups of people – the formerly married, the married, and "the rest." It is significant that he says "I command" only to the second group. This is the first explicit command of the chapter and it may be a result of the fact that Paul is drawing on some explicit teaching. It appears from what follows in verses 12 – 16 that Paul is directing his remarks in verses 10 – 11 to married couples, both of whom are Christians.

The problem we face in verses 10 – 11 is to determine the meaning of the verbs "to separate" and "to divorce." Does Paul mean the same thing by both verbs? Do they reflect the differences between a woman's and a man's rights in regard to the termination of a marriage in Jewish and some Greek contexts? If Paul means divorce by both of these terms, then he apparently knows a saying of Jesus similar to Mk 10.11 – 12; if by the first Greek verb he means separate, then he is closer to Mt. 5 and 19.

Beginning with the easier half of the problem, it is fairly certain that Paul is speaking of divorce when he refers to the husband's action. This means that in verse 13 Paul predicates divorce of a woman, a viable possibility in Corinth at that time. What then of the key verb "to separate" in verse 10? Perhaps a clue to its meaning is to be found in the fact that Paul does not see the marital bond being dissolved as a result of this action on the woman's part, for he goes on to say, "but if she separates, she is to remain unmarried or be reconciled to her husband." Another clue may be found in the fact that this conditional statement is predicated only of the woman, and in view of the way Paul has balanced male and female parallelism to this point, this departure may indicate that the activity of man and woman differs at this point.

That the woman is addressed first in verses 3, 10, 11, 16, and 39 may be because women were leading the movement to break up already existing marriages and prevent new ones. Favoring this conjecture is the view that the ''if'' clause should be seen as referring to an already existing situation – ''if she has separated herself.'' As J.K. Elliott has pointed out, the verb in question is used frequently in the New Testament simply to mean separate.[3] But these examples are not in the context of a discussion on marriage and there is evidence that this verb can mean divorce. There does not, however, seem to be any New Testament support for this translation, for in the only other passages where this verb is used in the context of a discussion of marriage – Mk 10.9, Mt. 19.6 – it may refer to the action of a third party, or even if it refers to the action of any human, it appears that the meaning is not divorce but actually put asunder, i.e. separate in an active sense of the word. Thus, separation or to make separate is the appropriate translation.

In verse 12, Paul begins to give advice for which he has no precedent in the teaching of Jesus. Who are ''the rest?'' Since Paul has no desire to speak about the situation of those who have no connection whatsoever to Christians or the Christian community (see 6.12), here he is addressing the situation of religiously mixed marriages (note reference to the unbeliever in verses 12 – 15). Paul advises that so long as the unbeliever agrees to live together with the believer, there should be no divorce. Far from the unbeliever contaminating the believer or making their progeny unclean, the believing partner has a sanctifying influence on the unbeliever and the children of such unions are holy.

In verse 15 Paul deals with a more difficult case where the unbeliever desires to separate, though apparently the believer wishes to prevent this. Paul, however, does not go on to say that these believers have the right to remarry, so it is doubtful that there is a ''Pauline privilege'' here. What Paul seems to mean is that the believer is not obliged to maintain the relationship against the will of the unbelieving partner. Rather, they should let the unbeliever leave since God has called believers to peace, not to the strife that would be involved in trying to keep a spouse against his or her will.

Is verse 16 to be taken as optimistic, pessimistic, or uncertain? The answer can only be determined by the context in which these questions occur. If verse 16 implies optimism about the conversion of the unbeliever, then why has Paul just advised the believer to allow the partner to leave? To take verse 16 in an optimistic sense requires one to see the peace referred to in 15c as the peace(?) that occurs when the Christian tries to prevent the dissolution of the marriage. This is too difficult and it is more natural to see here a reference to the peace that results when the unbeliever leaves and the tension in this mixed marriage is resolved. If verse 16 implies *uncertainty*, then verse 15c can be taken in its more natural sense and the sequence of the paragraph is logical. The believer cannot be sure whether or not the unbeliever will be converted. The outcome is in doubt. Humanly speaking, it seems most unlikely that unbelievers would be converted in a situation where they are being forced to maintain a relationship against their will. This is hardly a peaceful situation and thus Paul advises separation.

Verses 17 – 24 do not concern us in our present discussion except that we should take note of the principle that Paul maintains in verses 17, 20, and 24, a principle Paul says is a rule "in all the churches." In verse 17 as in verses 15 – 16 Paul has authorized a change of status if initiated by the non-Christian partner; he here goes on to reiterate that the Christian is not to attempt to make such a change. Rather, the Christian is to remain in the situation or status in which he or she was when called by God to be a Christian. The reasons for this advice begin to become evident in the next section.

1 Cor. 7.25 – 35

Now concerning the unmarried, I have no command of the Lord, but I give my opinion as one who by the Lord's mercy is trustworthy. (26) I think that in view of the present [or impending] distress it is well for a person to remain as he is. (27) Are you bound to a wife? Do not seek to be free. Are you free from a wife? Do not seek marriage. (28) But if you marry, you do not sin, and if a girl marries she does not sin. Yet those who marry will have worldly troubles, and I would spare you that. (29) I mean, brethren, the appointed time has been shortened; from now on, let those who have wives live as though they had none, (30) and those who mourn as though they were not mourning, and those who rejoice as though they were not rejoicing, and those who buy as though they had no goods, (31) and those who deal with the world as though they had no dealings with it. For the form of this world is passing away. (32) I want you to be free from anxieties. The unmarried man is anxious about the affairs of the Lord, how to please the Lord; (33) but the married man is anxious about worldly affairs, how to please his wife, (34) and his interests are divided. And the unmarried woman or girl is anxious about the affairs of the Lord, how to be holy in body and spirit, but the married woman is anxious about worldly affairs, how to please her husband. (35) I say this for your own benefit, not to lay any restraint upon you, but to promote good order and to secure your undivided devotion to the Lord.

Paul begins a discussion of a new topic at verse 25 and from the outset he makes plain that, as was the case with his advice to those involved in mixed marriages, he has no commands of the Lord to draw on in this case. Paul's advice to the "virgins" is the same as his advice to the circumcised and the slaves in verses 17 – 24: "remain in the state you are in." The reason he gives is found in verse 26 – "because of the present (or impending) crisis (or distress)." Here "distress" refers either to some impending and crucial event in the eschatological timetable, or to some sort of persecution that the Corinthians were facing or undergoing because of their faith.

What sort of "troubles" is Paul referring to in verse 28? Though Paul does use the word "troubles" in an eschatological sense of the tribulations that will befall Christians now that the end times have broken in, here he is surely referring to the worldly troubles that affect married people specifically. Thus it is more likely the troubles Paul refers to are those outlined in verses 32 – 5.

In verse 29, the word "shortened" is principally not a reference to a future event but to some past happening which has dramatically changed the state of affairs. Because of this, for the rest of the time Christians are to live differently from others. Their entire attitude toward all things that are part of this world – one's social position, one's race, one's marital status – must be different "for the outer form/pattern of the word is passing away" (verse 31). It is crucial to note the present tense of the verb "is passing away" in verse 31. Here Paul is not speaking of some future apocalyptic event but of an eschatological process already underway.

Paul's imperatives in 1 Cor. 7 are not grounded in what God has yet to do, but in the indicative of what God has already done and is doing in Christ. It appears in this case that the possible imminence of Christ's return only affects Paul's advice in this regard – it gives it greater urgency and causes Christians to strive with greater intensity to reach the goal – for the time has been shortened. Christ could return soon. If this is correct, then what we have here is an ethic that is grounded in the already of Christ's eschatological work, but gains urgency and is given a definite contingency because of what God is yet to do in Christ. It is an ethic affected by the possible shortness of the time left, but it is primarily determined by the eschatological events that have already transpired culminating in the death and Resurrection of Jesus.

Thus, the Christian must live realizing that all worldly things pale in significance in comparison to the Christ-event, but they are not made meaningless. One can no longer place ultimate value or faith in the things of this world, even human family relationships, for this world's form is already passing away. One can appreciate the things of this world, however, and use them as long as they are seen for what they are. These are the ideas that lie behind Paul's advice in verses 25 – 40.

Having stated his principle in verse 26 Paul then applies it in verse 27. In verses 27 – 8a Paul is probably addressing unmarried men, and in verse 28b he is addressing unmarried women. Thus, Paul is saying in verse 27, "Are you bound in a promise to a woman? Do not seek to be free of that commitment. Are you free of such a commitment to a woman? Do not seek a woman." In either case Christians are not to change their status.

In verses 29 – 31 the major point being made is that the Christian's existence is no longer to be determined by the "form of this world." Paul is not advocating withdrawal from or renunciation of the world, but that now the world is the sphere where the believer is called to obey God's will. The "as if" here does not reflect a tension between present and future but a dialectical relationship between a human being and the world. This is why we have present tenses in these verses. Bodily and worldly relationships have not become meaningless. Rather, they are the very spheres where Christ's Lordship and demands are asserted. "What God demands is not withdrawal from the world, but rather a new understanding of the world as the sphere of Christian responsibility" (verses 7 – 24).[4]

Paul does not say in verse 29 that those who are married are to abstain from marital relationships or the obligations of such relationships, indeed in verses 2 – 5 he says quite the contrary. Nor does he say that Christians should not make use of the world; indeed his advice in verses 30b and 31 is directed to those who are and will go on doing so. Their attitude, however, is to change. Those buying things must not act as though they possess things. Both the having and the not having are to be taken with equal seriousness and are to be thought of within a Christian perspective.

Paul's wish is that Christians be free from any sort of worldly anxiety that might distract them from the things of the Lord. The unmarried man has not such divided interests, but the married man strives to please both his wife and the Lord. His interests are clearly divided. Likewise, the formerly married woman and the virgin are concerned with the things of the Lord. But the married woman, like the married man, has divided loyalties or at least divided concerns which can distract her from giving proper devotion to the Lord. Significantly, Paul severely qualifies these statements in verse 35. They are not binding commandments but what could be called good advice from Paul acting as a pastor concerned that the Corinthians give proper and undistracted allegiance and devotion to their Lord.

1 Cor. 7.36 – 8

If any one thinks that he is not behaving properly toward his betrothed, if his passions are strong, and it has to be, let him do as he wishes: let them marry – it is no sin. (37) But whoever is firmly established in his heart, being under no necessity but having his desire under control, and has determined this in his heart, to keep her as his betrothed, he will do well. (38) So that he who marries his betrothed does well; and he who refrains from marriage will do better.

Verses 36 – 8 represent a considerable challenge to the biblical scholar. The main problem is to determine whom Paul is *addressing*: a couple engaged in a ''spiritual'' marriage, a father and his daughter, or a man and his betrothed.

The view that a man and his wife-to-be are meant in verses 36 – 8 makes the most sense in the context of Corinthian Christianity. A young man is engaged to be married; he is full of passion, but there are those in the Christian community at Corinth with ascetical tendencies who are advising him to refrain from marriage. He is thus of two minds: he wants to marry, and indeed he has strong feelings about his fiancée, but he does not know if his plans represent proper Christian behavior. Paul says that the marriage should go ahead – it is no sin. Indeed, if he marries he does well especially if he is already behaving somewhat improperly towards his fiancée. In such a case, it is apparent that his feelings are preventing him from remaining steadfast or from having complete control over his actions. He ought to marry.

Paul, however, wants to restate his preference that Christians remain unattached if they are not yet or no longer married. This is why he especially commends the behavior of the one who has decided in his heart not to marry but to keep his fiancée as she is. In Paul's view, this person does better. Again, Paul gives his audience more than one option and does not command any particular behavior if there is no necessity to move in any one particular direction. The motivation for what Paul commends appears to be based on his view that the unmarried person has more time for the things of the Lord.

1 Cor. 7.39–40

A wife is bound to her husband as long as he lives. If the husband dies, she is free to be married to whom she wishes, only in the Lord. (40) But in my judgment she is happier if she remains as she is. And I think that I have the Spirit of God.

Paul concludes his discussion of marriage with a statement about the obligations of a married woman and the options of a widowed woman. A married woman is bound to her husband as long as he lives; thus, Paul rules out any possibility of a Christian woman initiating an end to her marriage. On the other hand, if the husband dies she is free to marry again. Paul makes one proviso – "only in the Lord" – which probably means that she is not to marry someone who is not a part of the body of Christ.

Paul does not think it wise for a Christian to become involved in a mixed marriage, and it is notable that it is only in the case of a mixed marriage that Paul says that the believer is not obligated to try and prevent the unbelieving partner from separating. It may be significant that Paul, in counseling widows here, first says a widow is free to remarry before stating his preference for her to remain as she is (verse 40). Paul's parting remark on this subject may be his way of ironically saying to the spiritualists in Corinth that he too has the Spirit and thus his judgment is sound. Perhaps more likely it is his way of reassuring those in Corinth who are being influenced by the spiritualists that the spiritualists are not the only ones with the Spirit and the enlightenment He brings, and thus those Christians being advised by the spiritualists need not feel obligated to follow their counsel.

Conclusions

First, while it is certainly true that Paul expresses his preference for the Christian to remain single if that be his or her present condition, it would not be accurate to label Paul an ascetic. He neither belittles marriage nor sees it merely as a remedy for strong sexual desires. He says that those who marry do well, and he sees sexual intercourse as part of one's duty to the marriage partner. Paul appears to think that marriage is the normal state of affairs and that remaining single requires a special "gift."

These factors show that Paul did not think sexual relations or marriage were either evil (whether necessary or not) or even questionable. Both were seen as good within their proper perspective. Paul's advice to those unattached to remain unmarried is part of his more general advice to all Christians to remain in the situation or status to which they were called. His reasons for this advice are of a positive nature, not because of negative feelings against marriage and its consummation. In fact, his reasons for preferring the single state are specifically Christian in nature.

It is because the decisive Christ-event has already taken place that the Christian is called to live in such a way that he or she does not become attached to the things of this world in an ultimate way. This *detachment* gives freedom of choice – something Paul stresses in this chapter. This freedom also allows one to concentrate on the things that are of ultimate importance – the things of the Lord and how to please Him. Since Christ can save regardless of one's sex, race, or social class, there is no need to change status in order to improve one's standing in the Lord.

Paul speaks instead of the Christian's *attitude* toward his or her status changing (verses 29 – 30), and speaks of the ability of Christians to transform their situation. Christians have no need to draw back from or reject the world and its institutions, indeed they are called to be obedient witnesses to and in the world. Far from the world controlling a Christian's life and freedom, he or she influences a mixed-marriage situation in a positive way (verse 14), and even a slave can be said to be the Lord's free-person. It is only because the first priority of every Christian is his or her relation to the Lord and the obligation to serve the Lord that Paul allows a married couple to abstain from intercourse for a time in order to commit themselves to prayer. Thus, 1 Cor. 7 is both a criticism and a correction of various ascetical tendencies in Corinth! In essence Paul's view seems to differ little from that of Jesus (Mt. 19.1 – 12).

Secondly, Paul actively stresses the equality of male and female in 1 Cor. 7. He discusses the rights, responsibilities, and options of both sexes in regard to both the single and married state. This sort of mutuality is not commonly found or encouraged either in the writings of early Judaism or in non-Christian social codes. Both men and women are called to serve God in their situation. That Paul rejects divorce outright, following Jesus' teaching, means greater security for Christian women married in the Lord. That Paul advocates the single state, perhaps also following Jesus, for both men and women, gives women a choice of roles they did not formerly have in this Greek setting. The evidence of this chapter shows Paul to be a pastor sensitive to the needs and wishes of both the men and the women in his audience. He, in turn, expresses his own wishes, his strong advice, and his commands, taking care to allow Christians various options where a command is not required. There certainly is no evidence here to substantiate the view that Paul was either a chauvinist or a feminist.

Paul shows no bitterness towards those married or contemplating marriage, but he does show concern about their having to face troubles and distractions that might make difficult full devotion to the things of the Lord. Even if one does not accept Ephesians as Pauline, we have here enough evidence to show that Paul saw marriage as good, something that once undertaken should be a fully consummated relationship and not a spiritual marriage. As with all things, however, marriage for Paul must be seen within the perspective of the priorities of faith and must be lived out bearing in mind that the Christ-event has begun the process of eschatological change. This event calls for both a transformed attitude toward such worldly institutions as marriage and an unqualified allegiance to Christ. This is why Paul can say on the one hand, "the one who marries his virgin does well," and on the other hand, "the one not doing so does better."

Exclusive monogamy – Rom. 7.1–3

Do you not know, brethren – for I am speaking to those who know the law – that the law is binding on a person only during his life? (2) Thus a married woman is bound by law to her husband as long as he lives; but if her husband dies she is discharged from the law concerning the husband. (3) Accordingly, she will be called an adulteress if she lives with another man while her husband is alive. But if her husband dies she is free from that law, and if she marries another man she is not an adulteress.

It is not Paul's purpose at this point to speak on women or marriage. Nevertheless, Paul's argument would have no force if the illustration in verses 2–3 was not presumed by the apostle to represent something that was true about at least some married women in some first-century settings. The focus here is on a Christian's relationship to the law now that he or she is part of the body of Christ. Paul is drawing on a legal principle, probably Mosaic in origin, which was accepted as valid by the Christian community (or at least by Paul).

The principle ("the law is binding on a person only during his life") is stated in verse 1b, illustrated in verses 2–3, and applied in verse 4 to the Christian community as Paul draws his conclusion from the principle. The corollary of this is that death releases one from the law's obligations. This is true not only of the one who has died, but also of the surviving partner. Paul states in verse 2 that a woman "under the authority of a husband" is bound by law to her *living* husband. The word translated "under the authority of a husband" is found nowhere else in the New Testament. While it can simply mean "married," here it probably means "under the authority of a husband" because Paul is presenting an example whereby a woman is under the authority of the law. It also appears that Paul has Num. 5.20–9 (LXX) in view here where the matter of a wife's faithfulness or her being labeled an adulteress also comes up. If the husband dies, however, then she is released from the law concerning the husband and his rights. Thus, this key Greek word is used to describe the wife's legal position and does not refer to her voluntary yielding to her husband.

Paul, for the sake of illustration, speaks only of the obligation of the wife, but this does not mean Paul thought the husband did not have the same obligation to be faithful (see 1 Cor. 7; Eph. 5). Still, we have here expressed the expectation that the wife will be committed to exclusive monogamy and be bound to her living husband until death parts them. Implied also is that death (and only death) dissolves this marital bond, which agrees with the teachings of both Paul and Jesus (1 Cor. 7; Mt. 19).

Because what Paul has said in verse 2 is true, he can draw the consequences in verse 3 – that the wife shall be called an adulteress if she lives with another man while her husband is still living. Paul proceeds (verse 3b) to state the same thing he has said in verse 2b in a slightly different manner – if the husband is dead, then she is free from the law, and cannot be labeled an adulteress if she marries another man.[5] Paul thus recognizes the widow's right to associate with or even marry another man (so 1 Cor. 7.39), but the way he phrases it may indicate that in his view this was allowed though perhaps not encouraged or preferred. If this is the nuance of verse 3b, then we have similar views to those Paul expressed in 1 Cor. 7.39–40.

Rom. 7.1–3 while brief and complicated by several factors, gives us evidence about Paul's view of a woman's position in marriage. Legally she is under her husband's authority and should submit to the legal principle that she is bound to her husband as long as he is living. Because the marital bond is only dissolved by the death of one or both partners, a woman who associates with another man while still having a living husband is an adulteress. She has violated the law, though her act has not dissolved the bond. Once the first bond is dissolved by death, however, she is free, not only from the obligation to be faithful to her former husband, but also to marry another man. Verse 3b thus states her rights while verse 2 focuses on the husband's rights. Paul envisions a permanent bond, so long as both partners live, which entails the wife being under the husband's legal authority, and having no extra-marital sexual relationships.

Holiness and honor – 1 Thess. 4.3–8

For this is the will of God, your sanctification; that you abstain from unchastity; (4) that each one of you know how to take a wife for himself [or, to use the vessel that belongs to him] in holiness and honor, (5) not in the passion of lust like heathen who do not know God; (6) that no man transgress, and wrong his brother in this matter, because the Lord is an avenger in all these things, as we solemnly forewarned you. (7) For God has not called us for uncleanness, but in holiness. (8) Therefore whoever disregards this, disregards not man but God, who gives his Holy Spirit to you.

In 1 Thess. 4.3–8 Paul begins to address the Thessalonians on particular ethical issues. Paul's concern throughout this small section is that the Thessalonians conduct themselves in a sanctified manner in their personal relationships. The question is, what sort of relationships are we talking about, that of a man towards his own body or towards his wife?

This question requires that we determine the meaning of the key phrase in verse 4 translated literally "the vessel that is his." It is possible that Paul is referring not to the relationship of husband and wife, but to that of a man to his own body (with the possible implication that Paul is condemning homosexuality in this passage if verses 4–6 are taken together). The Greek word "vessel" can be used both literally of a thing and metaphorically of a person, and both uses are attested within and without the New Testament. Here we will advocate the view that "vessel" refers to a wife, bearing in mind that this debate has raged for centuries.

Paul's point in 1 Thess. 4.4 seems to be that "each of the men knew how to" do as Paul now advises and has previously advised, even if for some the advice no longer, or does not yet, or never will have applied. Generally speaking, the advice is valid for all men that Paul is addressing, but applicable only to "the some" who have the needs or problems Paul is discussing.

In view of modern concerns, it is worth noting that "vessel," when used by Paul of both male and female human beings, is not degrading when used in Rom. 9.21 – 3, and there is no reason to see it as degrading in 1 Thess. 4.4 if applied to wives. Those who argue that the reference to the wife as the "weaker vessel" in 1 Pet. 3 is degrading usually overlook that by implication the husband is also being referred to as a vessel. In any case, Paul's desire is that this vessel be honored, not dishonored and degraded. However, Paul could be using the term metaphorically of the wife perhaps to focus discreetly and somewhat euphemistically on her role in relation to her husband in marital intercourse.

If the key verb means "to have," or "to keep," or "to possess," then Paul would not be warning against marrying on the basis of the "passion of desire" but against relating to one's wife in a lustful manner, as if she could be treated merely as a sex object or a piece of property ("like pagans who do not know God"). Paul, in a discussion of what "your sanctification" amounts to so far as sexual relationships are concerned, after stating the general principle that it involves abstaining from sexual immorality (verse 3b), then proceeds to particularize how this principle is implemented in a positive way (verses 4 – 5, "you know how to take a wife ... in holiness and in honor; not in the passion of lust"), and then in a negative way ("that no man transgress, and wrong his brother in this matter"). He reinforces this appeal with a reference to his own previous exhortations about the Lord as a punisher of sins (verse 6b); implies that sexual immorality can happen in marriage if one possesses his wife in the passion of lust; reminds them that God's call was not for impurity but for holiness (verse 7); and finally underlines this appeal by referring to God's Spirit which is holy and has been given to the Thessalonians (verse 8). What then are the implications of these verses for Paul's view of women and their roles in the family?

God's will for His people is that they live sanctified lives which involves not only one's spiritual life but also one's physical and sexual life as well. Indeed, God's claim extends to every facet of human life – to the whole person and all that one is, says, and does. Living a sanctified life involves abstaining from any sort of sexual immorality, whether this involves the mistreatment of a wife in the passion of lust, or the defrauding of a Christian brother through an adulterous relationship with his wife. Paul thus warns the *men* in his audience that misconduct in marriage is just as much a sin as the offense of adultery.

Verse 4 probably refers to one's behavior in marriage. Such behavior is inconsistent with one's commitment to and knowledge of a holy God who calls His people likewise to be holy. This involves not only individual purity, but also the possessing of one's wife in a sanctified manner. From what follows in verse 5 it is clear that by holiness and honor Paul means that the wife is to be treated as an end in herself, not as a means to satisfy one's lustful ends. If the translation of ''so that'' in verse 6a is correct, then Paul does see one purpose of marriage as being the prevention of adultery. This comports well with what Paul says in 1 Cor. 7.2–5. It also indicates that Paul saw marital intercourse as the proper alternative to such sins and thus verse 4 intimates that marital intercourse is not merely a means of avoiding impurity, but something which can be done in holiness and honor. Though not stated, it is implied that Paul saw marital relations as good when performed in the context of honoring the marriage partner and relating to her in a sanctified manner. Far from being something which works against God's will, it is seen as compatible with the process of sanctification. But marriage and marital intercourse are things which must be undertaken in the full knowledge of what God requires of His people in all their relationships.

Paul's stress on sexual matters is not a result of his own personal preoccupation with such matters, but of his knowledge of how acceptable all sorts of sexual aberrations (including religious prostitution and relations with ''companions'') were in the Gentile world. Further, in a permissive society it is easy to see how the intimate fellowship of early Christians (who met in the confines of homes, shared in the Lord's Supper, greeted each other with a holy kiss, and allowed men and women to participate in all these activities) could lead to an intimacy of a wrong sort between certain members of the Christian family.

Paul thus enforces his commands with the strongest reminders that rejecting his teaching on these matters amounts to rejection of God. One's sexual and spiritual life are integrally related. Paul's instructions amount to a severe curtailment of a man's sexual freedom and thus would likely serve to improve a woman's position and security in marriage. Her position is further aided by Paul's statement that a wife is to be possessed not as a tool of sexual self-gratification, but in an honorable and sanctified manner. Thus, she is not to be treated as less than a person who deserves respect and morally correct treatment. It is just as wrong to abuse one's own wife in the passion of one's lustful desires as it is to seduce a brother's wife.

It is also clear that Paul is again advocating exclusive monogamy. Each should have his own wife and should not break into someone else's marriage. God has not called Christians to sexual impurity, but to sanctification. Thus, in a sense, Paul is here advocating holy wedlock to the exclusion of all other forms of sexual relations. Finally, we may note that this is probably the earliest evidence we have of Paul's views on marriage and sexual relations. That they are consistent with what we find in 1 Cor. 7 (especially verses 1 – 5) and other Pauline statements (Rom. 7.1 – 3; Eph. 5.21 – 33) leads one to suspect that Paul had formed his views on this subject at an early date, not in reaction to any particular situation (such as that at Corinth) but as a result of his Christian principles – instructions he took to be God-given (1 Thess. 4.8) and in some cases Christ-spoken (see 1 Cor. 7.10).

Mixed marriages – 2 Cor. 6.14 – 7.1

Do not be/become unequally yoked/mismated with unbelievers. For what partnership have righteousness and iniquity? Or what fellowship has light with darkness? (15) What accord has Christ with Belial? Or what has a believer in common with an unbeliever? (16) What agreement has the temple of God with idols? For we are the temple of the living God; as God said, "I will live in them and move among them, and I will be their God, and they shall be my people. (17) Therefore come out from them, and be separate from them, says the Lord, and touch nothing unclean; then I will welcome you, (18) and I will be a father to you, and you shall be my sons and daughters, says the Lord Almighty." (7.1) Since we have these promises, beloved, let us cleanse ourselves from every defilement of body and spirit, and make holiness perfect in the fear of God.

One of the most vexing problems in the Pauline corpus is that 2 Cor. 6.14 – 7.1 does not seem to fit naturally into its present

context, nor does it appear to be particularly Pauline in content. This
has led to various theories of interpolation or displacement as well
as to the idea that 2 Cor. 6.14 – 7.1 is a non-Pauline or possibly an
anti-Pauline fragment. There are good reasons, however, to doubt
this conclusion. Many biblical scholars have presented more or less
plausible explanations of how our passage fits into its context. Bearing
in mind Paul's well-known tendency to digress to a new but related
subject as it comes to mind, it is not at all unlikely that we have
another example of this phenomenon in 6.14 – 7.1.

It cannot be assumed that marriage is the subject here since
"unequally yoked" is used metaphorically like many other terms
in this passage, and since it is possible that not Lev. 19.19a, but Deut.
22.10 is the main Old Testament text that Paul has in mind at this
point. Further, Paul, in 1 Cor. 7, clearly allows religiously mixed
marriages and, far from seeing such an association as immoral or
defiling, claims that the believing partner in some sense sanctifies
the unbelieving partner. Since this is a theological principle, Paul
is not basing his advice in 1 Cor. 7.12 – 16 on purely pragmatic
considerations, and thus it seems unlikely that Paul would have later
given contradictory advice to a congregation (part of which was
already predisposed to separation from unbelieving partners) or
would have changed his mind on such an important subject. This
means either that 2 Cor. 6.14 is probably *not* referring to marriage
relations at all (possibly only alluding to immoral or idolatrous
associations), or the key verb is to be translated "become" and refers
only to entering into a new marriage with an unbeliever. Paul
believed that a Christian could only be equally yoked with another
Christian (Phil. 4.3); thus here he would be advising against
becoming unequally yoked with an unbeliever in marriage, or
possibly in some form of association.

Thus, if our text says anything about Paul's view of marriage
between believer and unbeliever, then it is little different from the
advice given in 1 Cor. 7.39 where Paul advises Christian widows
to remarry only in the Lord. It does bear witness, however, to the
fact that Paul recognized, as did at least some of the Corinthians (1
Cor. 7.12 – 16), that there was a certain tension or inequality between
the partners of a religiously mixed marriage. Despite this, Paul does
not counsel the believer to separate or divorce the unbelieving

partner, but he does allow believers to let the unbelieving partner do so. This latter part bears witness to Paul's recognition of the differences between Christian and mixed couples, and it is perhaps Paul's way of helping Christians out from under an unequal yoke without violating Christian principles.

Conclusions

Our study of Paul's views of a woman's status and roles in the physical family leads us to see that Paul does not fit neatly into the category of male chauvinist or feminist. Nor may it be argued that he is some amalgam of the two extremes. Paul's views are at one and the same time egalitarian and, in a carefully limited sense, patriarchal. His views are grounded in and grow out of his Christian principles. As was the case with Jesus' views on the subject, the cumulative effect of Paul's teaching on marriage was that women were given greater security in marriage and greater freedom to choose whether or not they would assume the roles of wife and mother. These effects result from Paul's views that the marital bond is not dissoluble by anything but death (Rom. 7.1 – 3), and that exclusive monogamy is the proper Christian practice (1 Cor. 7.2). His own personal preference for the single life and encouragement of other Christians to remain in the single state (1 Cor. 7.7 – 8, 40) would clearly have allowed unmarried or formerly married women to devote themselves fully to the things of the Lord and His community (1 Cor. 7.32 – 5).

In Rom. 7.1 – 3 Paul is addressing Christians and it is fair to say that he has only relationships between Christians in view even though he may be drawing on a principle from Mosaic law. If so, then we may draw the following conclusions. First, Paul saw marriage as a relationship that *only* existed while both Christian partners lived, and *always* existed while they lived. Secondly, apparently he believed that nothing short of death dissolved the marital bond, for a person who engages in relationships with another or others is commiting adultery if the spouse still lives. While Paul only deals with women who are married or commit adultery, it is illogical to assume that Paul thought that these conditions did not also apply to men. Thirdly, the word "vessel" is used to describe the woman's legal position. Probably it is pushing the term too far to deduce whether or not Paul's use of this term implies that he thought of the Christian wife as sub-servient to the husband in marriage. Fourthly, verse 3 probably implies that Paul allowed remarriage but did not encourage it or prefer it. There is nothing here that does not comport with Paul's teaching elsewhere on this subject.

If 1 Thess. 4.3–8 is dealing with conduct toward a wife, or the ways and motives for gaining a wife, then it reveals several key insights into Paul's thoughts on women and their marital roles. Clearly, Paul believes in exclusive monogamy. He also believes that the basis for marrying or relating to a marital partner should not be "the passion of lust." There is to be something distinctly different about Christian marriage; namely, it is to be holy. Partners are to be chosen or related to not as sex objects but as sexual persons. Paul here is concerned to limit Christian men in their sexual activity to the context of marriage. A by-product of this teaching is a greater security for the woman in the marital relationship. Equally significant is the fact that Paul does not see marrying or marriage as in-compatible with holiness or the process of sanctification. There is no evidence here of the view that marriage is a necessary evil or merely a remedy for lust, though it can be a means of avoiding impurity. Finally, if Paul is refering to an existing marriage, it is important to note that he is counseling against sexual abuse of the wife.

If 2 Cor. 6.14–7.1 is dealing with mixed marriages, then Paul's advice is *not* that Christians should never associate with non-Christians, but rather that it is ill-advised for Christians to enter into marriage with them. This advice then would vary little from what we find in 1 Cor. 7.39.

In the end, we see that this material expands upon some of the main points of Paul's teaching in 1 Cor. 7. Paul appears to be adopting certain traditional norms and a traditional family structure, but adapting such institutions to suit the higher standards of Christian faithfulness, lifelong commitment, and sanctified inter-relating which he sees as mandatory for Christians. The result would seem to have been more security for Christian women in marriage due to the restraint of male freedom in sexual relating, but also less freedom to change partners as was allowed in the Jewish, Greek, and Roman context in the first century.

9

PAUL AND THE HOUSEHOLD TABLES

Introduction

One of the most fascinating areas of New Testament studies is the examination of the household tables, codes which outlined the relationships and responsibilities between people in a household (Col. 3.18–4.1, Eph. 5.22–6.9, 1 Tim. 2.8–15, 6.1–2, Titus 2.1–10, and 1 Pet. 2.18–3.7). There are several prominent schools of thought about the origins, nature, and purpose of these codes. On the one hand, it is claimed that we have here material primarily Hellenistic in origin and not situation specific in nature (M. Dibelius, K. Weidinger). On the other hand, it is contended that this material owes its origins and substance primarily to Hellenistic Judaism and/or the Old Testament (E. Schweizer, E. Lohse, J. E. Crouch, W. Lillie). Yet a third opinion is that these tables are fundamentally Christian in origin (K. H. Rengstorf), and that their ethical ideas may go back to Jesus' teaching and example (D. Schroeder). Needless to say, there is no consensus on these matters, nor is there likely to be in the near future.[1]

Can we talk about a pre-New Testament household table that could be the oral source or even the literary predecessor of the New Testament tables? After a careful study I have come to the conclusion that while discussion of household management was a standing topic in antiquity, both before and during the New Testament era, I can find no direct evidence of a household table and certainly nothing like what we find in the New Testament with reciprocal pairs that are commanded directly. I agree with W. Lillie when he concludes, after his own survey: "I find myself unconvinced ... by the evidence presented by most writers on the subject that the early Church in any substantial way took over 'the ancient housetable patterns' ... when we examine the actual content of the house-tables, Jewish and Old Testament influences appear far more important.''[2]

It is important to distinguish between possible sources of ideas which influenced the New Testament authors and actual literary sources from which the household table pattern in the New Testament is derived. It is possible that the household table pattern as we find it in the New Testament originated with Paul himself though, of course, he would be drawing on a host of ethical material inherited both from his Jewish heritage and possibly from the surrounding pagan culture. As C. F. D. Moule points out, it is certainly not the case that we have here a slightly Christianized-Hellenistic or even Hellenistic-Jewish duty code.[3] There are some similarities between Philo and the New Testament household codes in that both side with the weak, the minor, and the slave, but this is part of the general Old Testament heritage and may reflect a common dependence on it.

While we hesitate to endorse the thesis that this material originates in the teaching of Jesus, or the view that the early Christian interest in the household was the cause of this material, there is nothing improbable with supposing that some early Christians did give this material its basic form by drawing on Jewish and Old Testament materials. Such a thesis comports well with the evidence of how much the sources from the Jewish heritage influenced other types of New Testament material such as the early Christian preaching evidenced in Acts or the apocalyptic literature in Revelation. Bearing all this in mind we are now prepared to examine the material in Colossians 3 and Ephesians 5.

The Colossian household table – Col. 3.18 – 4.1

Wives, be subject to your husbands, as is fitting in the Lord. (19) Husbands, love your wives, and do not be harsh with them. (20) Children, obey your parents in everything, for this pleases the Lord. (21) Fathers, do not provoke your children, lest they become discouraged. (22) Slaves, obey in everything those who are your earthly masters, not only when their eye is on you, as men-pleasers, but in singleness of heart, fearing the Lord. (23) Whatever your task, work heartily, as serving the Lord and not men, (24) knowing that from the Lord you will receive the inheritance as your reward; you are serving the Lord Christ. (25) For the wrongdoer will be paid back for the wrong he has done, and there is no partiality (4.1) Masters, treat your slaves justly and fairly, knowing that you also have a Master in heaven.

With good reasons, various commentators have suggested that Col. 3.18 – 4.1 is a pre-set piece inserted into its present context. It appears we have in Col. 3.18 – 4.1 one form of an early Christian household table that we find in a very different version in 1 Peter, but which existed in some form prior to the writing of either document. It is likely that Paul and others modified this household table to suit the needs of their own audiences. Thus, for instance, the author of 1 Peter seems to have expanded both the slave and wife exhortations, and Paul appears to have expanded the slave section in Col. 3 and the husband section in Eph. 5.

In an attempt to discover the connection between Col. 3.18 – 4.1 and what precedes it, Ralph Martin suggests that problems of order arose in the *worship* service which called for exhortations from the apostle (see 1 Cor. 14).[4] A closer explanation draws on the fact that the early Church met in homes and so there was an overlap between members of the house and the house church, and between behavior in the house and the house church. Since the house was the context for both daily life and worship, it is natural to address proper household behavior *in general* in the context of discussing worship *in particular*. A household that was not harmonious and unified in Christ would not be a good place for worship.

The material in Col. 3.18 – 21 may well be the earliest form of the household table we have. Several structural elements should be kept in mind. First, the subordinate member of each pair is addressed first – wives, children, slaves. Secondly, each exhortation consists of an address, an admonition, and in some cases, a motive or reason, sometimes a specifically Christian one. Thirdly, the groups are arranged from the closest relationship (wife/husband) to the least-close relationship (slave/master). Fourthly, note that the husband, father, and master all refer to the same person in the household, but the subordinate members of each pair refer to different household members. Obviously, the table is arranged to focus first and foremost on the role relationships of the subordinate household members to the head of the household. The duties of the head of the household are also addressed, but they are divided up according to the role he is assuming. G. E. Cannon suggests the following reasons why this material is included and arranged as it is:

The facts are that inordinate freedom and enthusiasm were major problems in Paul's mission and ministry. The special focus which he gave on the inclusivism of the gospel would have made the slave and women issue a very real threat to the orderliness of the church both in worship and in social issues. Paul's insistence that Jewish Christians should not expect Gentile Christians to live Jewishly, gave birth to an inclusivism that specially marked his development of the gospel in Romans and Galatians. The proclamation that in Christ there are no distinctions (Galatians 3:28; 1 Corinthians 12:12, 13; and Colossians 3:11) would understandably generate a longing for full acceptance in the church by slaves and women. The Colossians-type [household table] was especially appropriate for dealing with that problem. Later, when the Jew – Gentile issue faded in the life of the church, the Colossians-type [household table] was not as fitting and other forms of the [household table] became more useful.[5]

If Cannon is right, then this household table was intended as a corrective for problems perhaps created by a misunderstanding of the implications of Paul's teaching about freedom and oneness in Christ. The household table would function to qualify certain misunderstandings that may have arisen as a result of Paul's own teaching.

In verse 18 the women are addressed first and this must surely refer to wives. This means that Paul is not discussing the relationship of women to men in general or in worship in particular. He is not addressing single women or widows or female minors here – only wives. Further, what is said of wives applies to their relationship to their husbands. We are not told whether there is an analogy between the relationship of wives to husbands, and the relationship of women to male church leaders. Clearly, the focus is on family not church relationships. The structure of the family has a bearing on general church matters, and so it is included in a letter addressed to a church, but the focus of the table is on the structure of the family.

In the household tables the subordinate members of the family including the slaves are addressed as persons who are expected to be as morally responsible for their behavior as their husbands, fathers, or masters are. Further, Paul is only addressing a household in which *all* the members are Christians and so could all be addressed in a letter to a church.

The verb translated "be subject" in 3.18 is crucial and the tense suggests not only that this is a continual activity expected of wives, but also that it is something they must do themselves. Paul does not tell husbands to force their wives to submit. This verb was by no means widely used in Greek literature dealing with marriage. Nonetheless, the use of it in Plutarch, for example, shows it was sometimes used in non-Christian contexts in the first century. The verb in some form appears twenty-three times in Paul, but its most crucial use is to describe Christ's relationship to God, members of the congregation to one another, members of the household to its head, and even believers with prophetic gifts (1 Cor. 15.28, Eph. 5.21–2, 1 Cor. 14.32). The verb is also used of a child in relation to his parents (Lk. 2.51), of all believers in relation to secular authority (Rom. 13.1, Titus 3.1, 1 Pet. 2.13) and to church officials (1 Pet. 5.5), and finally of God or Christ (Jas. 4.15, 1 Pet. 5.5). It has been suggested that the New Testament use of the verb "submit" draws on the Septuagint usage where its usual meaning is "subject or submit oneself" or in the passive "be subjected or subordinated."

That the verb "submit" is even used of Christ indicates that it does not imply inferiority of the one submitting so far as their personhood or worth is concerned. Rather, it has more to do with following the example of Christ who willingly humbled Himself to the Father. Thus, Gerhard Delling may well be right that this verb conveys the idea of humility and servanthood as the believer models him or herself on the Christ.[6] What "submit" seems to describe here is the appropriate form of humility or service for the Christian wife in relation to her husband. She is to submit or subordinate herself to him. Unfortunately, we are not told what this submission actually amounts to in practice or how it works itself out in the day-to-day affairs of the household. Paul's audience presumably knew what was implied.

The phrase "as is fitting" implies ongoing action begun in the past, i.e. this action has been customary practice and is still fitting now. Lest it be thought that Paul intended this phrase to mean something like "as is fitting" in our day, or in this culture, or in light of human nature or customs, he adds "in the Lord." He sees this exhortation as behavior appropriate for Christians in particular, not society in general. In 1 Pet. 3.1 submissive behavior is urged in order to win a husband to Christ. Here Paul is probably addressing households where all are Christians. Further, Paul is not urging conformity to society's norms but conformity to Christ whose behavior was the ultimate norm and pattern for Christian behavior. Not only is there a new reason given for this exhortation about submission, but a new model may be implied by which to gauge one's conduct – the Lord. Elsewhere, Paul grounds similar advice in the creation order (1 Cor. 11), but here the basis for such conduct is that one is "in the Lord."

Turning to the parallel exhortation to husbands, we find the idea of *agape* love coming to the fore. This verb or its noun form is not unknown in antiquity prior to its appearance in the New Testament, but is not used in the discussion of household duties in Hellenistic literature. It is not a uniquely Christian word or one that only Christians used to refer to the relationship of husbands and wives. Interestingly, wives are nowhere exhorted to love their husbands in the New Testament household tables, perhaps because Christian husbands in particular needed this exhortation.

The phrase "do not be harsh with them" is meant to be a negative expression that is a corollary of the positive injunction to love. Both of these exhortations serve to make clear that the Christian husband is not free to do as he pleases with his wife. His actions and even his anger must be limited by love. What seems to be in view here is an ongoing anger or deep-seated resentment toward one's wife.

In verse 20, children, both male and female, are addressed and told to obey *both parents*. It is uncertain how much difference in meaning there really is between "to submit" and "to obey." Certainly, in 1 Pet. 3.5–6 Sarah's obedience is taken to be an example of subordination or submission. Perhaps we may say that obedience is one form that submission takes. However, in Col. 3.20 two things distinguish the exhortation to wives from that to children. First, in the exhortation to children, "obey" is in the active imperative tense which suggests absolute and unquestioning obedience. Secondly, the command is made comprehensive by the inclusion of the phrase "in all things." Since Paul has the Christian family in view, he can say "in all things" with the expectation that Christian parents would not demand their children to do something

contrary to Christ's or the Church's teaching. This imperative may
have developed out of the Old Testament commandment, also found
in the teaching of Jesus, to honor one's parents. It is also the case
that the non-Christian parallels demand honor, not obedience, of
the children. This then suggests that the Christian household table
injunction to children is not merely a reproduction of earlier
injunctions but a further intensification of them.

The motivation for the children to give such unconditional
obedience is: "For this is pleasing in the Lord." The Greek term
translated "pleasing" is used in a variety of contexts inside and
outside the New Testament to designate that which is proper or
acceptable. Once again we find the phrase "in the Lord" which
probably means "in the Christian community" or in the context
where Christ's Lordship and grace are recognized.

Verse 21 begins with words which could mean parents but more
likely has fathers in mind. If so, then we have a parallelism between
the subjects of the second member of each pair of exhortations –
husbands, fathers, masters all refer to the same group. Children are
called to obey *both* parents in all things, but the father has a particular
responsibility as the head of the family and perhaps as its main
disciplinarian not to provoke or be overbearing toward his children
lest he break their spirit. While it is true in the case of the Romans
and apparently in some contexts in Hellenistic Judaism that the father
had almost unlimited authority to do as he pleased with his children,
here Paul is specifically limiting that authority and privilege.

What conclusions may we draw from this material? First, we do
not find a total rejection of a patriarchal family structure, but a
modification and limitation of the husband – father – master's
authority and rights as head of the household. Notably, the husband/
father/master exhortations are not supported by specifically Christian
motivational phrases such as "in the Lord." Perhaps Paul felt that
the Church needed to know whether, in light of such pronouncements
as Gal. 3.28, subordination of wives and obedience of children
was appropriate behavior in the Christian community. Paul affirms
that such behavior is fitting in a Christian context or in the *locus*
where Christ's Lordship is most manifest and recognized. However,
the exhortations to husbands/fathers serve to limit the exercise
of authority and power of the head of the household and make clear

that he too equally with wives and children has extensive obligations to the others in his family. What we see here is not a mere adoption, but a reformation of the general patriarchal structure of the family prevalent everywhere in that era, and in some cases an intensification of the demands placed on children and even on husbands/fathers in the Old Testament and in Jewish contexts.

In various ways, then, this Christian household table presents something somewhat different from what we find either in contemporary Judaism or in Hellenistic contexts. Being in Christ requires a reforming of traditional social structures, not a mere reproduction or repudiation of them.

The Ephesian household table – Eph. 5.21–33

Be subject to one another out of reverence for Christ. (22) Wives, be subject to your husbands, as to the Lord. (23) For the husband is the head of the wife as Christ is the head of the church, his body, and is himself its Savior. (24) As the church is subject to Christ, so let wives also be subject in everything to their husbands. (25) Husbands, love your wives, as Christ loved the church and gave himself up for her, (26) that he might sanctify her, having cleansed her by the washing of water with the word, (27) that he might present the church to himself in splendor, without spot or wrinkle or any such thing, that she might be holy and without blemish. (28) Even so husbands should love their wives as their own bodies. He who loves his wife loves himself. (29) For no man ever hates his own flesh, but nourishes and cherishes it, as Christ does the church, (30) because we are members of his body. (31) "For this reason a man shall leave his father and mother and be joined to his wife, and the two shall become one flesh." (32) This mystery is a profound one, and I am saying that it refers to Christ and the church; (33) however, let each one of you love his wife as himself, and let the wife see that she respects her husband.

When we read Eph. 5.21–6.9 we see both similarities with, and differences from, Col. 3.18–4.1. First, the Ephesian household table has 324 words to only 117 in Colossians; however they share seventy words in common. Some 60 percent of the Ephesian household table is devoted to the husband/wife tandem. Secondly, both the Colossian and Ephesian household tables have the order of address as wives, husbands, children, fathers, slaves, masters. Thirdly, while both tables seem to be drawing on traditional material but giving it a

Christian setting and orientation, this is even more evident in Ephesians. In Ephesians Christ is clearly drawn upon as a paradigm for husbands (5.25, 29) and for masters (6.9), whereas this is at most implicit in the Colossians' usage of "in the Lord." Finally, Ephesians has several commonplace expressions such as "no one hates his own flesh" (5.29) which "soften" the text. By contrast, Colossians seems to have only terse exhortations.

The use of tradition along with Christ-centered phrases may suggest we are again dealing with a pre-set piece of material. If so, then the material has been significantly transformed, for in various ways it manifests the same theme as the letter as a whole – unity and union of all in Christ as well as the union of Christ with His Church.

At this point, several comments are needed to explain the limits of our discussion. In Eph. 5.21–33 we have a *comparison*, not an *identification*, of two different kinds of relationships – husband and wife, and Christ and Church. Everything that is predicated of Christ and Church cannot and is not predicated of husband and wife. That we are only dealing with an analogy here is perhaps most clearly shown by the fact that husband and wife are addressed as married persons, but Christ and the Church are described as bridegroom and bride, as betrothed ones preparing for the wedding and consecration of their relationship. This means that it is unwise to press the analogy beyond the clear points of contact made – love of Christ and love of husband which entails self-giving and self-sacrifice; submission of wife and submission of Church; headship of husband and head-ship of Christ; provision and care for wife like Christ's provision and care for the Church. Thus, the material in verses 26a–27c, the description of Christ's sanctifying work for and effect on the Church, while very interesting, is probably not meant to be a description of the husband's role or effect on his spouse.

Notice the flow of thought. While Paul *starts* with the husband–wife relationship, at various points after the analogy is drawn he moves *beyond* that relationship to reflect just on Christ and the Church, a major theme of this whole epistle. This is especially the case in verses 26a–27c, but we see it already in 23c. The husband is not called the savior of the wife. Thus, we will not deal with such verses as 23c and 26a–27c.

The direction of influence between these two pairs, husband – wife and Christ – Church, is not one way. By this I mean that the language and imagery of betrothal in Paul's day affects how he describes the relationship between Christ and the Church. It is also true that Christ's action for the Church in history conditions how Paul describes the headship role, not only of Christ but also of the husband. Likewise, the submissive and reverential response of the Church to Christ conditions how Paul describes the wife's response to her husband. Paul is well aware of the grounding that human marriage has in the story of Adam and Eve (verse 31a), but he is more concerned here to model Christian marriage on the pattern of the relationship of Christ and Church.

This new approach to marriage is Paul's deliberate attempt to reform the patriarchal structure of his day. Paradoxically, the effect was to ground that revised patriarchal structure involving the husband's headship and wife's submission in Christ. Yet how Paul describes headship and the way he prefaces the whole section with remarks about mutual submission so alters the usual thinking about husband – wife relationships as to make this a new teaching indeed.

Eph. 5.21 ("Be subject to one another out of reverence for Christ") has rightly been seen as an introduction to and central theme for what follows in verses 22 – 33. It is an exhortation addressed to *all* church members, male and female, and so it would be wrong to say it simply calls for mutual submission of marital partners. Rather, it calls for mutual submission of all Christians to each other which includes, of course, marital partners. This verse has been seen as a criticism of the traditional patriarchal household code. There is some truth in this suggestion, but if 5.22 – 33 is an attempt to go on and explain in one crucial context (the physical family) how that mutual submission works itself out, then it must be noted that there is no abandoning of the language of headship in what follows, nor is there any attempt to deny a certain difference in the way submission and service is modeled and rendered by husband and wife. In short, 5.21 does not lead the author to speak of totally interchangeable roles. There is a mutuality of submission, but this works itself out in different ways involving an ordering of relationships and exhortations according to gender. Eph. 5.22 – 33 qualifies and explains the transitional remark.

The phrase "in the fear of Christ" in 5.21 bears witness to what we have just concluded because this language is applied specifically to the wife in the household table itself at 5.33. If 2 Cor. 5.11 is compared to Eph. 5.21 it suggests that what is meant is a "fear of the Lord" in view of the fact that a Christian's conduct will come under the review of Christ when He sits on the judgment seat at the end of time. We must conclude that 5.21 is a general remark which perhaps, because of the use of "submit," triggers in the author's mind a desire to present the household table and so explain how mutual submission affects physical family relationships.

In Eph. 5.22 the subordinate member of the pair is addressed first and is called upon to subordinate herself to her partner. The phrase translated "your own" is important in three regards: (1) it indicates that husbands and wives are meant and not merely men and women; (2) it indicates that the subject here is family behavior and not the submission of women and men in worship or women to male church leaders in general; (3) it implies an endorsement of monogamy, something which is more explicit in 1 Cor. 7 and will become more explicit in this text especially when Gen. 2.24 is quoted.

The phrase "as to the Lord" probably means that the subordination of the wife to the husband is *like* that she offers to the Lord, though on a lesser and completely human scale. Verse 24b may in fact make more explicit what is meant – the wife is to submit to her husband "in all things," just as she submits to Christ in all things. This unconditional submission hinges on there being a Christian context. Paul is *not* dealing here with couples of mixed religion, nor does he envision the possibility that the Christian husband might ask something not in accord with Christian love or faith or ethics. He is simply dealing in general terms and even though we get a clearer picture as to what submission amounts to and why it is enjoined, we are still not told what it entailed on a day-to-day basis, nor is a specific division of labor outlined.

We must constantly bear in mind that the comparison of husbands to Christ and wives to Church is in terms of similarity in role not nature. Notice that the point of comparison lies either in the noun "head," a role one can assume only in relation to others, or in verbs such as loving and submitting. The comparison then speaks of relationships and activities.

Before examining verse 23a we must bear in mind that here as in Col. 3.18 – 4.1 both husbands and wives are addressed as persons responsible for their own conduct. It has been rightly stressed that Paul nowhere exhorts the husband to subject the wife or even order her to submit, nor is the wife told to urge her husband to be her head. Each party is addressed directly. This suggests that Paul expects compliance to be voluntary in the sense that the onus is on the wife to assume a subordinate position just as the onus is on the husband to assume the role of headship. The duties are expected to be undertaken without compulsion, but this does not mean that our author thought them to be optional.

The crucial term in verse 23a is "head," a term found elsewhere in this letter but only with reference to Christ (1.22 – 3, 4.15), and elsewhere in the Pauline corpus in connection both to Christ and the husband (or man?, see 1 Cor. 11.3). There is evidence that the term "head" can mean source, as in the source of a river (1 Cor. 11), but the question of origins or source is not at issue at this point. Here, "head" indicates one's role and/or behavior in an ongoing relationship. There is also evidence that Aristotle spoke of the head of the household. This seems closer to the usage of the household table in Eph. 5 where the point seems to be Christ's headship over the Church, His body. Notice that Christ's saving activity for the Church immediately follows the mention of His headship and this in turn is followed by a remark on the submission of the Church. This strongly suggests that "head" in Christ's case speaks of authority and power over the Church to which the Church is to respond by submission. The "as" in verse 23 suggests an analogous view of the husband's headship, for the wife like the Church is called to subordinate herself in all things to her head. When Paul wishes to talk about roles or functions he speaks of headship and submission. When he wants to talk about "spiritual" union between Christ and Church or husband and wife he speaks of head and body (4.15).

What we learn from the analogy beginning in verse 25 is that headship for the husband means "go ahead" and take the initiative in active loving and self-sacrificial serving as Christ has done for the Church. Head would then mean head servant, and we are reminded that the definition of "the one who would be greatest" is the one who serves (Lk. 22.24 – 7).

Verse 28 begins, "In the same manner also/even so." This phrase refers back to the example of Christ's love for the Church. Thus, the husband's duty to love his wife is compared with Christ's love for the Church, not his natural love for his own body. The wife is to be considered and loved as being his own body (flesh is substituted for body at verse 29). At first it would appear that Paul has a rather degrading view of the wife – she is merely the husband's "body." However, the change to "flesh" in verse 29 is probably a result of the quotation in verse 31 of Gen. 2.24: "For this reason a man shall leave his father and mother and be joined to his wife, and the two shall become one flesh." Paul's imagery thus revolves around the organic unit between husband and wife – they are one flesh. Further, as verse 33 makes clear, what Paul has in mind is loving the wife "as yourself," not merely as a part of one's self, in particular, the physical part. Verses 28 – 9 are dealing with imagery reflecting the "one flesh" union; they are not a comment on a woman's nature or purpose.

There is no question but that Paul interpreted Gen. 2.24 to refer to some sort of organic or at least spiritual union of husband and wife. For Paul, sexual intercourse is no mere momentary physical pleasure but an act which creates a bond between two people. In fact, it appears that in the case of a Christian husband and wife we are talking about a bond indissoluble except by death. It may be that Paul felt free to draw an analogy between husband and wife, and Christ and Church precisely because he assumed that both relationships were intended to be irrevocable during this life.

A great deal of ink has been spilt trying to decide what "mystery" Paul is referring to in verse 32. Is it the hidden meaning of the text, or the mystery of Christian marriage, or the mystery of Christ's relationship with the Church, or the mystery of the analogy between the relationships of Christ and Church and husband and wife? Paul does tell us that he is at least speaking about Christ and the Church. Verse 33 serves as a return to the initial topic of discussion – husband and wife – by way of contrast with what has just been said in verse 32. In any event, Paul is not likely to be suggesting that marriage is a sacrament. Indeed, it may be even more probable that the mystery is the mysterious one flesh union which exists between husband and wife and by analogy in a transferred sense between

Christ and His Church. It is the latter union that Paul says he mainly wishes to speak to in this passage and epistle.

In verse 33 Paul returns once more to speak of human relationships. It should be seen as a resumption of the original topic after a digression and so we translate, "in any case, individually each one of you must love his wife as himself." This is a *command* to love. That Paul can command love suggests that he is talking about loving *actions*, not feelings. Actions can be commanded; feelings cannot. By contrast, the wife is urged to "fear/respect the husband." The point is not that the wife should cower, or be afraid of her husband, but that she should respect his God-given position as head. Thus, it is not conditional anymore than her reverence for Christ ought to depend on performance or circumstances. Perhaps Marcus Barth best sums up the matter when he says:

She can have many *good* reasons to fear her husband, and can fear him in a way that does not degrade her in her own or in his eyes. When a husband loves his wife with a love inspired by Christ's love and (however feebly) resembling it, she would be a fool to prefer or seek autonomy apart from him or sufficiency in herself, or a dominant position over him ... Instead of attempting to move him in the manner or by the tricks by which she may be able to move other men, she will be moved by him. Instead of shaping and changing him after her heart's desire, she will feel thoroughly changed by him. Instead of bringing him under control, she will be overwhelmed by his love. No less than the sunburned Shulammite from one occasion to another, she awaits her lover's coming and the ever-new experience of his love with fear and trembling. A woman moved by *this* "fear" will by no means seek to make herself autonomous in relation to him who loves her and she will receive him as one who in his own imperfect way reminds her of the true head of all the world, the church, her lover and herself: Jesus Christ ...[7]

Conclusions

Paul's teaching addressed to married women is striking in many regards. He treats wives, equally with husbands, as responsible human beings who deserve to be addressed, exhorted, and encouraged as full members of the Christian community. In both 1 Cor. 7 and Eph. 5 Paul stresses the reciprocal nature of the privileges and responsibilities of husband and wife. Though their roles or functions may sometimes differ, their commitment to each other "in the Lord" is to be total. It is significant that Paul stresses that both husband and wife belong to each other bodily and have an obligation to meet each other's sexual needs, in view of the fact that some rabbis argued that only the wife had a right to sexual pleasure and only the husband had an obligation to procreate. Even more striking is the absence of any mention of an obligation to "raise up a seed." Thus, marital intercourse was not to be seen as merely a means to the end of producing children but a means of marital communion between husband and wife. All of this could only serve to improve a woman's status in marriage, for she could no longer be treated as simply a necessary means to the end of continuing the family line. She was to be seen as an end in herself – indeed, the husband's alter ego (Eph. 5.28).

Besides Paul's warnings against illicit sexual relationships of various sorts, Paul's positive statement that the husband is to love his wife as Christ loves the Church implied a standard of self-giving and fidelity that precluded the husband from even contemplating having any sexual partner other than his wife. Further, to love the wife in this way clearly implies not treating her as a mere sex object or appendage (1 Thess. 4.4–5 and Eph. 5.22–33). The husband is to honor and love his wife because she is "his own" body, "his own" vessel. He is to treat her in a sanctified manner. There could be no devaluation of her personhood, her value in the family, her importance to the husband's life, both physical and spiritual. If it is right to see Eph. 5.21 as an announcement of the theme of what follows in verses 22–33, then we can see that husband and wife are called to a mutual self-giving that is to be total and rules out the idea that one member is superior to the other. It does not preclude the husband's headship or the wife's submission, but it does so define those roles that the husband becomes the chief servant, like Christ, and the wife an example of one who responds to her serving lover with loving submission as the Church does in relation to Christ. This is what it means for a wife to fear her husband – she acts in a way that recognizes and respects the role and responsibility given to her husband.

Whether a Christian woman was married or single she is "in the Lord" and as such she is subject first and foremost to the call to loyalty

10

WOMEN AND THE FAMILY OF FAITH

Our discussion of the Pauline material thus far has been limited to family relationships. Now we will investigate Pauline material dealing with women and their involvement in worship, evangelism, and other aspects of church life.

Rites and rights for women – Gal. 3.28

There is neither Jew nor Greek, there is neither slave nor free, there is neither male nor [and] female; for you are all one in Christ Jesus.

The first thing we need to note is some interesting parallels. In 1 Cor. 12.13 we read, "For by one Spirit we were all baptized into one body – Jews or Greeks, slaves or free – and all were made to drink of one Spirit." And in Col. 3.11 we have, "Here there cannot be Greek and Jew, circumcised and uncircumcised, barbarian, Scythian, slave, free man, but Christ is all, and in all." The repetition of pairs suggests that Paul is working with a pre-set piece in Gal. 3.28. Paul could be adopting and adapting material formulated at an earlier time and by someone other than himself. In particular, the argument that this is part of an early baptismal liturgy is very impressive.[1] If so, then it makes sense that this text is a commentary on entrance requirements, or the lack thereof, and about the fact that neither social, sexual, nor ethnic differences should affect whether one can be or remain in Christ.

According to Paul, these differences should not be used to divide the body of Christ or to calculate one's position in the body. This does not mean that the distinctions are obliterated by some sort of spiritual transformation, but that they no longer have any significance so far as salvation is concerned. Paul states this strongly

in order to com   made by the Judaizers that
some are "mo   is perhaps likely that Paul
is combatting t   s were creating by insisting
on things that   and sexual distinctions.

The second   nterpretation of Gal. 3.28
is adequate wl   t Paul breaks the parallel
structure by sa   This could be an allusion
to Gen. 1.27 ("   d them'') which, along with
the creation stor   es behind Paul's arguments
in 1 Cor. 11. Since the duty to procreate was so widely held, Paul
had to clearly affirm his teaching that there is a place for the single
person in Christ (1 Cor. 7). Women and men do not necessarily have
to be coupled in Christ, contrary to what Paul's opponents seem to
have insisted.

Thus, this text does have social implications for women in Christ.
First, it implies that they may remain single if they have the ''gift''
to do so. This means they could be free to concentrate wholly on ''the
things of the Lord'' (1 Cor. 7.34). Secondly, it implies that sexual,
social, and ethnic distinctions cannot be used to determine whether
one may be or remain in Christ. Thirdly, it implies that such
distinctions, while they still exist, should not be used to determine
one's standing in Christ. Baptism into Christ means that one should
use his or her social, sexual, or ethnic conditions to glorify God and
build up the body of Christ. Accordingly, Paul combats a misuse
of such distinctions. This does not lead to an agenda of obliterating
or ignoring such distinctions and their relative advantages. Indeed,
Paul is willing to argue that there still are advantages to being Jewish
(Rom. 9.4ff.), and that it is still important to publicly recognize
gender differences (1 Cor. 11.2 – 16). It is just that these distinctions
do not have the significance for one's spiritual status that Paul's
opponents seem to be claiming.

An unveiled threat? – 1 Cor. 11.2 – 16

I commend you because you remember me in everything and maintain the
traditions even as I have delivered them to you. (3) But I want you to understand that the head of every man is Christ, the head of a woman is her husband [the man], and the head of Christ is God. (4) Any man who prays

or prophesies with his head covered dishonors his head, (5) but any woman who prays or prophesies with her head unveiled dishonors her head – it is the same as if her head were shaven. (6) For if a woman will not veil herself, then she should cut off her hair; but if it is disgraceful for a woman to be shorn or shaven, let her wear a veil. (7) For a man ought not to cover his head, since he is the image and glory of God; but woman is the glory of man. (8) (For man was not made from woman, but woman from man. (9) Neither was man created for woman, but woman for man.) (10) That is why a woman ought to have a veil on her head, because of the angels. (11) (Nevertheless, in the Lord woman is not independent of man nor man of woman; (12) for as woman was made from man, so man is now born of woman. And all things are from God.) (13) Judge for yourselves; is it proper for a woman to pray to God with her head uncovered? (14) Does not nature itself teach you that for a man to wear long hair is degrading to him, (15) but if a woman has long hair, it is her pride? For her hair is given to her for a covering. (16) If any one is disposed to be contentious, we recognize no other practice, nor do the churches of God.

Paul spent perhaps eighteen months in Corinth from the spring of 50 to the fall of 51. The Corinthians had numerous occasions to hear Paul preach or teach on the new freedom in Christ – but freedom can be abused. Apparently, not all the implications of what this new freedom meant were clear, both generally for women and particularly in the Christian worship.

Corinth was a major commercial center with a constant influx of people from all over the Mediterranean. Paul's letters suggest that the Christian congregation there was composed of city dwellers who were a cross-section of the social and economic classes living in Corinth. There were a few well-to-do people who could house the meetings (e.g. Stephanas, 1 Cor. 16.15), a variety of artisans (Aquila and Priscilla), and the poor, both freedmen and slaves (1 Cor. 11.22). There is no reason to dispute Paul's remarks that among the converts there were "not many wise ... not many influential ... not many of noble birth" (1 Cor. 1.26).

This is of real importance to our study for several reasons. First, customs regarding head coverings in rural areas will not be useful in discovering the meaning of our text. Secondly, customs that could only be practiced or afforded by the well-to-do are also of little relevance for Paul specifically says he is addressing "all men and women" (1 Cor. 11.4–5). Thirdly, Christian meetings took place in people's *homes*. Thus, the question to be raised is, what did Paul see as appropriate "in house," specifically in worship in the house? It appears that it is behavior in worship that is Paul's particular concern in 1 Cor. 11.2–26, not merely behavior in the home, but how much the two overlap is difficult to say. Apparently there were certain customs and apparel that were especially appropriate for women in Corinth and elsewhere in Greece and the Mediterranean world in *ritual* contexts (i.e. weddings, funerals, religious processions, festivals, and worship).[2]

The matter of the "pneumatics" or "spiritual ones" must also be addressed before looking more closely at 1 Cor. 11.2–16. Paul spends much time in this letter dealing with the problems caused in Corinth by the "spiritual ones." J. Painter explains:

The problem of the *pneumatikoi* of 12.1ff. is related to the background of the Corinthians in pagan ecstatic religion, 12.2, and Paul indicates that an outsider coming into their community would interpret what he saw and heard in those terms, 14.23. The evidence suggests that Paul saw the problem in terms of the influence of the pagan mysteries on Corinthian Christianity.[3]

1 Cor. 11, like 1 Cor. 14, deals with those who prophesy and so Painter's remarks can be applied to both. It is plausible that various of the Corinthian women who were prophesying were behaving in the same fashion in which they had seen men and women behave in the mystery cults; for example, in the Cult of Isis women participated in the processions and rites with a bare head. The specific evidence we have for Corinth, however, indicates that this was not the usual practice in most religious contexts.[4]

The evidence seems sufficient to show that the wearing of a head covering by an adult woman in public and especially in a ritual context was a traditional practice known to Jews, Greeks, and Romans alike. This may be contrasted with the evidence that girls, maidens, harlots, and immoral wives were in various contexts expected to be bareheaded. Paul was not likely to impose any alien or uniquely Jewish customs on the ethnically mixed group in Corinth. He may, however, have been endorsing a traditional Greek and Corinthian practice that he found theologically significant and useful, a practice some of the female "spiritual ones" may have abandoned. But what sort of head covering is Paul arguing for in our text?

In the descriptions of a Greek woman's attire, H. Licht points out that a veil was distinguished from a cloak.[5] In 1 Cor. 11.5 Paul argues that a woman's long hair has been given her in place of a cloak. Paul's analogy is appropriate only if "covering" means cloak, not veil, for the latter comes across the face and covers it except perhaps for the eyes, whereas a woman's hair may cover the back or side of her head or even her shoulders but not her face! Paul says that nature should tell the woman that her long hair is her glory – given to her instead of a cloak. The point is that even nature suggests that a woman should have a lengthy head covering. This is simply another argument to bolster the general contention – women ought to wear a head covering in worship.

In terms of the flow of Paul's argument, we find that he appeals to tradition (verses 2, 16), scripture (verses 7 – 12), human judgment (verse 13), and nature (verse 14). In short, he pulls out all of the stops to make his case. The bulk of Paul's argument is made on the basis of the creation story in Gen. 1 – 2, but his final word is about church tradition which he has passed on and which is the custom of the "churches of God." Paul has not created this teaching on the head covering out of his fertile imagination.

After the general introduction in verse 2, Paul gives us some sort of chain of being or chain of command in verse 3. How we view verse 3 will be determined by how we interpret the word "head," here used metaphorically. The word can be used to denote supreme or superior rank, or to indicate the source of something (such as the head of the river). Note that Paul does not use the term "lord" here; thus, he is probably not talking about a ruler – servant chain of command. Bedale has cogently pointed out how well the meaning "source" or "origin" fits our text.[6] In the first place, Paul goes on to talk about the source of man and woman in verses 8 – 9. Would it not make sense then to talk about Christ as the source of all men, by being the true agent of creation (an idea expressed in 1 Cor. 8.6)? Further, there would seem to be little problem for Paul in talking about God being the origin or source of Christ whether this refers to God's sending of the Son at His human birth (Gal. 4.4) or His pre-mundane origin as the wisdom of God (1 Cor. 1.30, 2.7). I conclude that Paul is using "head" here to mean source or origin. Verse 3 seems to indicate that this is a new teaching Paul is offering.

As the argument proceeds, the possibility that "man" means husband, and "woman" means wife, becomes increasingly difficult to maintain. It appears that already in verse 3b when Paul says "the head of the woman is the man," the man he has in mind is not her husband but Adam. He is the ultimate source of woman.

Paul's injunctions in verses 4–5 should be read together for they are comprehensive, referring to all adult men and women in the Corinthian congregation. Verses 4–5 indicate a contrast – what is proper apparel for the woman is the opposite of what is proper for the man. Clearly, the reason for this is gender, but it also has to do with the source of each gender. It is doubtful that Paul is referring to the natural head covering of hair in verses 4–5. It follows from this that verse 5b means the effect of the uncovered head is the same as if the woman were shaved, a clear sign of disgrace for a woman. The two deeds are not identical but they have an equivalent effect.

Note also that Paul may already be using "head" as a *double entendre* in verse 4b (his head = the man's physical head = the source, Christ), but not in verse 5b (her head = her physical head). Verses 6–7 favor the view that verse 5b only refers to a woman's physical head since that is Paul's focus in these two verses. In verse 6a Paul is arguing that if a woman is going to be uncovered in worship, then let her also be close cropped – she might as well go all the way with her disgraceful deed! In verse 6b he takes it for granted that the Corinthians would see a short hair cut or a shaved head as disgraceful. In short, Paul is linking a deed that must have been seen by the Corinthians to be disgraceful with the deed of going without a head covering in worship. If the linkage is accepted, then the conclusion must be "let her head be covered."

Though it appears Paul's main concern is to correct the behavior of the Corinthian women, it is striking how he alternates between speaking of the men and then the women in verses 7–10. Notice how Paul begins by saying what men ought to do but concludes in verse 10 with what women ought to do. The use of the verb "ought" suggests a moral obligation on the part of the Corinthians. This does not mean Paul was hoping an inner sense of obligation by the individuals in question could be or become the motivating factor.

In verse 7 we are finally given a theological motivation for a man not wearing a head covering – he is the image and glory of God from the beginning. There is presumed to be a clear and historical connection between the first man, Adam, and all ensuing men who are likewise the image and glory of God. We might paraphrase here, ''man ought not to cover his head because he has always been (from the beginning of the race) the image and glory of God.''

Verse 7 indicates that by contrast the woman is the glory of man. Paul is *not* suggesting that women are not also made in the image of God; indeed, everything else about this passage suggests that Paul thinks they are. Not only does he address women in the same breath and on the same terms as men, but he expects them to relate to God in worship as men do.

Woman is the glory of man because woman came forth from man (clearly a reference to Gen. 2), while man did not originally come from woman. The source or origin of man and woman differed, but now in verse 9 we will be told they differ somewhat in their purpose, their reason for being. Man was not created for the sake of woman, being made before her according to Gen. 2, but woman for the sake of man. In light of verses 7 – 9 there can be little doubt that Paul took the Gen. 2 narrative as a story about historical events.

In verse 10, the phrase, ''to have an *exousia* on/over her head'' is a notorious one. The key Greek word here can mean power or authority but there is no evidence that it can mean authority exercised by someone else over the person in question. Indeed, as long ago as W. M. Ramsay the idea that Paul had in view an authority to which a woman is subject was said to be a ''preposterous idea which a Greek scholar could laugh at anywhere except in the New Testament.''[7] More recently, Morna Hooker has demonstrated that most of the usual interpretations of this word, including the subordinationist one, are unlikely if not impossible.[8] We are talking then about an authority which women had to have in order to do what they were apparently doing in worship – praying and prophesying. Paul is willing to insist that women should have this authority which must be seen as an authorization to do something which she would otherwise not be able to do. It is also likely that Paul is implying that this is a new authority, at least for Jewish Christian women, for there is evidence women were expected to be silent in the synagogue.

As one proceeds through this difficult argument it becomes apparent that Paul would not have gone to all this trouble if he had not accepted and affirmed a woman's authority to pray and prophesy in Christian worship. His argument demonstrates that he is concerned to regulate how, not whether, they may properly do these things.

Because of the order and nature of human creation as male and female, a woman ought to wear a head covering in worship. In verse 10b, Paul adds a subsidiary reason – "because of the angels." Now it is clear that Paul thought of angels as observers of the created order (1 Cor. 4.9), and perhaps also of the proper order in worship. But why mention the angels at this point? As Hooker argues forcefully, only God's glory must be in evidence in Christian worship. If a woman is man's glory, and Paul will also argue that a woman's hair is her own glory, then there is good reason why a woman's head should be covered. Neither a man's nor a woman's glory, but only God's glory (symbolized by the uncovered head of the man), should be in evidence in the midst of Christian worship.

The wearing of a head covering by the woman has a dual function: (1) it preserves the order in worship – only God's glory is to be revealed there, and (2) it authorizes women to pray and prophesy without denying the creation order distinctions. Paul considered it important to recognize and to symbolize the creation order distinctions in Christian worship. New creation for Paul does not obliterate the original creation order distinctions – men are still men, and women are still women. Other differences in origin and purpose should be reflected even in worship. What the new creation does accomplish for women, however, is the granting of new freedom, roles, and responsibilities in the community of faith. Paul is attempting to endorse the new freedom of women while maintaining in a transferred and transformed sense the old creation order distinctions.

Verse 11 begins with "nevertheless" which breaks off the preceding discussion and offers a qualification: in the Lord there is neither man without woman, nor woman without man. The point is that it is not merely a matter of women being dependent upon men, but rather a mutual dependency of each gender upon the other. Paul reasons that though woman originally came from man, now all men come into the world through women, but all things ultimately come from God. "In the Lord" probably means "in the church" or "in the body of Christ." Men and women stand together, mutually dependent upon each other, not only in creation but also in the Lord. This means that both men and women are equally necessary and important to each other for their ongoing existence. Thus, verses 11 – 12 make abundantly clear that Paul does not wish to imply the inferiority or lesser importance of women in comparison to men.

The arguments in verses 13 – 15 must be seen as subsidiary and corroborative. For our study it is unnecessary to examine them in detail, but it is worth noting that verse 14 indicates that Paul saw certain signs of gender distinction as natural and indeed indicated by nature. These distinctions are not obliterated but are reoriented in the Lord. Finally, at verse 16 we have a reiteration of the appeal to tradition or to what is customary in all the other churches. If the Corinthian women had been arguing that their hair was a sufficient head covering, using it instead of a cloak, Paul's response could easily have been, "we have no such custom of women using only hair as a head covering in worship." It would be very surprising if Jewish Christian women did not have the custom of wearing a head covering.

At this point we can say that Paul allows both men and women to do some sort of speaking in worship. It would be natural to see praying as speaking to God, and prophesying as speaking to fellow believers. If so, then it is a significant departure from Paul's Jewish heritage especially in regard to women addressing men in worship. This should not be glossed over because Paul spends much time explaining how these activities may be performed properly by both men and women. In any case, we hear in this passage both the old (creation order reaffirmed) and the new (women praying and prophesying in worship). Paul here is delivering a received church custom or tradition; however, he does not wish it to be interpreted in such a way that women are silenced in Corinthian worship.

There is certainly nothing un-Pauline about the content or form of argumentation in 1 Cor. 11.2 – 16. Perhaps we have shown that Paul can be exonerated of "male chauvinism" in this passage without the radical surgery suggested by those favoring some form of an interpolation theory. Women were a threat to the traditional creation order *not* because they prayed or prophesied but because they went without the required head covering.

Silence in all the churches? – 1 Cor. 14.33b – 36

As in all the churches of the saints, (34) the women should keep silence in the churches. For they are not permitted to speak, but should be subordinate, as even the law says. (35) If there is anything they desire to know, let them ask their husbands at home. For it is shameful for a woman to speak in church. (36) What! Did the word of God originate with you, or are you the only ones it has reached?

Verses 34–6 have been taken by an increasing number of scholars to be a clear case of interpolation of non-Pauline material into this Pauline letter. However, our working hypothesis will be that this material is Pauline and can be explained in terms of its immediate context – the discussion of prophecy and the judging of the prophecies found in chapter 14 – and the larger context – the discussion of abuses in Corinthian worship caused by the "spiritual ones" (chapters 11–14). Some of these "spiritual ones" were women prophetesses who seem to have been imitating some of the practices of women involved in the mystery cults. The result was disorder in Corinthian worship.

Let us first consider Paul's views on prophecy before we tackle the text itself. Paul thought of prophecy as an important gift that could be used to build up the Christian community (Rom. 12.6; 1 Cor. 12.10, 13.2, 14.6; 1 Thess. 5.20). It is not by accident that Paul lists this gift ahead of *glossolalia* (speaking in tongues) in the gift lists of Rom. 12.6 and 1 Cor. 12.10. Indeed, Dunn points out that if one looks at all such lists in the Pauline corpus the only constant member is prophecy or prophet.[9]

Paul indicates that prophecy is not only a desirable gift but also one which the Corinthians should seek (14.1). Far from being a learned art, it depends on the receiving of revelation from God which must then be delivered (14.30). 1 Cor. 14.19 suggests a contrast between speaking with the mind and speaking in a tongue (*glossolalia*). This means that prophecy is an intelligible communication that even non-believers can hear and be convinced by (1 Cor. 14.24–5).

Christian prophecy does not need interpretation, but it may need "weighing." This means that the prophecy given could be some mixture of the word of God and human words. Apparently, the greater one's faith and openness to the source of revelation, the more nearly the utterance could be completely a word of God. This would explain why the prophecy spoken of in 1 Cor. 12–14 had to be weighed or sifted – because its content might be three parts inspiration and one part imagination.

Paul indicates that the prophet(ess) had conscious control over his or her utterances, i.e. the prophecy could wait until another finished (1 Cor. 14.29–32). Apparently, the Corinthians thought they could not wait and several were blurting out prophecies at one time with the result being chaos and confusion.

It is clear that not all were prophets (1 Cor. 12.29), and 1 Cor. 14.37 suggests that we should not talk about an appointed office of prophet(ess). In short, there were only certain individuals who perceived themselves as prophets, who believed that they were inspired by the Spirit to stand up and give a word of prophecy to the congregation.

The implications of all this are important to our study of 1 Cor. 14.33b–36. First, it suggests that women were not only allowed to engage in prophecy but also in the weighing of the prophecies if the latter was a separate gift also exercised by prophets. Secondly, prophecy offered by women in Corinth was only authoritative to the degree it was inspired. Thirdly, prophesying may be distinguished from teaching and preaching, though there would be some overlap in regard to the audience and function of these gifts. Prophecy, preaching and teaching are addressed to the whole congregation which includes the men. Since prophecy involves authoritative exhortation or a new word of God for the congregation it clearly has a teaching function. It is not merely a personal testimony or word of witness. Paul ranks prophets immediately after apostles but before teachers (1 Cor. 12.29, Rom. 12.6–7). There is nothing in 1 Cor. 12–14 to suggest that prophesying, teaching, or preaching were gender specific gifts. How then do we interpret the silence of women in 1 Cor. 14.33b–36?

It is evident from what precedes and follows 1 Cor. 14.33b–36 that Paul is concerned that proper order be maintained in Christian worship. To re-establish the proper order of things in Corinth, Paul begins by citing the rule of order followed in all the churches (or all his churches?). When Paul uses the phrase "in all the churches" he is not referring to the behavior of God in all the churches but rather he is trying to establish a rule of behavior, his rule or the rule of all the Christian churches for the Corinthians. Further, the word "*ekklesia*" translated "church" is crucial in Paul's vocabulary and theology. It is almost a proper name and his concept of church is such that: "If anyone is despised in such a gathering ... if people come together in it ... if women are to keep silent in it ... if it is not to be burdened ... these things apply to the church as a whole and not merely to a local congregation."[10]

The crucial phrase is, of course, "the women should keep silence in the churches." From our historical study we have learned that there were temples to Dionysius, Isis, Serapis, and others in which women took important roles and were free to speak. Women also achieved the prophetic rank of sybil in the mystery cults. Possibly, then, the Corinthians were surprised at Paul's silencing of women. Apparently, he is not drawing on conventional Corinthian or Greek views of the role of women in worship. Nor is he merely drawing on his own Jewish background when he discusses the role of women in worship in 1 Cor. 11 and 14. Why would he allow them to pray and prophesy as he does in 1 Cor. 11.5? More likely, in 1 Cor. 14.33b – 36 Paul is dealing with a specific problem in the Corinthian worship service and we should therefore look for particular reasons why Paul silences women here and what the scope of this prohibition is.

It does not appear that Paul thought the women were violating a relatively minor church rule; his reaction is too strong for that to be the case. Indeed, he musters five authorities to persuade the Corinthian women to adhere to this ruling. He says that their behavior is out of line with:

(1) general church practice;
(2) the law;
(3) common conventions of what is proper or disgraceful;
(4) the word of God;
(5) his apostolic authority (if we apply verses 37 – 40).

This piling up of authorities seems to be a Pauline practice when he felt something important was at stake.

In verse 34 when Paul says women are "not permitted to speak" it appears that the passive tense points back to an already valid rule. It must be asked why they had no permission to speak and where the rule banning their speaking in Christian worship originated. It would seem that if the problem was simply a matter of decency or order (e.g. 14.1 – 33a), then Paul would not have banned women from speaking but reinstructed them how to do it properly. Note also that the Greek word *aner* can refer to man in general or husband in particular, likewise the Greek word *gune* can refer to woman in general or wife in particular. From the context of 1 Cor. 14.33b – 36 the translation of husband and wife is the more appropriate. Paul is addressing the particular problem of wives in relation to the prophets, whether the prophet is their own husband or another man in the church.

Two words are important to our study. First of all, the word "to speak" can refer to: (a) inspired speech – as in prophetic utterances; (b) uninspired speech – as in questions or even idle chatter; (c) an authoritative word of wisdom – as in a moral discernment or judgment. Which of these options is most appropriate depends on the nature of the silence that Paul is imposing. The key is in the inter-relationship between silence and subordination. Secondly, the word "subject oneself" or "be subjected" or "be subordinated" is here used to describe the relationship of the wife to the husband (see also Eph. 5.22; Col. 3.18; Titus 2.5). This then would be a further teaching about husband/wife relationships. But why would such an exhortation be needed at this point?

It may be the case that wives were asking questions in such a manner as to stand in judgment over the prophets or, even more likely, that they thought themselves to be prophetesses with the gift of interpretation or weighing of prophecy. The problem would then be as follows:

(1) some Corinthian wives were prophetesses who thought they had the gift of judging the prophecies of others in the context of Christian worship;
(2) the others in this case just happened to be either their own husbands or some men who were also prophets in the congregation;

175

(3) Paul had apparently said before and is reiterating now "the spirit of prophets is subject to prophets;"

(4) these wives, who thought they were spiritual, were asking leading questions of their own husbands or others in such a way as to judge what they were saying (in other words, they were presuming to speak in an authoritative way over what their own or another husband had said);

(5) thus, these wives, in trying to subject the men's prophecies to their judgment were themselves not being subordinate to their husbands or men by so doing. Indeed, they were exercising authority over them by their "authoritative speech" and consequently were violating the marriage or male/female creation order hierarchy.

The merits of such an interpretation are several. First of all, it in no way negates a woman's right to pray or prophesy in church but only restricts her from judging prophecy by men or speaking in some manner so as to lord it over either her husband or men in general. It fits well with what precedes and follows our passage contextually. If Paul is speaking of the judgment of prophecy, then this would certainly be a natural outflow of 1 Cor. 14.29–30. Paul would be turning from a more general exhortation to orderly procedure (verses 32–3) in regard to the matter of weighing prophecy, to the more specific case of women weighing or questioning prophecy. If women were judging their husbands' prophecy and, by implication, questioning the veracity of their own husbands or other men in regard to prophesying, then they were creating a situation where the Corinthian worship service might become a family feud. A natural way for Paul to deal with this problem would be to reassert that women or wives, rather than being dominant over men or their husbands as in this instance, were to be subordinate and to show their subordination by asking their husbands their questions at home. This is Paul's word on how to practically apply the principle of subordination and thus remedy the violation.

If "submit" in this context refers to the subordination of wives to their husbands, then we need to see how this qualifies or clarifies why Paul tells women to keep silence in the worship service. Of various Old Testament passages the one which seems to have the closest connection with our passage is Job 29.21 which involves the silence of respect for a teacher, the silence of someone who is a learner. There are no real New Testament parallels to our passage except 1 Tim. 2.8ff.

There is another view, however, which has some different nuances even though it is not radically different from the one just described. If the reason for the counsel to silence and submission is caused by disorder in the worship service, not disorder in family relationships, then this explains why "submit" is used here in the absolute form. Women are not being commanded to submit themselves to their husbands so much as to the principle of order in the worship service, the principle of silence and respect shown when another is speaking, especially when another is speaking the word of God to you! The Corinthians should have known that even the Old Testament speaks about a respectful silence when a word of counsel was spoken (Job 29.21). The scenario we envision is as follows: during the time of the weighing of the prophet's utterances, some of the wives, who themselves may have been prophetesses and entitled to "weigh" verbally what was said, were asking questions that were disrupting the worship service. The questions themselves may have been disrespectful or they may have been asked in a disrespectful manner. The result in any case was chaos. Paul's ruling is that questions, or at least questions of this sort, should not be asked in worship. The wives should ask their husbands at home. Worship was not to be turned into a question and answer session.

This solution has the merits of fitting the context, but also takes seriously that "submit" has no personal object here. At this point we are able to conclude that verses 34–5 cannot be taken as a prohibition of a woman praying or prophesying or for that matter teaching or preaching in a worship setting. "Speak" here then most likely refers to uninspired speech, i.e. questions. The alternative Paul gives these women is simply to ask in another context. Paul is not ruling out the use of proper speech in worship but he is ruling out a form of insubordinate speech. The silence has to do not with all speech but with a specific kind indicated by the context, just as in verse 30 there is a command for a prophet to be silent if another begins to speak. Thus, verses 34–5 fit well into their present context. The problem dealt with in these verses is an example of what is spoken of in verse 29b – a problem arising during the weighing of the prophecies. Verse 29a is spoken about further in verses 30 – 33a; verse 29b is spoken about further in verses 33b – 36.

As a final point, one may ask, why then are women singled out in verses 34 – 5? The answer is that they were the cause of the problem, the ones needing correction. But Paul includes that correction in a letter to all the Corinthians and addresses them all so they too may avoid this abuse.

I conclude that the creation order or family order problem was not at issue in this passage, but rather a church order problem caused by some women in the congregation. Paul corrects the abuse not by banning women from ever speaking in worship, but by silencing their particular abuse of speech and redirecting their questions to another time and place. Paul, after all, wishes the women to learn the answers to their questions. This passage in no way contradicts 1 Cor. 11.5, nor any other passage which suggests that women taught, preached, prayed, or prophesied in the churches.

Conclusions

The first and most important conclusion to be drawn from Gal. 3.28 is that women are given equal standing before God, as equal members of the body of Christ. Secondly, Gal. 3.28 is probably a dictum serving the same function for women in Paul's audience as Matt. 19.10 – 12 did for Jesus, i.e. allowing women to remain single for the Lord, a condition Paul clearly prefers (1 Cor. 7). This opened the possibility of women being involved in roles other than the traditional ones of wife and mother.

In 1 Cor. 11.2 – 16 we discovered that Paul allows women to pray and prophesy. The latter was seen as crucial by Paul, a word of God for a specific situation whether as a proclamation, an exhortation, or a message to build up the congregation. Prophecy, given its origin solely in the Spirit's prompting, could be distinguished from *glossolalia*, teaching, and preaching. Perhaps in its content, prophecy also served the purpose of edification.

In 1 Cor. 11.2 – 16 we also hear Paul affirm the distinction of the sexes in the context of Christian worship, reaffirming the creation order in the Christian community. New creation has not obliterated the distinctions that came by way of creation, so that as long as the creation order is recognized and affirmed Paul does not prohibit women from speaking in the congregation. Above all, only the Lord is to be glorified in the worship service. Thus the head covering serves the functions of preserving the worship order – only God's glory is to be revealed there – and authorizing women to pray and prophesy without denying the creation order distinctions.

1 Cor. 14.33b – 36 is to be seen as an attempt to correct a specific problem in the Corinthian church caused by wives judging the prophets whether their own husbands or another man. Instead of disrupting the service, they should ask questions of their husbands at home. I conclude that submission refers more specifically to church principles of order and decorum in worship, not generally to husbands. Weighing of prophecy is not ruled out, but neither is it to be done in such a way as to disrupt the worship service or deny the authority structure of the home. Wives were singled out because they were the source of the problem in the Corinthian church.

The family of faith is central for Paul, as it was for Jesus, and this means the structure and roles of the physical family would be affected, and in some ways transformed, by the transcending practices of the family of faith. Paul walked a difficult line between reaffirmation and reformation of the good that was part of the creation order, and the affirmation of new possibilities in Christ. In our next chapter we will see how this works itself out as women took on missionary roles in the family of faith.

11

PAUL AND HIS FEMALE CO-WORKERS

Paul relied on many Christians all over the Mediterranean to help him continue his ministry to the Gentiles. But what was the relationship between Paul and his co-workers? How and in what way did they function? Were they also itinerant missionaries or was their sphere of influence primarily local? What was the relationship between Paul's co-workers and the local church leaders in various places? To ask these questions is also a way of asking, What was Paul's vision of the Christian community and its structure, and what roles could women play in that community? If we are to assess such texts as Phil. 4.2 – 3 and Rom. 16.1 – 16, which speak of women who were Paul's "co-workers," we must first ask how the Pauline communities were structured and what roles various parties assumed.

The church – spirit and structure

Traditionally the Greek work *ekklesia* has been translated as church or churches, but this is debatable. The Old Testament word likely in the background is *qahal*, a term used of either the assembling or assembly itself of God's people. This is also its meaning in the writings of Philo and the historian Josephus. Paul is flexible in his usage and can speak of the church/assembly of God meaning the whole Church, the church/assembly in a particular locality (Thessalonica, for example), the church/assembly in a particular household, or the church in a particular region.

The term *ekklesia* always refers to people, not buildings, and the meeting place was usually in a household. We find, for instance, the phrase "the assembly of God's people in someone's house" (1 Cor. 16.19, Col. 4.15). Possibly Paul uses "in the house of" to distinguish individual household-based groups from "the whole assembly of that place.'' We conclude that for Paul *ekklesia* in the singular can refer to an individual unit of believers meeting in a household (the church), a particular local or regional church, or the Church corporately world-wide. In the plural it can refer to the latter two, but not to the first. Doubtless, this usage reflects Paul's view of the nature of the church/assembly. Meeks suggests, ''One peculiar thing about early Christianity was the way in which the intimate close-knit life of the local groups was seen to be simultaneously part of a much larger, indeed ultimately worldwide, movement or entity.''[1] We may also conclude that the basic unit of Christianity, the individual house church/assembly, overlapped with what was seen as the basic unit of society, the household and the usually extended family that dwelt in it.

There is plenty of evidence in Paul and Acts that one of the main ways the Church grew was by the principle of household inclusion/conversion into the faith (1 Cor. 16.15, Rom. 16.10b, 11, Acts 16.31ff.). Perhaps partly because of its meeting in households and because of the overlap with the household structure, the church was called the household of God, and Christians were seen as a family – brothers and sisters if you will. These factors also explain in part the use of household codes (Col. 3.18–4.1, Eph. 5.21–6.9) for ordering the Christian household, and to some extent the Christian church. One might conclude that the church must simply have adopted the hierarchical structure of the families, and applied it to the Christian family, and also the Christian church as family. However, spiritual gifts, social/intellectual status, and a host of other factors affected how the church was structured. Meeks adds,

The head of the household, by normal expectations of the society, would exercise some authority over the group and would have some legal responsibility for it. The structure of the [house] was hierarchical, and contemporary political and moral thought regarded the structure of superior and inferior roles as basic to the well-being of the whole society. Yet ... there were certain countervailing modes and centers of authority in the Christian movement that ran contrary to the power of the paterfamilias, and certain egalitarian beliefs and attitudes that conflicted with the hierarchical structure.[2]

It was not at all common in Judaism or in pagan groups to call one's fellow believers brothers or sisters, but it does seem fundamental to the early Christian churches. A related concept can be found when Paul discusses fathers and mothers in the faith, terminology that seems to indicate who was the agent of one's knowledge of Christ and/or the nurturer of that faith. For instance, in Rom. 16.13 the phrase "his mother and mine" probably means a hostess or patron of Paul, and it possibly implies a spiritual debt in the faith Paul owed to a woman.

When Paul calls himself the father (1 Cor. 4.15) or mother (1 Thess. 2.7) of certain Christians and calls them his children (1 Cor. 4.14) he seems to imply a certain family relationship in the Lord, and a certain authority structure and responsibility Paul has over those who came to know Christ through him. Paul does not use the term father of the minister or local church leader but of the evangelist or apostle through whom one is converted.

Notice how in 1 Cor. 3.1, Paul talks about converts as infants, and at 4.14 he sees them as his children. Yet, he also calls them brothers (2.1, 3.1, etc.) implying a certain equality. Could the Corinthians outgrow the need for Paul's fatherly direction while growing up into spiritual adulthood and pressing on to become sons of God? It appears that the structure and functions of Paul's communities were complex and grew gradually, but there is no indication that Paul ever saw a time when his communities would be so mature that leadership would prove unnecessary. There is, however, no radical clergy/laity distinction. There are several reasons for this. First, Paul makes clear that all members of the body are given gifts of the Spirit for the common good (1 Cor. 12.7). Since being "gifted" implies using that gift in the service of the body, Paul intends that all members of the body be ministers, using their gifts to minister to one another. Secondly, when Paul discusses gifts and functions in the Church (Rom. 12.3ff.) he is addressing the whole Church, not just some ministerial class. Thus, how (not whether) a person ministers in the community is determined in part by what gifts and graces the Spirit has imparted. In a sense, it is the Spirit that determines who does what in Paul's communities. It is clear from 1 Cor. 12.28 that there are authority figures in and for the community. Paul seems to rank them (in order of authority?) as follows: apostle, prophet, teacher, miracle worker, and others. Again, at Gal. 6.6, a structure is implied – there are local instructors in the word whom the local church is to heed and to feed, i.e. share all good things (which may also imply housing, etc.). In 1 Thess. 5.11–15 the job of exhortation and building up the body is for everyone, but there are some who have specific leadership tasks as "overseers" of the rest of the church. As Allan Chapple says, "The responsibility of each believer is for his brother; the responsibility of the leaders is for the church … Those who lead the church in this way are seen by Paul … as associated with him, as participating in his mission."[3]

At this early stage in Paul's ministry it does not seem there is any systematically ordered ministry or process of ordination. Some people single themselves out, take the lead, and devote themselves to the work. In addition, there are functions such as church discipline which the whole Church is to exercise when it meets (1 Cor. 5.4–5), as well as mutual service and exhortation. It is also clear from 1 Cor. 12–14 that prophecy was a gift of the Spirit that empowered various sorts of people to assume a ministry of the word, remembering that 1 Cor. 11.5 implies that women were involved in this ministry.

As for the deacons (*diakonoi* – Phil. 1, Rom. 12), if they were not the church's financial officers/treasurers, then it appears their tasks were to see to the physical needs of the community including food, shelter, and clothing. Paul uses the term "overseer" (*episkopos* – Phil. 1) to refer to a leader or pastoral supervisor of a church. Providing a place to meet seems to have been the function of a well-to-do member or patron/ess (Acts 16.15). At Rom. 16.2, the Greek word *prostatis* probably does not designate an office, but rather a patron or presiding officer. Finally, the term "co-worker" which in its secular usage originally meant a person who shared the same trade, seems to refer to one who helps Paul in his missionary work.

It appears Paul's co-workers had a wide range of functions including assisting in letter writing (1 Thess.), checking up on and encouraging fledgling Christian communities (1 Thess. 3.2, 6), carrying apostolic messages to a church (1 Cor. 4.17, 16.10), providing a location for and management of a local house church, as well as instructing and evangelizing in the area (Acts 18, Rom. 16, 1 Cor. 16). We must avoid thinking that the churches developed at the same rate or with the exact same structures. Nor can we make hard and fast distinctions between the itinerants and the local leaders.

It still remains to ask about the local church leaders and their range of authority and functions. 1 Thess. 5.12 tells us about local church functions – laboring, administering, verbal discipline, acting as a patron or protector. In this last category, were those at the higher end of the socio-economic and educational scale who were able to provide certain benefits such as meeting places, financial support, protection, lodging, etc. These functions seem to have been both practical and pastoral. Now this is interesting precisely because Paul, while not abolishing all social or natural distinctions (ethnic, sexual), does use them in service of the Church. Previously, social and sexual distinctions were used to create religious barriers. Paul tries to use such distinctions and people to build up and knit together the Church and provide it a place to exist in safety. Robin Scroggs has argued that "Paul wanted to eliminate the *inequality* between the sexes, while the gnostics wanted to eliminate the *distinctions* between the sexes."[4] I think this conclusion is fundamentally correct, but the elimination of inequality was not Paul's main agenda. It was something that Paul assisted in bringing about in the course of preaching the Gospel of Jesus Christ and working out its social implications. Paul's over-arching criteria for assessing a leader or a gift were: Does it build up the Church? Does it or do they serve or sever the body of Christ? For Paul, service is the key. It guides how one uses one's wealth, gifts, possessions, etc. Thus, the community is not purely structured by the Spirit and His gifts. One's authority could come from revelation, from a spiritual gift, from being appointed, from one's closeness to Paul and his dictates, from one's knowledge and use of Scripture and authoritative traditions, or from one's experiences as a Christian. In some cases who housed the church was determined by who was financially able, and who first led a house church was in part determined by who was first converted. If one embodied Christ and His lifestyle one should be heeded. In the end, however, all offices/functions/leadership roles functioned in the context of the ministry expected of all Christians everywhere.

The hierarchy of leadership that emerges from all this seems to be the following: (1) apostles; (2) Paul's traveling fellow workers who were over or involved in several congregations (Priscilla, Aquila, Timothy, etc.); (3) local leaders. What is significant is that women were a part of the general ministry of all in the Pauline community, *and* in the specific ongoing ministry of Paul as his "co-workers."

Trouble in paradise? – Phil. 4.2 – 3

Therefore, my brethren, whom I love and long for, my joy and crown, stand firm thus in the Lord, my beloved. I entreat Euodia and I entreat Syntyche to agree in the Lord. And I ask you also, true yokefellow, help these women, for they have labored side by side with me in the gospel together with Clement and the rest of my fellow workers, whose names are in the book of life.

Paul's favorite description for one who aided him in his ministry is not brother, deacon, or apostle, but co-worker. Of thirteen uses of this term in the New Testament all but one (3 Jn 8) are in the Pauline corpus. Notice how at 1 Cor. 16.16, 18 the Corinthians are urged to be subject to all those who are co-workers and laborers. Clearly, this implies that they have some leadership role in the Corinthian community. 1 Thess. 5.12 speaks of workers who are "over you in the Lord and admonish you" which clearly implies a leadership function involving some form of authoritative speech. It is hard to say whether this means preaching or teaching or both, but it likely involved at least one of these, and it appears unlikely that Paul simply has prophesying or its weighing in view here since he uses none of that sort of language to describe what these laborers did.

It is on account of this evidence that Phil. 4.2 – 3 becomes so illuminating. In the first place, Paul is clearly dealing with two women in this passage. Secondly, unless the problem between these two women was significant enough to affect the Philippian church, it is unlikely Paul would have addressed it in a letter to the whole church. Thirdly, "in the Lord" may mean "in the Christian community" in which case we are definitely dealing with a personal problem affecting the community. It required the church leaders to intercede and bring about reconciliation and unity "in the Lord." We simply do not know who Paul's yoke fellow was (although the words must surely argue that it was a man) but Paul is apparently calling upon someone he felt was trustworthy and in authority.

Paul says of these two women that "they struggled together with me in the gospel along with Clement also and the rest of my co-workers.'' The key verb in verse 3 is drawn from athletic terminology used of the pagan games or gladiatorial matches, and could easily be translated ''fought together side by side with.'' This hardly suggests a passive role in the spreading of the Gospel, but rather one that involved real activity, difficult struggles, and noteworthy sacrifices (Phil. 1.27). That they are ranked alongside Clement and Paul's other co-workers strongly suggests that the two women engaged in the spreading of the Gospel with Paul.

This should not surprise us since we have noted the somewhat liberated status various Macedonian women had even before Paul's day; in fact, the Macedonian church was founded when Lydia was converted (Acts 16). Both Philippians and Acts suggest that women took leading roles in the Philippian congregation. One wonders if this had any bearing on the fact that the church in Philippi was apparently Paul's most beloved and least troubled group.

An ancient greeting card? – Rom. 16.1–16

I commend to you our sister Phoebe, a deaconess of the church at Cenchreae, that you may receive her in the Lord as befits the saints, and help her in whatever she may require from you, for she has been a helper of many and of myself as well. Greet Priscilla and Aquila, my fellow workers in Christ Jesus, who risked their necks for my life, to whom not only I but also all the churches of the Gentiles give thanks; greet also the church in their house … Greet Mary, who has worked hard among you. Greet Andronicus and Junia(s), my kinsmen and my fellow prisoners; they are men of note among the apostles, and they were in Christ before me … Greet those workers in the Lord, Tryphaena and Tryphosa. Greet the beloved Persis, who has worked hard in the Lord. Greet Rufus, eminent in the Lord, also his mother and mine … Greet Philologus, Julia, Nereus and his sister, and Olympas and all the saints who are with them. Greet one another with a holy kiss. All the churches of Christ greet you.

Phoebe is commended and called both deaconess and a protector (helper). She was the former in the church at Cenchreae, the eastern point of Corinth, and the latter for many including Paul himself. How then are we to evaluate these two assertions? Rom. 16.2 and possibly 1 Tim. 3.11 are the only two places in the New Testament where women are given the title deaconess. It may be possible to trace the development of this church function from some of the passages in Acts we will explore later in this book, through Rom. 16.1 to Phil. 1.1 and finally to 1 Tim. 3.8ff. It seems clear that this term was used for those devoted to "the practical service of the needy." Cranfield points out that Paul's formulation, "deaconess of the church," suggests we are at the stage where deacon(ess) was a definite church office or recognized ongoing function.[5] This fits well with the description of Phoebe as a protector (helper). If one examines Rom. 12.8 it appears we are talking about a person in charge of the charitable work of the church. In addition, she may have protected Paul and others by providing sanctuary in times of trouble.

Later we will discuss in detail Priscilla and Aquila, a husband and wife ministry team whom Paul calls his co-workers. Here we are being told they even "risked their necks" for Paul. The end of verse 4 suggests the large impact this team had on the Gentile church as a whole. Between Acts and Paul's letters, we hear of them playing important roles in the churches of Ephesus, Corinth, and Rome. One gets the impression they were some of Paul's closest and most reliable workers and it is likely that they were involved in a wide range of activities from providing hospitality for Paul, to church planting, to teaching and preaching (notice the mention of churches in their home, Rom. 16.5, 1 Cor. 16.19, Acts 18.1–3). Clearly they were a major factor in the Gentile mission.

In verses 6–7 we hear of a Mary who has been a hard worker for Paul's audience. The name may be a Jewish one, and it is possible that not only Aquila, Priscilla, and Mary, but also various of the others named here, were Jewish Christians. This is significant because Jewish women in particular would have seen the new religious roles allowed them in Christianity to be in stark contrast to the synagogue or Jewish home. If laborer and co-worker have virtually identical meanings, Mary's work cannot be limited to hospitality or charitable work.

What then do we make of Andronicus and Junia(s)? Are these two men, or a man and a woman, perhaps a husband and wife? While possibly Junia(s) is a shortened form of the name Junianus, probably it is a common Roman female name, Junia. Besides the fact that there is no evidence for the male name Junia(s) in this form, the patristic evidence (especially from John Chrysostom) supports the view that a woman named Junia is meant here. We must reckon with the possibility that another Christian husband and wife ministry team is in view here. Paul calls this pair his kinsmen which probably means they are fellow Jews who converted to Christianity. They too had been imprisoned, perhaps with Paul.

We are told that Andronicus and Junia(s) were "outstanding" "*among* the apostles." If this is the correct translation, then we have a reference to a woman apostle. The question becomes, what did "apostle" mean for Paul? Apparently, there are four ways the term apostle is used in the New Testament. First, it could refer to the original twelve charter members of Jesus' group of followers as in the phrase the Twelve Apostles. Secondly, it could refer to a person who had seen the Risen Lord and was commissioned by Him for some special ministry. It is in this sense that Paul saw himself as an apostle, and it appears Paul identified apostles of this sort by the phrase "apostles of Jesus Christ." Thirdly, it could refer to an emissary or missionary sent out by a particular church to perform particular tasks. Fourthly, it could be a term meaning a missionary.

It would appear that Paul means that Andronicus and Junia were engaged in evangelism and church planting as itinerants. That Paul says they are outstanding may imply that their work had borne fruit, prompting the recognition of the Church in various places. Paul adds that these two were converted before he was, suggesting that they were some of the earliest converts at the beginnings of the Church and could have had a decade or two of ministry behind them. The idea of Christian missionary couples (1 Cor. 9.6) could be a variant on the Jewish practice of sending out two yoke fellows, a practice Jesus may have adopted (Lk. 10.1). This practice would have allowed the women to reach fellow women and children which would have been difficult if not impossible for men to do, at least in Jewish contexts in the first century. Paul, however, says nothing here about a gender specific ministry.

Two more Christian women, Tryphaena and Tryphosa, probably sisters, are called workers in the Lord. Persis, a name which may mean the Persian woman, is called beloved and said to have labored hard "in the Lord" (another example where "in the Lord" likely means "in the Church"). Finally, at verse 15 we have greetings for what may be another Christian couple, Philologus and Julia, depending on how we punctuate the sentence.

The overall impression one gets from Rom. 16 is that a wide variety of women were involved in the work of the church, and that they were doing a variety of things including acting as missionaries, carrying letters, serving in charitable tasks as deaconesses, providing aid or shelter for traveling apostles, etc. If Rom. 16 was originally sent with Phoebe and the rest of this letter to Rome, we see here a picture of a vibrant, multifaceted church at the heart of the Empire using the gifts and graces of both men and women to further the spread of the Gospel and the Church. We noted earlier that in traditional Roman religion women did not have such a variety of roles, and it is not surprising that Christianity should have been viewed by pagan Romans as another Eastern cult like the Mysteries that was affecting a considerable number of Roman women and giving them active roles to play. Rome's cosmopolitan nature was such that people from all over the Empire came there to settle, or to stay on business, and this led to numerous contacts and converts for Christianity at the hub of the Empire. During the Empire period, people were a great deal more mobile than we might have expected, and there is no reason why Aquila and Priscilla could not have returned to Rome after Claudius' edict fell into abeyance. In any event, Paul realized his indebtedness to both men and women in his ministry and it is significant that he felt it important to address both before he came to Rome. This can only witness to the crucial roles women played in the house church in Rome (or less probably Ephesus).

One final conjecture is worth pondering. In the undisputed Paulines we have seen evidence of husband and wife team ministries such as Aquila and Priscilla, or possibly Andronicus and Junia. Did Paul make any distinctions between what roles wives could play as opposed to single women in ministry for Christ? In the later Paulines, we will see that widows apparently played a specific role. But there is no evidence in the undisputed Paulines that women had to be married to play a significant role in a house church, or any particular role for that matter. The conjecture that wives, under the authority of their husbands, might be allowed to do more for the Lord than single women has no basis in the material we have examined. If anything, 1 Cor. 7 suggests Paul thought being single was preferable for Christian women to give them more time for "the things of the Lord."

Conclusions

Both Phil. 4.2–3 and Rom. 16 indicate that many women were involved in some form of ministry, though we cannot know the full extent of their service. The use of the terms co-worker, deacon, and apostle of service indicates that Paul was receiving assistance from women in ministry not only in practical ways, but also in the ministry of the word. There is certainly nothing in the undisputed Paulines that would rule out a woman from teaching or preaching. Paul, however, did apply restrictions when new roles in the Christian community were taken to imply a repudiation of women's traditional roles and the importance of maintaining sexual distinctions.

12

THE PASTORAL EPISTLES

Behavior at worship – 1 Tim. 2.8–15

I desire then that in every place the men should pray, lifting holy hands without anger or quarreling; (9) also that women should adorn themselves modestly and sensibly in seemly apparel, not with braided hair or gold or pearls or costly attire (10) but by good deeds, as befits women who profess religion. (11) Let a woman learn in quietness with all submissiveness. (12) I permit no woman to teach or to have authority over men; she is to keep silent. (13) For Adam was formed first, then Eve; (14) and Adam was not deceived, but the woman was deceived and became a transgressor. (15) Yet woman will be saved through bearing children, if she continues in faith and love and holiness, with modesty.

Whether the Pastoral Epistles were written by Paul or by a later Paulinist, in all likelihood they represent a development of Pauline thought and practice. The question that the Pastorals raise is, are they a legitimate development of or a development away from the Pauline preaching and practice? This question becomes especially acute when we examine 1 Timothy 2 which seems to be a development of 1 Cor. 14, but also seems to go beyond, if not against, Paul's teaching in 1 Cor. 14.

Note the parallels between our text and 1 Cor. 14.33b–34:

As in all the churches of the saints, the women should keep silence in the churches. For they are not permitted to speak, but should be subordinate, as even the law says.

It appears 1 Tim. 2.8–15 is a modification of the same sort of argument we find in 1 Cor. 14.33b–34 to meet a later and different situation. In both texts it appears we are talking about behavior in the worship service, not behavior in general.

The author is attempting to deal with some specific problems affecting worship. Thus, at 1 Tim. 2.8 we hear about contention and grumbling among the men, and at 5.14 – 15 about backsliding or apostasy among the women. These problems may be traced to the influence of the false teachers who seem to have been espousing a "proto-gnostic" form of Jewish Christianity. Their teaching apparently involved some form of dualism that saw the physical side of human existence as having little or no significance in terms of salvation. As they argued, one could either refrain from or indulge in sexual activity without it affecting one's status before God in a negative way.

This would account for both the libertine and ascetic qualities that were part of the problems addressed in these letters. If 1 and 2 Timothy are concerned with Christians in a cosmopolitan city like Ephesus, where there was a wide variety of religious influences, then it is not surprising that from a practical point of view a clear and conservative policy about both theological and ethical matters was necessary. Christianity wanted to be a good witness to those who might be drawn to the faith, but at the same time wanted to protect the new Christians from slipping back into familiar pagan ways or a syncretistic compromise of the faith.

About the problems involving women we have the following hints. First, there were problems of a sexual nature involving young women, perhaps young widows (1 Tim. 5.11 – 16). Secondly, there were women weak in the faith, guilty of sin, and perhaps looking for an easy theological way out (2 Tim. 3.6 – 7). Thirdly, women were involved in (if not teaching) myths and endless genealogies and speculation involving the law (1 Tim. 1.3).

The tone of 1 Tim. 2.8 – 15 is indicated by verbs such as "I wish" (verse 8) and "I don't permit" (verse 12). The author has the authority to command, but the tone is somewhat milder than this, perhaps because the letter is directed to a faithful colleague. It appears the author is talking about men and women as groups, not husbands and wives.

In 1 Tim. 2.8 the author is calling the men to worship "without anger or quarreling." There were apparently some tensions between the men in this or in several of the house churches in Ephesus. We do not know what these disputes were about but the important thing to realize is that the author is dealing with abuses in worship. Likewise the author is calling for women to come to worship with modest apparel and without extravagant hairstyles. There is abundant evidence from secular literature of what the author is criticizing. J. B. Hurley explains:

He refers ... to the elaborate hair-styles which were fashionable among the wealthy and also to the styles worn by courtesans. The sculpture and literature of the period make it clear that women often wore their hair in enormously elaborate arrangements with braids and curls interwoven or piled high like towers and decorated with gems and/or gold and/or pearls. The courtesans wore their hair in numerous small pendant braids with gold droplets or pearls or gems every inch or so, making a shimmery screen of their locks.[1]

The author is arguing for modesty in dress and against ostentatious hairstyles that would attract the wrong sort of attention and so compromise the moral witness of the Church. Women who profess religion should instead be "clothed" with good deeds.

In verse 11 women are exhorted to "learn in quietness." The phrase suggests the correct behavior for one who is learning; it is unlikely to be a prohibition of all speaking. The focus is on *how* one should listen and learn, not whether or not one may speak in worship. Besides learning quietly, women are to learn "in full submission." This parallels "in quietness" explaining how women should learn and should be contrasted with the teaching and other activities mentioned in verse 12. This means that "in all submission" describes her proper attitude towards the teaching. This is probably not an attempt to make a comment on the relationship of husbands and wives. It is, however, being contrasted with an attempt to teach and domineer the men present at the worship.

Verse 12 indicates women are to learn in quietness and all submission but *not* to teach. The verb should be rendered, "I am not permitting." There are no examples in the Septuagint or New Testament where this verb tense implies a perpetual ordinance; rather, a timely and specific permission (or prohibition) is involved. Of course, only the context can ultimately determine such a matter. We have already seen that the author is dealing with specific problems in worship and there is no reason to doubt he is doing so here. Whatever verse 12 may mean, it would not rule out: (1) women speaking in worship; (2) women speaking in the course of their duties as a deaconess; and (3) possibly women teaching their children including males or other women in the faith. In short, there appear to be some hints in 1 and 2 Timothy of how the verb "I am not permitting" is to be qualified.

That verses 11 and 12 are addressed to women in general and not to those who may have been causing difficulties, suggests the author felt there was a sufficient problem in the congregation to impose a general, though possibly temporary, ban. The verb "to teach" is a general one and does not suggest a particular kind of teaching, such as "authoritative" preaching or teaching. The only apparent limitation from the context is that the author is talking about what all women should and should not do in worship.

The real crux of the matter hinges on how one interprets *authentein*, a word found only here in the New Testament. If one surveys all the extra-biblical and patristic evidence, it seems clear that the verb is a strong one. I conclude that the author of 1 Tim. 2.12 means that women are not permitted to "rule over," "master," or "play the despot" over men. If indeed 1 Tim. 1.3–7 includes a warning about some women (and men) trying to teach different doctrines, desiring to lay down the (Mosaic) law in the house church(es) in Ephesus, this correction of the problem in 1 Tim. 2.12 is quite understandable. It is advice given to correct a problem, but it also suggests the author did not favor a matriarchal power structure in the church (at least he did not favor a woman domineering or playing the despot over men). Once again, however, the dictum applies: "abuse does not rule out the proper use of a privilege." One cannot assume that the prohibition here would extend beyond the period of the abuse, or beyond other cases where a similar abuse might arise. There is then no universal and unqualified prohibition of women teaching and preaching in this text.

The author backs up his qualified restrictions with an appeal to Scripture in verses 13–15. It is important to ask whether the "for" in verse 13 introduces an appropriate example or whether it is giving the reason for the prohibition. If it is the latter, then it might be implying "Women should not teach because they are more susceptible to deception, as Eve was." However, it is not *all* women, but only weak and guilty women, who are said to be susceptible to being led astray. Notice that the author's solution for these trouble-some women is that they remarry, have children, and "rule the house" (1 Tim. 5.14). It is unlikely, therefore, that our author is trying to pass some universal judgment on women's susceptibility to temptation and deception. Only some women in Ephesus were manifesting that problem. Others were believing and trustworthy women who could be assigned tasks to do for the church (1 Tim. 5.16, 2 Tim. 1.5–6). Thus, verses 13–15 suggests that women should continue in faith and love and holiness with modesty, and not follow the example of Eve.

The use of texts in Genesis to teach women a lesson was common among Jewish expositors. Note that the curse on Eve was not childbearing but pain in childbearing, and the husband "lording it over the wife." Gen. 3.15 suggests that bearing children will be a blessing in that it will provide a "seed" who will combat and over-come the tempter, the serpent. Gen. 3.20 indicates Eve would be called mother of all living and 4.1ff. indicates she saw that God helped her to have a child. In short, Eve's being a mother was not a curse but a blessing from God.

Verse 13 speaks of the order of creation; verse 14 the order in the fall. What is interesting about verse 13 is the suggestion that Eve was made as was Adam, only second. Now this suggests not only an order in creation but an identity in it. Adam and Eve were made in like manner. The author makes no capital out of this assertion but presses on to the real nub of the issue – Eve was first in the fall, being deceived. There is nothing in this exposition which implies Eve's sin was sexual. Our author is considerably more constrained in his assertions than some of his rabbinic counterparts.

Verse 15 indicates that Eve's transgression is not without a remedy. Women in Ephesus are not to emulate Eve in being deceived and transgressing (listening to false teachers) but rather are to work out their salvation. How? Not by attempting to rule over men or engage in harmful teaching, but by being married, having children, and helping them continue in faith, love, and holiness.

Character of a deaconess – 1 Tim. 3.11

The women likewise must be serious, not slanderers, but temperate, faithful in all things.

This verse is set in the context of rules and behavior for the office of deacon. Though the women of 3.11 could possibly be a reference to deacons' wives, or even single women, whether widows or unmarried women, it is more probable that we see here a development of what we found clearly at Rom. 16.1 – a female diaconate.[2]

Unfortunately, it is not made clear what a deacon or deaconess did, only what character they must have. Whatever the tasks were, they may have involved practical service and charitable works such as those mentioned at 1 Tim. 5.9–16. It is difficult to say whether or not 1 Tim. 5.9–16 indicates there was already an order of widows when the author wrote. 1 Tim. 5 makes clear that women could serve active and useful roles in the church community beyond the raising of a family.

Finally, note that Priscilla and Aquila are mentioned at 2 Tim. 4.19. If this is a genuine greeting and this ministering couple was in Ephesus, then we know that there was at least one woman who had taught and probably continued to do so. This makes it all the more likely that 1 Tim. 2.8–15 is situation-specific advice. From all this we conclude that women were not banned from meaningful work in the Christian community.

Conclusions

In our study of 1 Tim. 2.8–15 and 3.11 we found no universal prohibition of women speaking in church but the author dealing with some serious problems that caused him to ban women from teaching and domineering over men in Ephesus. We conjectured that this was a response to women being involved in false teaching and being led astray into apostasy. The remedy offered was a reaffirmation of women's traditional roles in the family. There is nothing in this material any more than in 1 Cor. 14.33b–34 that suggests a permanent ban on women engaging in the ministry of the word. However, when certain isolated verses, such as 1 Tim.

2.11 – 12, are taken out of their historical context, it is understandable how such a ban could arise. It must be admitted that the material in the Pastorals is much more tradition-oriented and in this we may see a more conservative position than in earlier Paulines. Perhaps we should say this is a development of one side of the tension that Paul maintained between freedom and obligation. There is nothing in the Pastorals that clearly repudiates or contradicts Paul's earlier affirmation of both sides of the tension, but there is more emphasis placed on one side of the tension – the traditional one.

In the next part of our study we will examine how the tension between new freedom for women and traditional roles is presented in some of the Gospel material from the last quarter of the first century.

PART IV

WOMEN AND THE EVANGELISTS

13

WOMEN AND THE THIRD EVANGELIST

Women in the ministry of Jesus

Lk. 4.16–30 indicates that the liberation of the oppressed and poor is an essential part of any ministry modeled on that of Jesus. Luke structures some of his Gospel material to illustrate the fulfillment of Isa. 61.1–2 in the ministry of Jesus: preaching to the poor, giving sight to the blind, setting the oppressed free, and proclaiming "the acceptable year of the Lord." He stresses again and again that women are among the oppressed that Jesus came to liberate.

Another structural element in Luke–Acts is Luke's interest in male–female parallelism. This is evident both in Luke's noted pairing of parables, one about a man and one about a woman, and in his selection of special material about women. As Flender concludes: "Luke expresses by this arrangement that man and woman stand together and side by side before God. They are equal in honor and grace; they are endowed with the same gifts and have the same responsibilities ..."[1]

A good deal can be learned about Luke from the way he edits his Markan and sayings source material, for here we are able to compare the source material and its redaction. For instance, at Lk. 18.29–30 (Mk 10.28–30) we read: "Truly, I say to you, there is no man who has left house *or wife* or brothers or parents or children, for the sake of the kingdom of God, who will not receive manifold more in this time, and in the age to come eternal life." Luke's addition of "or wife" intensifies the cost of discipleship. Luke's concern for a woman's condition is also evident in what he adds to the Markan story of the widow and her two coins (Lk. 21.1–4/Mk 12.41–4). Only Luke says she was poor and stresses this woman's good example. More than any other Evangelist, Luke emphasizes Jesus' concern for widows, a particularly disadvantaged group of women.

Luke suggests that a woman's chief blessedness is in her response to God's word rather than her traditional gender-specific roles (11.27–8). Luke's portrayal of Mary and Martha (10.38–42), unique to his Gospel, implies a similar criticism of any attempt to suggest a woman's traditional roles were more important than hearing and heeding the word of Jesus. The "one thing needful" for women as well as men is a response to the Word, the "best portion."

Omissions from his Markan source also give us clues to Luke's interest as is shown in the way he handles the difficult material in Mk 3.21, 31–5 (Lk. 8.19–21). Luke not only deletes Mk 3.21, which implies a serious misunderstanding by Mary of Jesus, but also softens the contrast between Jesus' physical family and the family of faith. In Lk. 11.31 (Mt. 12.42) a prominent woman, the queen of the South, is praised at the expense of certain male Jewish leaders who ought to be setting a good example (see also 7.36–50 and 13.10–17, both uniquely Lukan). All of this demonstrates an editorial tendency by the Third Evangelist in favor of women.

Women in the Resurrection narratives

Although there is no great stress on women or their roles in the Lukan Resurrection narrative (Luke 24), there does appear to be a notable structural example of male–female role reversal and a stress on the validity of a woman's word of witness about the Resurrection events. When the women visit the tomb on Easter morning, Luke highlights the angel's words to the women: "Why do you seek the living among the dead? Remember how he told you, while he was still in Galilee, that the Son of man must be delivered into the hands of sinful men, and be crucified, and on the third day rise" (24.5–7). Luke implies that the women were with Jesus in Galilee and were taught these prophecies, for they were among His disciples. In this "call to remember," the women are being summoned to be true disciples. There is no future element in the angel's words or any commissioning of the women to go tell the disciples. Thus, the women are treated

202

not as emissaries to the disciples but as true disciples who are worthy of receiving special revelation about Jesus.

Finally, Luke gives the reader a list of those involved in the death, burial, and Resurrection events: "Mary Magdalene and Joanna and Mary the mother of James and the other women with them" (24.10). This placement of presumably known names at a climactic point may be Luke's way of validating what he previously recorded. If so, we again see Luke emphasizing the equality of women and their worth as valid witnesses to all three events. The women announce the Good News to the men and even to the Apostles, whose future it would soon be to make such proclamations.

Luke appears to make a deliberate contrast between the women witnesses and the men who receive the witness. He says that their words seemed to be nonsense to the Apostles who refused to believe their report. This reaction is typical of the common Jewish male prejudice against a woman's testimony; however, Peter is portrayed as taking the women seriously enough to go and inspect the tomb (24.12). It has been suggested that verse 12 is Luke's apology to his female readers for the Apostles' refusal to believe the women's witness about the empty tomb. Peter's wondering at what had happened is reminiscent of the women's visit. The parallels are perhaps Luke's way of informing us that the initial reaction of both women and men to the empty tomb is not faith but doubt and uncertainty.

Unlike Matthew and John, Luke does not recount a Resurrection appearance to one or more of the women. However, in Luke's main appearance story, the encounter on the Emmaus Road, there is evidence of male – female role reversal and contrast even though the story does not feature women. In 24.23 – 4 we see reversal whereby the supposed idle tale of the women is confirmed by some of the men. In the same verses there is male – female contrast; i.e. the women faithfully reported that the angels said Jesus was alive, while the men insisted they would have to see to believe. The irony reaches its peak here since it is Jesus who is being told all this, and thus the men are made to look very foolish indeed. We also see in Luke's main appearance narrative a vindication of Jesus' female followers at the expense of some of His male followers. The women had seen the angel and reported accurately the empty tomb and Easter message. The men could only confirm the report of the empty tomb and did not see Jesus or anyone else.

Women in the birth narratives

It is Elizabeth and Mary, not Zechariah and Joseph, who are first to receive the message of Christ's coming, who are praised and blessed by God's angels, and who are first to sing and prophesy about the Christ child. Luke presents these women not only as witnesses to the events surrounding the births of John and Jesus, but also as active participants in God's Messianic purposes. Perhaps they are also the first examples of the lowly being exalted as part of God's plan of eschatological reversal that breaks into history with, in, and through the person of Jesus.

Mary is introduced as a virgin engaged to Joseph of the house of David. At 1.28 the angel Gabriel greets Mary with the words: "Hail, O favored one, the Lord is with you!" Probably F. Danker is right in saying,

Gabriel's greeting is unusual, for women were ordinarily not addressed in this way ... That Gabriel, one of the highest members of the heavenly council, should come to the insignificant village of Nazareth and present himself before this girl – this is a miracle of the New Age and presages the announcement of the Magnificat, that the mighty are brought low and the humble exalted (verse 52).[2]

Mary should rejoice because she is highly favored by God – she is to be graced with the privilege of giving birth to the Messiah and of being the first person to call His name. Luke appears to give Mary the same status as the First Evangelist gave Joseph (Mt. 1.21).

The crux of the annunciation story is to be found in Mary's response in verse 34 – "How shall this be, since I have no husband?" Mary, unlike Zechariah who questioned the "whether," is asking "how" can this conception and birth take place considering her abstinence from intercourse during the betrothal period. She is seeking clarification not proof (for which Zechariah was punished). The angel's response is an explanation of how Mary will conceive prior to marital consummation – she will conceive by the Holy Spirit.

The similarity between the angel's response to Mary at 1.35 and Acts 1.8 is striking – both speak of the coming of the Holy Spirit. Mary is present at the birth of Jesus and at the birth of the Church (Acts 1.14). In both cases, there is a promise that "the Spirit will come upon you." Luke may be intending us to see Mary as a key link between the life of Jesus and the life of the Church.

Mary's reaction to Gabriel's explanation is the classic expression of submission to God's word and will: "Behold, I am the handmaid of the Lord; let it be to me according to your word" (1.38). The meaning of 1.38 is toned down by the translation "handmaiden," for the actual meaning is "Behold the slave of the Lord." Thus, Luke portrays Mary as binding herself totally to God's will, giving up her plans and desires for the future. Her response was one of submission in full recognition of what effect this act of God could have for her social position and relation to Joseph. We see the Evangelist presenting Mary as one who is willing to give up betrothal and reputation for God's purposes, the sort of self-sacrifice which, in Luke's Gospel, is the mark of a disciple.

Mary goes to visit her kinswoman, Elizabeth, and receives from her a two-fold blessing. In 1.42 we read: "Blessed are you among women, and blessed is the fruit of your womb". First we learn that Mary is blessed among women because she is "the mother of my Lord," i.e. because the fruit of her womb is blessed. This is a derived honor, for it is the fact that she bears Jesus that makes her favored. The implication seems to be that motherhood and the blessedness it involves are affirmed and hallowed, for God has chosen this means to bring His Son into the world. Mary's blessedness in her role of mother is what Elizabeth first remarks upon, and yet Mary could not have been the mother of God's Son had she not first believed and submitted to God's word. Elizabeth's second blessing is rather different. In verse 1.45 we read: "And blessed is she who believed that there would be a fulfillment of what was spoken to her from the Lord." In a sense, Luke intimates the resolution of the tension between physical and spiritual blessedness – it is the blessedness of believing in God's promise that leads to the physical blessings. Luke, however, indicates that Mary must yet wrestle to obtain a proper perspective on both. Her difficulty will be in learning and understanding both her own priorities and her Son's priorities which must be first with His spiritual Father and family, and secondly with His physical family. In the Lukan narrative, Mary has declared herself the Lord's slave, but she has still to learn that this entails her being Jesus' disciple first and His mother second.

What is the nature of The Magnificat? In its present context it has become a song of promise, prophetic protest, and powerful deliverance by the Lord of the poor and oppressed. It is Jewish in nature and similar to the Psalms and the Song of Hannah. While rooted in the Old Testament past it sheds light on the New Testament present and future as God begins to do new things. Mary is thus portrayed by Luke as a type of Old Testament prophetess who proclaims Old Testament hopes as the salvation of God breaks in; however, she differs from the Old Testament prophetesses in that she herself helps bring in salvation. She represents the Israel that obeyed God's commands, one of the lowly and poor upon whom God has bestowed unmerited favor. She is not merely a representative symbol of Israel's collective need and response, for the song is about her individuality. She as an individual fulfills her people's hopes by being the vehicle through which God's salvation and Messiah comes.

But it is wrong to suggest that Luke casts Mary in the role of a venerated saint. Rather, Mary recognizes that she is insignificant and of lowly estate. Her blessedness is in what God has done for her, and thus it is God, not Mary, who receives praises in this song. It is precisely because Mary is not portrayed as a sinless and angelic figure that she can be a model and a sign of hope for other believers.

The theme of Mary as "the servant of the Lord" assumes greater proportions and importance when we note with W. Grundmann, "The fact that God has regard to the lowly estate of his handmaiden gives rise to the hope that His eschatological action ... is now beginning ..."[3] Mary is seen as a forerunner of a Christian disciple, one who reveals what God will do for those who accept God's will in regard to the new thing He is bringing about.

In order to obtain a more holistic perspective on Mary's role in Luke's infancy narratives, we must examine her role in light of Elizabeth. Luke presents a somewhat developed picture of Elizabeth, but he takes pains to cast her in the shadow of Mary (just as Elizabeth's son is cast in the shadow of Mary's Son). The stories about Elizabeth and Zechariah are uniquely Lukan, though he may have found these narratives in his source and shaped them to show that both men and women are objects of God's salvation and subjects who convey His revelation. Let us see how Luke works out this schema.

After the prologue, Luke's Gospel begins in similar fashion to the First Evangelist – an angel appears to a man and speaks of a miraculous birth. In Luke the angel tells Zechariah of the birth of John; Zechariah expresses doubt; and Elizabeth expresses faith. She says, "The Lord has done this for me ... in these days He has shown His favor and taken away my disgrace among men" (1.25). She speaks both as a typical Jewish woman and as one who has been liberated by grace to sing God's praises. Her response anticipates Mary's, "I am the Lord's servant ... may it be to me as you have said" (1.38), and her "for He has been mindful of the humble state of His servant" (1.48). Elizabeth is portrayed as the forerunner of Mary. As Luke presents things, Elizabeth's miraculous conception serves as a reassurance to Mary that the angel's word is true.

Elizabeth in her relation to Mary reminds us of her son John's role in the Gospels in relation to Jesus. When Elizabeth is visited by Mary she says, "Blessed are you among women and blessed is the child you will bear! But why am I so favored, that the mother of my Lord should come to me?" (1.42–3). Compare this to the Lukan form of John the Baptist's words: "He who is mightier than I is coming, the thong of whose sandal I am not worthy to untie" (3.16, see Mk 1.7). Both texts convey the sense of unworthiness and the clear distinction between the lesser and greater person.

Luke certainly portrays Elizabeth, not Zechariah, as a person of faith. To the surprise of all the relatives and neighbors, Elizabeth gives their son the name John as the angel told her. It is only when Zechariah concurs with Elizabeth's words that he is freed from his dumbness and is able to praise God. Even when he does speak, his song in many ways is an echo of Mary's.

Just as Elizabeth is given more prominence than Zechariah, and is cast in a more favorable light as a model of faith, so too is Mary in relationship to Joseph. There is little mention of Joseph until after the major prophecies and songs have been given concerning Jesus. It is Joseph, like Zechariah, who is silent in Luke's Gospel in contrast to Mary's silence in Mt. 1–2. In his way, perhaps Luke gives notice of the new freedom, equality, and importance of women in God's plan, in contrast to the prejudices and limitations they often faced in Judaism. Luke does indicate, however, that it is Joseph who leads and guides the family on a journey, and it is to the town of his family line that they go to register. While Luke's vision of the New Age does include the idea of equality for women in service and importance to the Lord, there is no indication that he is rejecting patriarchy outright in his infancy narrative.

To this point we have seen that through the prominence of Elizabeth as Mary's forerunner and by the absence of Joseph, Mary is cast in a central role in this infancy narrative. This becomes more apparent when we examine Mary's relationship to Anna and Simeon in the Temple.

Anna and Simeon are representatives of the old order of Jewish piety and of the longings of their people for the Messiah. Simeon is described as one who has been looking for the "consolation of Israel," a term for the salvation that would come to Israel in the Messianic era.

Luke has Simeon bless both Joseph and Mary to indicate God's endorsement of them in their roles as mother and father. However, Simeon turns to Mary with the fateful words: "Behold, this child is set for the fall and rising of many in Israel, and for a sign that is spoken against (and a sword will pierce through your own soul also), that thoughts out of many hearts may be revealed" (2.34–5). The sword has been seen as a reference either to Mary's doubts about Jesus at the cross, or to her co-suffering with Jesus beneath the cross, or to the word of God as a sword piercing Mary. Luke, however, makes no mention of Mary at the cross; therefore, views involving the cross are probably inconsistent with the Evangelist's purpose. The sword is probably symbolic of the cause of Mary's anguish, i.e. seeing her Son spoken against and rejected by her own people. She is part of true Israel, yet she is being divided between Israel and her Son. Mary's sword of rejection may also entail Jesus' apparent turning away from her (see Lk. 8.19–21), even as early as the next scene in Luke's account (2.41–52).

Luke frames the infancy narrative with men and women who are connected closely with the Temple (1.5–25, 2.22–40). The woman who completes the second half of the parallel structure is Anna.

She, like Simeon, is old and devout. In view of other parallels noted between Lk. 1 – 2 and Acts 1 – 2, it is possible that we should see in Anna a foreshadowing of the pouring out of the Spirit of prophecy on men and women (Acts 2.17). As a prophetess she stands in the line of such Old Testament figures as Deborah and Huldah, and Luke's shaping of the material may be the cause of her resemblance to Judith, a heroine in inter-testamental Jewish literature. Possibly, Luke mentions her because she is the second and validating witness to testify of Jesus' significance. If so, then Luke is placing a high value on the witness of a woman. Once Anna arrives and sees Jesus she goes forth to witness to the rest of the righteous remnant who long for the Messiah. She is presented as both a prophetess and a proselytizer for the Messiah.

Alfred Plummer has made an interesting comparison of Anna and Simeon. Simeon comes to the Temple under the influence of the Spirit, while Anna is always there. The sight of the Messiah makes Simeon happy to encounter death, while Anna goes forth to proclaim what she has discovered.[4] Do these two represent respectively for Luke the Old Testament prophetic order satisfied to see the Messiah and die out, and the New Testament proselytizing plan that goes forth proclaiming the new thing God is doing? If so, then it probably reveals how Luke has carefully cast his material in such a way to bring out the theological themes he desires.

Luke does wish to show that true Israel (Zechariah, Elizabeth, Simeon, Anna) recognizes the Savior, even when Jesus' own parents do not fully understand. Mary is put in perspective as one potential disciple (among many) who does not always have the clearest insight among those who are "true Israel." This lack of complete understanding on Mary's part comes out at several points in the narrative (1.29, 34, and 2.33). In 2.50 it is explicitly said of Mary and Joseph that "they did not understand the things he said to them." Luke does not paint an idealized portrait of Mary, but is willing to reveal both her insight and her lack of understanding. We also have affirmations by Luke that Mary neither forgot nor failed to ponder Jesus' words (2.19, 51). Thus, we see that Luke is presenting Mary as an example of a person growing toward full understanding. The point is that it will take time for Mary to understand all that happens in the course of Jesus' earthly life. Raymond Brown says,

... Luke's idea is that complete acceptance of the word of God, complete understanding of who Jesus is, and complete discipleship is not yet possible. This will come through the ministry of Jesus and particularly through the cross and resurrection. It is no accident that the final reaction of the parents of Jesus in the infancy narrative is very much like that of the disciples of Jesus after the third passion prediction: "They did not understand any of these things, and this word ... was hidden from them" (18:34). But Luke does not leave Mary on the negative note of misunderstanding. Rather, in 2.51 he stresses her retention of what she has not yet understood and (implicitly – see 2:19) her continuing search to understand.[5]

In the story of the boy Jesus in the Temple (2.41 – 52) the tension between the claims of the physical and spiritual family on Jesus are made evident when Mary speaks of Jesus' father (Joseph) and he replies in terms of His real Father (God). The Evangelist draws a parallel between Mary and Jesus by stating that Jesus grew in wisdom and stature, while Mary stored up information and gave it careful consideration. Thoughtful learning is a characteristic mark of the growing disciple (8.15, 18 – 21, 10.39). Luke may wish to make clear that while Mary recognizes Jesus' miraculous birth, she does not understand what it may imply in regard to His life work and mission. In this she would be like other disciples who do not fully understand until after the Resurrection (24.45 – 7). For the Lukan audience, Mary is a very approachable model of faith.

Women in the primitive church – The Book of Acts

Luke does not feature women in his Book of Acts to the same degree as he does in his Gospel. Nevertheless, there are certain traces of Lukan male – female parallelism, and perhaps male – female role reversal in the material not directly focusing on women, and women figure prominently in some of the editorial summaries. It is no accident that in the few texts where Christian women do receive attention, Luke gives us something of a survey of the different roles they played in the earliest days of Church history.

Incidental references

In terms of male – female parallelism, Ananias and Sapphira (Acts 5.1–11) are in some respects negative counterparts to Priscilla and Aquila, even though they apparently were members of the Christian community. Luke takes pains to show that both husband and wife were equally culpable, the former attempting to deceive Peter, the latter lying openly to him. The actions of this couple stand in contrast to the exceptional generosity and honesty of the only other Christian couple to whom Luke gives significant attention – Priscilla and Aquila. Perhaps Luke chose to present Christian couples who were polar opposites in order to provide examples for Christians to avoid or to emulate. Luke stresses the parallels in intention and activity of the male and female members of both couples.

It is also noteworthy that Luke gives examples of male – female partnership outside the Christian community, especially when he refers to governing authorities (Felix and Drusilla, Agrippa and Bernice). Luke's mention of Agrippa and Bernice three times (25.13, 23, 26.30) is hard to understand since they play no real part in the story. Perhaps Luke has a concern to show that the Word goes out to men and women of all social classes, and that prominent women who hear the Gospel sometimes heed it.

An examination of Luke's summaries reveals that he wishes to stress both male – female parallelism and the reception of the Gospel by prominent women. For example, in the process of recording the swelling tide of conversion, Luke points out specifically that more and more men *and* women came to believe (5.14). When Saul decides to persecute the Christians in Damascus, he plans to seize both men *and* women. This should imply to Luke's readers that the women were significant enough in number and/or importance to the cause of The Way that Saul did not think he could stop the movement without taking women as well as men prisoners. We find this sort of parallelism at 17.34 as well where Luke gives us the name of one male (Dionysius) and one female (Damaris) who were among those converted at Athens.

Luke's interest in prominent women converts is seen in the phrases "women of the first rank not a few" (17.4) and "a number of prominent Greek women" (17.12). These women are apparently among those who "searched the Scriptures" (17.11), even though Jewish women (or God-fearing proselytes) were normally not allowed to study the Old Testament. Thus, Luke may be pointing to the new freedom given to women by the Gospel even as they were in the process of accepting it. In each passage it is the women, not the men, who are qualified by words indicating their importance.

One of the major themes in Luke's Gospel is the idea of reversal of roles or expectations (the last become first, the first become servants) which to some extent he carries over into his second volume. Stephen and Philip, both prominent preachers and teachers of the Word, are among the seven chosen to supervise the food distribution to the widows. Thus, leading men are chosen for a task that normally a male servant would fulfill in a Palestinian Jewish setting, or a woman would fulfill in a Hellenistic or Roman setting. In the eyes of the Hellenists, for a prominent man to fulfill such a task would be demeaning and a reversal of roles with a man doing a woman's or servant's work.

Prominent women converts

Jesus often relied on the system of standing hospitality which implies an endorsement of certain roles commonly assumed by women. Perhaps we may hypothesize that this reliance and Jesus' instructions to His closest friends to rely on this system (Mt. 10.15 – 32; Lk. 9.2 – 5, 10.1 – 16), not only set a precedent for the traveling missionaries in the early Church, but also established a practice from which came the house church. If this is correct, then it explains why prominent women are mentioned wherever house churches are mentioned in the New Testament. Women converts of some means who were offering occasional lodging and hospitality to fellow Christians became the Christian equivalent of a "mother of the synagogue" as their homes, originally hostels for traveling Christians, became regular meeting places of the converts in their areas. In a sense, the Church owed its continuing existence to these prominent women who provided both a place for meeting and the hospitality required by the community. A woman's customary role of providing hospitality to visiting guests became a means by which they could support and sustain the Church.

Luke's interest in lodging and hospitality has long been a recognized feature of both his Gospel and Acts. D.W. Riddle suggests that these people and places are mentioned, not in order to historicize an otherwise non-descriptive narrative or to give it the feel of authenticity, but to recognize those who helped in the transmission of the Gospel in those early days.[6] Luke's second volume is about the spreading of the Gospel and those who made it possible; these places of lodging and hosts are mentioned as vital supports to that movement. However, it is not just a matter of these families providing temporary lodging for traveling Christian preachers and prophets, but a matter of providing a place where the Gospel could be preached and oral and written traditions could be collected. Thus, we may see hospitality not only as the physical support that kept the message going, but also as the medium in which the message took hold and was preserved.

These examples of hospitality suggest that the custom may account for a notable phenomenon of those days: the acceptance of the travelling preacher's message by entire households ... That the primitive churches were house-churches is a detail of this, and an aspect of early Christian hospitality.[7]

Christian hospitality was a vital factor both in the intensive (home becomes house – church) and the extensive (home-as-lodging for missionary and the Word) growth of the early Church. Inasmuch as women were mainly responsible for the hospitality of that day in a situation where the house was the center for the Church, women quite naturally were in the forefront of providing for Christian life and growth, and the spread of the Gospel. Probably, it is no accident that at the only two points in Acts where Luke clearly tells us of a church meeting in a particular person's home (12.12, 16.40), it is in the home of a woman. Perhaps Luke chose these examples in order to point out the role women, particularly prominent well-to-do women, played in the growth of the early Church.

Mary, mother of John Mark

As has been the case throughout this chapter, we are not concerned to raise or answer the question of the historical value of this material. Rather, we wish to ask how Luke is using his source material and what sort of teaching he is providing for his audience. Nonetheless, though our focus will be elsewhere, there are few reasons to doubt that Luke presents several narratives about women that have high claims to historical authenticity.

Luke tells us at Acts 12.12–17 that Peter went to the house of Mary, the mother of John called Mark. Luke portrays Mary as a widow whom Luke's audience would know primarily because of her son. Mary is financially well-to-do; her house has an outer court-yard gate and a servant girl named Rhoda. Mary's house is portrayed as a place for gathering and praying implying that it was a regular meeting place. Perhaps this is a woman's prayer meeting since (1) a woman answers the door in the middle of the night, and (2) Peter's words make clear that James and "the brethren" are not at the meeting. If so, then it is significant that Peter entrusted his parting words to a group of women.

This prayer meeting may have included Rhoda, the servant girl, for she came to answer the knock at the door. Rhoda's audience thought she was mad when she told them Peter was at the gate. Possibly Luke is providing an example of latent prejudices against a woman's, particularly a female servant's, word of witness. Nevertheless, Rhoda's perseverance pays off, her word is vindicated, and a crucial message is passed to the Christian community to be sent on to its leaders. Thus, the witness of a woman is shown to be trustworthy, and Luke presents Rhoda as an example for his audience.

That Mary would hold such a meeting in a time of mounting opposition to the Christian movement is evidence that Luke is portraying one woman's courageous contribution to the community of faith. Perhaps Luke intended a rebuke to those in his audience who had a tendency to devalue the word or work of women.

Lydia

Women were allowed to play a significant part in Macedonian society from the Hellenistic age onward. It is not surprising that Luke would relate a story about a prominent Macedonian woman who was converted to Christianity and assumed an important role in the Christian community.

As elsewhere in Acts, Luke chooses representative examples of conversions in the area covered by his narrative. It is probably not accidental that he focuses primarily on the conversion of one woman (16.12–15, 40) and one man (16.23–39). Luke's intention is once again to convey a certain male–female parallelism in order to stress the equality of man and woman in God's plan of salvation, and their equal importance to the new community.

The structure of Acts 16.12–40 is important for it reveals how vital it was that Lydia provide a meeting place for Christians. Luke is at pains to show that the Gospel and its followers can exist within the confines of Roman authority by creating its own space "in house." That Luke portrays a woman, Lydia, providing such a meeting place for Christians in the city is crucial. Thus, he shows that the faith, while not subservient to Rome, is not fundamentally at odds with the Roman Empire or its authorities.

The story of Lydia is extraordinary in many regards. In some ways she should not be seen as a typical Macedonian woman, for Luke portrays Lydia as having come to Philippi from her native city of Thyatira, famous for its production of clothing goods with a distinctive and very popular royal purple dye. Perhaps she had moved to an environment where she could better take advantage of imperial Roman tastes and needs.

One of the significant messages Luke is apparently trying to get across is that Paul, in contrast to his Jewish background, is willing to begin a local church with a group of women converts. That women could constitute the embryonic church, but not the embryonic synagogue, reveals the difference in the status of women in the two faiths at that time, and it seems likely that Luke intended for us to draw this contrast by mentioning the "place of prayer" (16.13) and the church meeting (16.40).

Luke tells us that on the sabbath, Paul and his companions went down to the riverside outside the city gates, sat down (assuming the posture of a Jewish rabbi), and taught the women gathered at the place of prayer. Among them may have been some Jewesses, but there was one prominent Gentile God-fearer who had also brought along members of her household. Just as Paul's coming to Macedonia was due to revelation, so Lydia's conversion is to be seen as God's work. Luke intimates that God intended Lydia and her household to be the first converts in Macedonia so that the initial European church would have a good home. Lydia responded to God's work in her life by begging Paul and his company to take advantage of her hospitality, basing her plea on Paul's acceptance of her as a sincere convert to Christianity. Luke intimates that faith was the only door she had to pass through to be accepted as a disciple and a hostess of disciples.

Lydia's significance was not confined to her being a disciple or hostess to traveling disciples. Luke wishes us to understand that what began as a lodging for missionaries, became the home of the embryonic church in Philippi. This is suggested by the fact that when Paul and Silas emerge from prison they go to Lydia's house to encourage the brethren (16.40), rather than to the Philippian jailor's house where they had also been entertained (16.34).

Once again, we see how a woman's fruitful role of providing hospitality played an integral part in the establishment and continuance of a local church. The manner of Luke's telling of this story clearly reflects his interest in showing the advantages of embracing Christianity even for various underprivileged groups. Here a woman progresses from being a marginal member of a Jewish circle in which she could never receive the covenantal sign, to being a central figure in the local Christian church and the first baptized convert in Europe.

Women as deaconesses

No one is certain when the office of deaconess began in the Church. At the very least it seems probable that the office had its origins in apostolic times, and perhaps the first traces of its existence may be found in the New Testament at Rom. 16.1 and 1 Tim. 3.11. What seems more certain is that in New Testament times women were performing the functions later associated with the office of deaconess.

Possibly we find Luke's development of the idea of women serving the community by providing material aid in Acts 9.36–42.

In Acts 9.32–42 we note a sequence of two miraculous deeds by Peter, one performed for a man and one for a woman. The account of the healing of Aeneas is very brief (verses 32–5); perhaps Luke included it merely to create a certain male–female parallelism which reveals how the Gospel ministers equally to both sexes. In Acts 9.32–42 there is a clear crescendo in the miraculous – whereas Aeneas is healed of paralysis, Tabitha (Dorcas) is raised from the dead. In other respects as well, the story and person of Tabitha are presented in a more positive light than the story and person of Aeneas. While it appears that Aeneas was a Christian, he is not specifically called a disciple as is Tabitha. Further, there is no real interest in Aeneas himself, only in the fact of his healing. By contrast, the story of Tabitha relates in a specific way what she did and why she was important to the community. Finally, the story indicates that Peter recognized how important she was to the community, for he makes a point of presenting her to the disciples. This story may be taken as an example of the Lukan interest in giving a woman more prominence than a man.

Perhaps the main reason for the Tabitha story is that Luke wishes to reveal how a woman functioned as a deaconess – as a very generous supporter of widows. We are told that Tabitha was a "female disciple" and literally "full of good works." She gave money or material aid to the needy, probably to community members only (verse 36). Some of her good works involved making outer and under garments for needy women. That Tabitha's service was to all the widows indicates a specialized and ongoing ministry, not just an occasional good deed to friends or neighbors. The description of Tabitha is reminiscent of Lk. 8.3 and Acts 6.1–7, and thus it seems that Luke depicts Tabitha as fulfilling a task similar in kind to the work of The Seven.

Possibly, Luke paints a portrait of a woman commissioned for ministry, for Tabitha's efforts are depicted as an ongoing concern directed to a specialized group of recipients. It is possible that Luke intimates that Tabitha is in charge of an order of widows. Thus, she should be presented as a model of one who builds up and maintains the community by her service and living example of the power of the Gospel. It is the presentation of Tabitha as a model disciple that differentiates this story from that of Aeneas.

Women as prophetesses

Luke's passing reference to Philip's daughters (Acts 21.9) seems to be made partly because of his interest in the theme of fulfillment. In the daughters of Philip, Luke presents to us the first recognized and recorded examples of Christian prophetesses in the apostolic age. But what sort of prophetesses are portrayed here? Were they of the sort we find in Paul's correspondence with the Corinthians (1 Cor. 11.5), and thus perhaps involved in ecstatic utterance? Or, are we to see them as female counterparts to Agabus (Acts 11.28, 21.10 – 11), and thus a continuation of the type of prophet we find in the Old Testament? Or, are we to see them as a combination of these two types?

A survey of all Luke's references to prophets and prophesying in his two volumes leads to the following conclusions:

... Christian prophecy in Acts is represented as an eschatological power of the Holy Spirit from God ... or from the risen Jesus ... Although prophecy is a possibility for any Christian, it is primarily identified with certain leaders who exercise it as a ministry.[8]

As Ellis suggests, Philip's daughters are probably depicted as included among these leaders, since they appear to be more than just occasional prophesiers.

It is not clear how we should take the Greek work *parthenoi*. If it means virgins then Luke may be attempting to say that early on there was an order of single women who had a certain ministry to the Church. Because of the stress on "*virgins* prophesying" it would seem that Luke is not making an irrelevant statement about the virginity of Philip's daughters. These are the two main facts he relates about these women and it seems natural to suppose that Luke gives us these facts because they are related to their roles and their spiritual example for the Church. The participial form, prophesying, points to an activity or gift rather than an office, but it is doubtful that Luke deliberately tried to avoid calling them prophetesses. Perhaps we should not make too rigid a distinction between these women's functions or gifts and their office. However, it may be that Luke intends his audience to see a connection between these women being virgins and their having particular gifts and roles. It is probably not coincidental that most of the women we find in Acts playing a significant role were either single or widowed.

Women as teachers

In Acts 18.1 – 3, 24 – 6 we have a story about a husband and wife team of Christian missionaries and teachers. Luke's concern is not so much with *what* Apollos was taught by Priscilla and Aquila, or the results of that teaching, but that he was taught "more accurately" by this couple. This suggests that his concern is not doctrinal but personal, i.e. he may wish to indicate the role of this couple, particularly Priscilla.

Four of the six times the two are mentioned in the New Testament, Priscilla's name comes before Aquila's and it is unusual in antiquity for a woman's name to precede her husband's. Luke notes that Aquila is a Jew from Pontus, and implies that Priscilla was from the city they had recently left – Rome. Thus, Luke probably intends his audience to think of Priscilla as of higher social rank, or of more prominence in the Church, or both, than her husband.

There are good reasons for thinking Luke depicts Priscilla and Aquila as being Christians before they met Paul. As E. Haenchen remarks, "That a Jewish couple expelled because of the conflict with Christians in Rome deliberately gave a Christian missionary work and shelter is far more improbable than that Paul found lodgings with Christians who had fled from Rome."[9] If Luke expects us to think of Priscilla and Aquila as already being Christians, then we also see why Paul immediately leaves them in Ephesus – to lay some foundations for his later evangelistic work in that city. Haenchen adds, "the interest which the author obviously takes in Aquila and Priscilla ... shows that they were so important to the history of the Christian mission that Luke could not overlook them."[10]

What role do we find Priscilla and Aquila taking? Though Priscilla and Aquila's teaching may have included various matters of Christian doctrine, it is probable that it pertained to instruction in the Christian practice of baptism, since the one deficiency in

Apollos' knowledge clearly indicated in the text is that he knew only the baptism of John. "The way/road of God" likely involves a matter of practice, probably Christian baptism. This is to be contrasted with "the things concerning Jesus" which refers to the story of Jesus. If so, then Apollos was a Christian who needed some advanced instruction primarily on a matter of practice – the "way" of Christian baptism.

We can now discuss Priscilla's part in these matters. It is stated that both she and Aquila instructed Apollos and her name is mentioned first, so that if anyone is indicated by Luke as the primary instructor it is Priscilla. By "more accurately" Luke depicts Priscilla as expounding the matter further than basic Christian teaching, or at least in a way that involves the whole panorama of Christian teaching, so the place of the part would be seen in relation to the whole. Apollos is depicted as already having a correct framework and knowledge about "the things concerning Jesus." Further, Apollos is not just any convert to the faith but a man "well versed in Scripture" and this presupposes that Luke wants his audience to see that Priscilla and Aquila were also knowledgeable enough in Scripture to teach Apollos in such a fashion that he would accept it from both a woman and a man.

Since Luke does not care to expound on exactly what was taught, it is the fact of the teaching and the identity of the teachers and pupil he wishes his audience to note. There may be special considerations involved, i.e. Priscilla and Aquila are portrayed as a team and perhaps a team ministry is different from a woman acting alone. However, Luke depicts Priscilla as taking the initiative here, and her being married does not seem to be a determining factor.

Not all the implications of Acts 18.24 – 6 are clear, but certainly Luke portrays Priscilla as a co-worker of Paul in the Gospel. As John Chrysostom says, "He sailed for Syria ... and with him Priscilla – Lo, a woman also – and Aquila. But these he left at Ephesus with good reason, namely, that they should teach."[11]

Conclusions

In this chapter we are not so much concerned with historical issues as with the motives behind Luke's selection of stories for his Gospel and Acts. Given the material unique to Luke, and the addition and

220

omission of phrases from his source material, we see in his editorial style an attempt to present women in a new light, as an oppressed group "set free" by the fulfillment of Isa. 61.1 – 2 in the ministry of Jesus.

In the Resurrection narrative, Luke masterfully re-emphasizes some of his key ideas about male – female relationships. In 24.1 – 11 we see the new prominence of women as valid witnesses, worthy of being named as such in the Gospel story. We also noted evidence of male – female contrast and role reversal, for it is the women, not the men, who receive the more complete revelation and have the less inadequate understanding of the significance of the Easter events. We also see Luke's reassertion of the primacy of the community's male leadership. In a sense, Luke 24 presents a microcosm of his views on these matters and prepares us for the equality of relationship of male and female, the new prominence of women, and the reassertion of male leadership which we find in Acts as accepted facts.

The birth narratives in particular feature women at the expense of men. Elizabeth, Mary, and Anna are all presented in a more favorable light than Zechariah, Joseph, and Simeon. Mary's central role in the birth narrative is striking. Note the following:

(1) the Evangelist composes a scene where Mary, not Joseph, receives revelation;
(2) she sings the Magnificat;
(3) by Elizabeth's own words Mary is shown to be a more crucial figure than Elizabeth herself;
(4) Simeon addresses Mary specifically;
(5) Mary alone speaks for the family;
(6) while many wonder at the events surrounding Jesus' birth, twice Mary is said to ponder their significance;
(7) Mary in a unique way will feel the effects of Israel's rejection of her Son;
(8) in Lk. 1 Mary links the various sections of this infancy narrative while in Lk. 2 Joseph and Mary link the events.

Mary reflects the overlap between the old and new ages – she continues to fulfill the requirements of the law, but believes in the new things God will do through her. Lk. 1 – 2 reveals that in the context of Judaism, God can and does reveal the equality of male and female as recipients and proclaimers of God's revelation. True Israel is called to believe in what God is doing, and to see the blessedness of the motherhood of Mary. By presenting Mary as an example of true Israel, Luke is able to describe, through one individual, both the struggles of relating a Jewish heritage to God's eschatological activities, and the struggles of relating material blessing and the physical family to spiritual blessing and the family of faith. Significantly, from the beginning of his Gospel, Luke stresses that physical and spiritual blessings are both part of the new thing God is doing. It is not a case of being either Jesus' mother or His disciple, but of orienting her motherhood to the priorities of faith in God's new activity through Jesus. Her struggles in this emerge in Lk. 2.41–52. As part of Luke's presentation of the reversal the Gospel brings about, Luke stresses the way women rejoice and are liberated as God acts. Elizabeth is liberated from the curse of barrenness and the reproach of Jewish men; Mary is liberated to sing and prophesy even in a situation where she would appear to be of questionable character; Anna is motivated to witness to those looking forward to the redemption of Jerusalem. The male characters in this narrative, however, either remain silent (Joseph), are struck dumb (Zechariah), or ask to be dismissed in peace (Simeon).

Luke does not feature women to the same degree in his second volume as he did in his first. His five stories about Christian women are interesting because they reveal the variety of roles Luke intimated women could, and perhaps did, assume in the primitive community. In the mother of John Mark and in Lydia we see women assuming the role of "mother" to the fledgling Christian community in Jerusalem and Philippi respectively. This involved providing both the home and the hospitality needed for the local Christian missionaries passing through. Thus, Luke implies that women who do such things aid both the intensive and extensive growth of the Christian community.

The role we see Tabitha playing in Acts 9 is similar to that of Lydia and the mother of John Mark in that it entails providing material aid to the believers. In Tabitha's case, it appears to be a ministry to widows. We conjectured that because of the specific and ongoing nature of her good works, Luke may be suggesting that women should be, and perhaps were, commissioned by the local community as deaconesses in the primitive Church. Tabitha is depicted as serving in capacities later associated with that office so that even if she was not labeled or commissioned as a deaconess, Luke may still be presenting her as a prototype of a deaconess. That Luke calls her a "female disciple," may be his way of indicating that her actions are exemplary of how Christian women ought to be and act. Nevertheless, he shows no desire to confine women to roles that only involved providing material assistance, for he also mentions women who prophesied and women who taught.

Luke's mention of Philip's prophesying daughters is tantalizingly brief, but sufficient enough to indicate that Luke affirmed women were involved in this important activity that had its roots in Old Testament practice but also manifested the new gift of the Spirit (Acts 2.17). Prophesying was not the activity of every early Christian and a good case has been made for seeing it as primarily identified in Acts as the task of certain Church leaders. If so, then perhaps the reference in Acts 21.9 to the fact that Philip's daughters prophesied is more important than it might at first appear. We also learned from Acts 21.8–9 that Philip's daughters were virgins. Possibly Luke mentions this because he thought that in a woman's case being single was a prerequisite for the task of prophesying, or the office of prophetess, or, less likely, because he intended to depict Philip's daughters as being part of an order of virgins. Here we also see Luke indicating that roles other than the traditional ones of wife and mother were possible and appropriate for Christian women, and perhaps in Philip's daughters we may see early examples of the sort of roles these women were assuming.

Perhaps most important of all is Luke's reference to Priscilla in Acts 18. Apart from Jesus' mother, she alone among the Christian women mentioned by name in Acts is referred to in several other places in the New Testament. Priscilla is presented as a teacher adept enough to give Apollos, a leading male Evangelist, "more accurate" instruction, possibly about the important matter of Christian baptism. By including this story, Luke reveals the new roles he believed women ought to be assuming in the Christian community. Luke's portrayal of Priscilla is very positive, thus, it is fair to assume that Luke is presenting her as a model for the behavior of at least part of his audience.

By the very fact that Luke portrays women performing these various roles, he shows how the Gospel liberates and creates new possibilities for women. In Jerusalem, Joppa, Philippi, Corinth, Ephesus, Thessalonica, Beroea, and Athens, we find women being converted or serving the Christian community in roles that normally would not have been available to them apart from that community. Thus, Luke chronicles the progress of women as part of the effects of the Christian Gospel. Though it is not perhaps one of his major themes in Acts, nonetheless he takes care to reveal that where the Gospel went, women were some of the first, foremost, and most fruitful converts to the Christian faith.

Why then did Luke go to such lengths to stress and indeed support the role of women in the earliest Christian churches? It is a reasonable hypothesis that when Luke wrote in the last quarter of the first century there was still considerable resistance to such ideas among his audience, and so the case had to be made in some detail. Though we have not seen evidence in this chapter to warrant the conclusion that Luke totally rejected the patriarchal framework of his culture, he is exercised, like Paul, to stress a transformed vision of such a framework and to uphold a model of servant leadership. At the same time, however, Luke stresses the viability of women performing various tasks of ministry for the community. Luke and Paul stand together in maintaining a tension between the reformation of the old order and the affirmation of the new ''in Christ.''

14

WOMEN AND THE EVANGELISTS
MATTHEW, MARK, AND JOHN

The literature covered in this chapter is diverse both in its generally accepted date and in its audience. Mark's Gospel may have been written as early as A.D. 66–8 in and for a Roman congregation. The Fourth Gospel may date to as late as A.D. 96–100 and could hail from an Asian province. The First Gospel probably dates between these two extremes and if it is dependent upon Mark then we should date it at least to A.D. 76. Finally, the Gospel called Matthew has a certain Jewish Christian flavor and may have been written to a Syrian audience. To anticipate our conclusions, it appears that: (1) Mark has only a moderate interest in women and their roles; (2) Matthew has some interest in this theme but also wishes to stress informed and reformed male leadership for the community that follows Jesus; and (3) John has a real interest in portraying certain key women as models of awakening faith and as witnesses of the Christian community. Again, our interest is not on thorny historical problems but on how the Evangelists present material that bears on the question of women and their roles in the earliest churches.

The Gospel of Mark

Women in the ministry of Jesus

This Gospel appears to reflect little interest in women and their roles in the early Christian community. Indeed, Mark can be accused of painting a negative picture of Jesus' mother, brothers, and sisters (3.21, 31–5, 6.1–6). However, Mark's critique of Jesus' family could be part of his overall attempt to distinguish clearly between the physical family and the family of faith. The Evangelist has nothing against mothers and sisters being in the Kingdom, but the family of faith must take priority over the physical family (see 10.29).

Mark does record how Jesus gave loving attention to women and their needs. In 1.30 – we find Jesus healing Peter's mother-in-law and in 5.25 – 34 he takes time to heal a suffering woman and makes the point of telling her that her faith has made her well. Mark 5.35–43 recounts the raising of a little girl. More importantly, we have a woman being praised for her faith (5.25 – 34), a foreign woman being commended for her response to Jesus (7.24 – 30), and a widow being set up as an example for others to follow (12.41 – 4), while the Twelve are being criticized for their lack of understanding and belief (4.40, 6.52). This is particularly telling because Mark normally focuses on the Twelve as *the* disciples of Jesus who receive extra, private instruction. To them are given the "secrets of the kingdom." Yet they do not respond in faith even as well as a woman who probably had "magic-tainted" faith in the supposed healing properties of Jesus' robe!

Notice how Mark's arrangement of teaching strengthens the physical family. Mk 10.1 – 12 rules out divorce and gives a more secure place to wives in Christian marriages. Children are affirmed in 10.13 – 16, and the audience is reminded to "Honor your father and mother" in 10.19.

On the matter of clean and unclean, Mark's point in 7.1 – 23 is to show that only moral impurity defiles a person. If such teaching can be understood to mean that ceremonial uncleanness was not a problem, then women could not be banned from worship during the time of their monthly period but could have full participation in Christian worship. We know that this sort of ceremonial uncleanness was considered a major impediment to a woman's full participation in synagogue worship.

The Passion and Resurrection narratives

In the Passion and Resurrection stories we discover that Jesus' women friends, not the Twelve, become the primary witnesses to these crucial events in Jesus' life. Let us focus on some of the main features of Mark's story.

First, Mark presents the anointing narrative (14.3 – 9) which serves as a prophetic foreshadowing of Jesus' death and burial.

The author indicates that her act of devotion will be proclaimed in memory of her throughout the world. Secondly, Mark recounts that Judas betrayed Jesus, that Peter denied Jesus, and that the Twelve abandoned Jesus, thereby stressing the failure of the male leadership. Thirdly, Mark focuses on the role the women played at the cross and the tomb before and after Easter. He goes to some lengths to mention their names not once but three times (15.40, 47, 16.1) to the complete neglect of the male disciples.

It would seem that Mark wishes to establish the credibility of Jesus' female disciples for they would become the validating witnesses of the most crucial elements in the Christian story – Jesus' death, burial, and Resurrection. These women provide the link between these events because they are mentioned by name as authenticating witnesses.

Precisely for these reasons it seems unlikely that Mark intended to end his Gospel at 16.8 – on a note of fear and flight which would invalidate the trustworthiness of Mark's female witnesses. All that Mark carefully builds from the Crucifixion, to the burial, to the empty tomb in regard to the women's word of witness is called into question. I agree with many scholars that Mk 16.9 – 20 is not the original ending, and I lean toward the theory that the original ending can be found in Mt. 28.9 – 10 and possibly 16 – 20. Matthew takes over virtually everything he finds in Mark including many prominent motifs. Mt. 28.9 – 10 implies that the women reported what they saw, brings to light the Galilean appearance promised in Mk 14.28 and 16.7, and contains the recommissioning of the Twelve intimated in the pre-Resurrection narrative of Mark. Though only a theory, the addition of these verses continues the pattern of justifying the role of women at the Resurrection developed by Mark. Let us examine their witness in detail.

E. L. Bode states, "The only Easter event narrated by all four evangelists concerns the visit of the women to the tomb of Jesus."[1] This observation indicates that all four Gospel writers saw this event as essential to their Resurrection narratives.

Mark's version begins by telling us that Mary Magdalene, Mary the mother of James, and Salome brought spices the day after the Sabbath in order to anoint Jesus. They were going to perform a devotional anointing of the dead, not to receive a revelation.

Upon discovering that the stone had been rolled away from the tomb, they entered and were greeted by "a young man ... dressed in a white robe" (16.5). He explains, "Do not be amazed; you seek Jesus of Nazareth, who was crucified. He has risen, he is not here; see the place where they laid him" (16.6). Thus, the women become "ear witnesses" as well as eye witnesses to the reality of the empty tomb and the Resurrection. Apart from revelation, the empty tomb is open to various interpretations, not all of them positive. Thus, the women had both heard and seen. They could testify not only to an empty tomb but also to a risen Jesus.

The revelation continues with a command: "But go, tell his disciples and Peter that he is going before you to Galilee; there you will see him, as he told you" (16.7). The women's task was specific and limited. In Mark's scheme the purpose of the women's commission was to restore and reinstate the disciples so that they could become the authoritative witnesses to the world. This does not disparage the women's witness, but it does indicate Mark's endorsement of the view that the male leadership of Jesus' community, particularly Peter, is recommissioned by divine command despite their failure to stand by Jesus during the Passion events.

The women go to the tomb to perform a role that was traditionally theirs – anointing a corpse. But they left the tomb charged with performing a most untraditional role – relating to Jesus' disciples the Easter message and the command to go to Galilee. Once again, the first become last and the last first. Mark's narrative is bound together and given continuity by the triple mention of Mary Magdalene, Mary the mother of James, and Salome who validate the death, burial, and Resurrection events. However, while Mark intends this passage to give precedent for women to bear witness to the Easter events, and affirms the worth of women witnessing to men, at the same time the commission given to them may actually reaffirm their subordinate positions in relation to the male leaders. The women's witness is an indispensable foundation for the Gospel tradition, but the Apostles are the official witnesses to the world.

The Gospel of Matthew

The First Evangelist's interest in Peter and especially in church matters is well known. He alone tells us that the Church is founded upon Peter. Yet, almost exclusively among the Evangelists, he characterizes the male disciples as being ''of little faith.'' By contrast, he says of only one person in this Gospel ''your faith is great'' – a foreign woman (15.28). Thus, the theme of male – female reversal is somewhat in evidence even in the most Jewish of all the Gospels.

The birth narrative

Mt. 1 seems to focus on Jesus as the Son of David and Son of God, themes present elsewhere in Matthew. As Raymond Brown argues, Matthew probably composed his infancy narrative as an integral part of his Gospel, not as an afterthought.[2]

Joseph is the main focus in the birth narrative, but various women do play secondary roles. The first mention of Mary is found in the genealogy: ''Jacob begat Joseph the husband of Mary of whom Jesus was born, who is called Christ'' (1.16). The First Evangelist is suggesting that Jesus is legally in the line of David through Joseph but that physically Mary is Jesus' only human parent. What is also unusual about the Matthean genealogy is that it mentions not only Mary but also four other women: Tamar, Rahab, Ruth, and Bathsheba. There are a number of theories as to why they are included but perhaps the best is because they were involved in ''irregular'' sexual unions and yet were vehicles of God's Messianic plan. If so, then the First Evangelist calls attention to Mary as an instrument of God's providence. The genealogy also points out Jesus' indebtedness to both men *and* women for his Davidic ancestry, and to Mary especially for His humanity.[3]

As Matthew develops the theme of Jesus as Son of David he focuses almost exclusively on Joseph. However, when we turn to the second theme, Jesus as the Son of God, Mary comes to the fore through her relationship with Joseph and her role as Jesus' mother. Even here, however, the story is couched in light of what has happened to Mary, but is focused on Joseph's reaction to Mary's pregnancy. Let us now see how Mary's role and her virginal conception were viewed by Matthew.

Mt. 1.18 states that Mary was betrothed to Joseph, but before they consummated their marriage she was found to be with child by the Holy Spirit. This phrase is mainly a way of explaining that God alone was responsible for Mary's conception and that Jesus is the result of God's, not Joseph's, creative act. Thus, Jesus as a Son of David and as the Son of God is seen as a fulfillment of Old Testament prophecy. Mary is seen as fulfilling the role which would be a Jewess' greatest honor – being parent to a first-born son who is the Davidic Messiah. Through her, Israel's national destiny is fulfilled.

But it is Joseph, not Mary, who connects the sections and ties this infancy narrative together, a role Mary plays in Luke's infancy narrative. Mary is seen as submissive to Joseph's leading into and out of Egypt; in fact, she is not only submissive but also silent. Thus, the Evangelist reaffirms the traditional Jewish roles of headship and subordination despite the fact that Mary is singularly honored by a special relationship with God and His Son.

Women in the ministry of Jesus

A familiar theme in Matthew is Jesus' intensification of the law through a return to the spirit of the law. In the Sermon on the Mount we repeatedly hear, "You have heard that it was said ... but I say unto you." In each case extra responsibility is placed on the male leadership of the community for maintaining its moral integrity. For instance, in the material on adultery and divorce in 5.27–32 Matthew rails against male aggression and the attitude that makes women scapegoats for sexual sin. For Matthew, male leadership means more responsibility, not more privilege. Part of this responsibility is to remain either married or single for the sake of the Kingdom (19.10–12).

The Matthean editing of various Markan stories involving women gives little or no indication of any attempts to highlight women or their roles. Further, he is not averse to adding material that reflects negatively on women. Thus, at Mt. 20.20–2, it is not James and John but their mother who requests the special seats in the Kingdom for her sons (compare Mk 10.35 – 40). The parable of the wise and foolish virgins, unique to Matthew, represents both positive and negative impressions of women – the wise virgins are prepared for the coming King and His Kingdom while the foolish virgins are not.

The Passion and Resurrection narratives

In the Passion narrative Matthew seems to highlight even more than Mark the failings of the Twelve, but he does not highlight the women at the cross as does Mark. Nonetheless, Matthew features women as witnesses at the tomb more than Mark, and presents a more positive portrait of the women's involvement in the Easter events.

How has Matthew modified his Marcan source for the Resurrection narratives? Mt. 28.1 specifically says "Mary Magdalene and the other Mary" went "to see" the tomb – no mention is made of spices and anointing. Already, Matthew seems to be hinting at the witness theme he will develop and some even suggest they were witnesses to the opening of the tomb and the Resurrection.

The appearance of the angel stuns the guards but the women apparently take it in their stride. He addresses them only with the words:

Do not be afraid; for I know that you seek Jesus who was crucified. He is not here; for he has risen, as he said. Come, see the place where he lay. Then go quickly and tell his disciples that he has risen from the dead, and behold, he is going before you to Galilee; there you will see him. Lo, I have told you.   (28.5 – 7)

The reaction of the women to the angel's words is both similar to and different from Mark's account. In both, the women leave the tomb rapidly but Matthew adds "quickly" and omits "they fled." He tells us the women left *with* fear and great joy, not *because* of it. Their emotions are mixed and their running is not only out of fear of their experience at the tomb but also from a desire to "tell his disciples."

Surprisingly, Jesus Himself meets them and says, "Hail ... Do not be afraid; go and tell my brethren to go to Galilee, and there they will see me." When the women meet Jesus they eagerly grasp His feet and worship Him; when the men later meet Jesus in Galilee they worship Him but some doubted (28.17). Note also that once again the seeing and witnessing themes are emphasized. Interestingly, Matthew does not include Mark's account of the disciples' reaction to the women's message – perhaps he wished to spare them at this point.

In comparing Mt. 28.9–10 to 16–20 we see that only the women followers of Jesus are portrayed as models for the Evangelist's audience. Their devotion is sincere, their joy great, their obedience perfect, their worship spontaneous. By contrast, there is no outward expression of devotion by the men in Galilee. Here again we see male–female contrast. In the actions of Jesus, the Evangelist presents male–female parallelism, i.e. Jesus appears first to the sisters, then to the brothers, and gives a commission to both groups. However, the women are given a temporary task in service to the community of disciples, while the men are given the permanent task and authority to make disciples. The commissions affirm new roles for women, but reaffirm the headship role for the Eleven.

In conclusion, the Matthean Passion and Resurrection narratives prove to be an interesting combination of motifs involving male and female disciples. On the one hand, we have a pattern of reversal in which the women are presented as better models of discipleship than the men, and the women receive the first appearance of Jesus. Though they are given the unusual task of instructing the male leaders, this task is limited in nature and serves only to reassemble the male leaders. The men take over at that point as they alone are commissioned as evangelists with authority to make disciples of all nations.

The Gospel of John

The Fourth Evangelist presents us with the most-developed picture of women and their roles among those who responded to the call of the Gospel. He presents several women as more perceptive spiritually than certain men, and shows their progress toward a fully formed Christian faith.

Mary, mother and disciple

At the marriage feast of Cana (John 2) we see the tension between Jesus' physical family and the family of faith – a theme noted in Mark. Consider Jn 2.4: "O woman, what have you to do with me? My hour has not yet come." Not only is Jesus' mother called "woman," not "mother," but His response to Mary's request for help with the wedding refreshments should be seen as His disengagement from her parental authority (a theme we also see in Lk. 2.41–52). Mary must learn to see Jesus first through the eyes of faith, and then with the eyes of a parent.

Jn 19 should be seen as the Evangelist's way of saying that beneath the cross the family of faith and the physical family can be reconciled. The beloved disciple is representative of the community of faith and Mary will become a spiritual mother to that community. Some suggest that Mary and the beloved disciple are archetypal disciples, male and female, standing together beneath the cross as examples for all.

The Samaritan woman

John 4 presents the progress of a soul toward an adequate faith in Jesus. In the end, she seems to fulfill the role of disciple better than any of the Twelve for she goes forth to share the Good News about Jesus. She alone provides Jesus' real spiritual food, while the disciples can only bring back physical food from the village. Here is a clear example of male–female role reversal. John 4 is striking because it portrays *positively* a Samaritan woman who would be considered unclean and unacceptable to Jesus' Jewish disciples. If this Gospel is indeed directed to non-Christians, then the author is probably showing his audience how they should respond to Christ – using a woman as an example!

Mary and Martha

The portrait of Mary and Martha in Jn 11–12 is similar to that found in Lk. 10.38–42. In John 11 Martha is the crucial figure for she is depicted as having a dialogue of faith about Jesus. She is said to believe that even after Lazarus' death, Jesus can still help him. Her confession of faith "Yes Lord; I believe that you are the Christ, the Son of God, he who is coming into the world" (11.27) is the best to this point in the Gospel. Martha is certainly on her way to becoming a full-fledged disciple. Discipleship implies servanthood. In John 12, sister Mary is depicted as a model servant who performs a prophetic burial act by anointing Jesus with expensive ointment. Her act is defended by Jesus Himself.

The Passion and Resurrection narratives

John 18–19 does not emphasize the witness of women to the Passion, but there is a witness list mentioned at 19.25 which includes "[Jesus'] mother, and his mother's sister Mary the wife of Clopas, and Mary Magdalene." Unlike the Synoptics there is no mention of the women witnessing the burial. Unlike Mark especially, John does not seem concerned to link the women's authenticating witness to all three of the crucial elements in the Creed – death, burial, and Resurrection.

Jn 20.1–2, 11–18 relates how Mary Magdalene went from (1) a state of sorrow and preoccupation with the dead body of Jesus, to (2) a sudden state of euphoria because Jesus was alive which led her to cling to Jesus' physical nature in a way that limited her understanding of her Lord, to (3) a state of understanding so that she was able to leave her preoccupations behind and become an "apostle to the Apostles."[4]

In verses 11–18 we see this gradual transformation. Mary stoops to look into the tomb and sees two angels sitting like bookends where Jesus was laid. There is a void between them, but it is not devoid of meaning. They indicate that Jesus' body is no longer in the tomb and thus one should no longer focus on the past, the tomb, or Jesus' dead body. Significantly, it is only when Mary turns from the empty tomb (and the past) that she sees Jesus, but she does not recognize Him until He calls her by name: "the sheep hear his voice, and he calls his own sheep by name … and the sheep follow him, for they know his voice" (Jn 10.3–4).

In 20.17 we have Jesus' cryptic response, "Do not hold me [stop holding on to me], for I have not yet ascended to the Father; but go to my brethren and say to them, I am ascending to my Father and your Father, to my God and your God.'' Apparently, the wrong sort of clinging to Jesus' physical being is involved which assumes that relating to Jesus after the Resurrection is only a matter of renewing pre-Resurrection relationships. It is not a case of Mary being irreverent; rather, she still looked at the past and must be led to a higher, more spiritual way of holding on to Jesus. Mary learns that it is not a knowledge of where Jesus is, but where He is going, that truly leads to finding Jesus and to having a permanent grip on Him.

Knowledge of Jesus' true destination gives her the freedom to play a part in revealing the destiny of Jesus and His followers. Just as Jesus must journey to the Father before His disciples can journey to the nations, so too Mary must learn of Jesus' journey to the Father before she can journey to the disciples. Mary is given the role to bear witness; she is to be an ''apostle to the Apostles.'' The words ''Mary Magdalene went proclaiming to the disciples'' effectively tell us that she is looking forward to the task at hand, knowing that the Jesus she left at the tomb will not go away and leave her comfortless again. Ironically, Jesus has begun to reestablish fellowship with His ''brothers'' by first establishing fellowship with one of His ''sisters.'' It must be added that this Evangelist also affirms the ongoing male leadership of the community. Jesus breathes the Spirit on the male disciples (20.21 – 2), gives them power to forgive sins (20.23), and recommissions Peter as *the* tender of the sheep (21.15 – 17).

There is little doubt that the Fourth Evangelist wishes to portray Mary Magdalene as the first true witness of the Resurrection and thus as a positive image and model of women whose testimony was valid and valuable. Perhaps this was the message John's audience needed to hear in the last decade of the first century, due to the frequent disparagement of women as valid witnesses in various social contexts.

Conclusions

This survey has revealed that the First and Fourth Evangelists, as well as Mark, all manifest some of the themes we noted in Paul and in Luke – Acts, e.g. male – female parallelism, male – female role reversal, use of women as exemplars of faith, or as legitimate witnesses to the Gospel events. However, we noted that at the same time the male leadership of the community is still reaffirmed even after their despicable behavior during the events recorded in the Passion narratives. Even before the Resurrection material, there are hints that it is a reformed patriarchy the Evangelists have in mind, one that means more responsibility, not more privilege.

Matthew seems to be the most tradition-oriented of all, perhaps due to his Jewish – Christian audience, but even he does not endorse sexual stereotypes, and holds up women as examples of faith, even at the expense of some male disciples. Mark's material places special stress on women as the validating witnesses of the crucial doctrines of the Creed.

The Gospel of John, probably written last, places special stress on various women as models of the process of developing a fully formed Christian faith. Perhaps of these three writers, only for the Fourth Evangelist is this as much a crucial part of the agenda as it is for Luke.

Once again, it is plausible that the reason why these authors feel it is important to give attention to women and their roles is because when they wrote there was significant resistance to such ideas perhaps especially among Jewish Christians. If this resistance was indeed a pervasive reaction to women assuming vital roles in the earliest churches, then it is to the Evangelists' credit that they did not try to obscure the important roles of women, indeed, they often focused on them. This sort of honesty and commitment was to be almost universally lacking in the post-New Testament literature that led up to the Council of Nicea in A.D. 325.

CONCLUSIONS

Our study of Jesus' words and deeds leads us to conclude that in many regards Jesus differed from His Jewish contemporaries. This is more remarkable when we note that Jesus probably never left His immediate Jewish environment and directed His mission specifically to His fellow Jews.

Jesus' outright rejection of divorce would have offended nearly everyone of His day. His view that the single state was a legitimate calling for those to whom it was given, went against prevailing views about a man's duty to marry and procreate, but nowhere more so than in His native Palestine. This teaching made it possible for women in Jesus' community to assume roles other than those of wife and mother.

The fact that Jesus did not endorse various ways of making women "scapegoats," especially in sexual matters, placed Him at odds with other rabbis, though doubtless even many Gentiles would have thought that Jesus' rejection of the "double standard" was taking equality too far. Further, we do not find negative remarks about the nature, abilities, and religious potential of women compared to men on the lips of Jesus in contrast to various Jewish authors. There is also reason to believe that Jesus' estimation of the worth and validity of a woman's word of testimony was higher than that of most of His contemporaries.

Jesus' teaching that the claims of the family of faith take priority over the physical family also led to some circumstances that both Jew and Gentile would have found objectionable. For instance, what husband (Jew or Gentile) would willingly have let his wife leave home and family to become a follower of an itinerant Jewish preacher? This teaching did not lead Jesus to repudiate either the traditional family structure or the patriarchal framework which existed to one degree

237

or another in all Mediterranean cultures of that day. Jesus' teachings on the matter of corban, on honoring parents, on divorce, and on children make clear that He was not advocating a rejection of the traditional family structure. Rather, Jesus reaffirmed the responsibility of the husband and male leaders to be moral examples for the community. Jesus' choice of twelve men to be leaders of His new community also leads one to think that He was attempting to reform, not reject, the patriarchal framework under which He operated.

Certain of Jesus' words and deeds, such as His teaching on the laws of uncleanness, His healing of a woman on the Sabbath, and His willingness to converse with a strange woman in public, while obviously offensive to His fellow Jews, would probably not have raised many eyebrows outside Jesus' native context. Then, too, Jesus' attitude toward a woman's right to religious training and to be a disciple of a religious leader, while no doubt shocking to Jews, would not have seemed radical to many Romans or Greeks of that day.

Jesus' views of women and their roles do not fit neatly into any of the categories of His day. He was neither a Qumranite nor a traditional rabbi, though He had certain things in common with both groups. His use of women, both fictitious and real, as examples of faith for His followers, and His teaching on honoring parents, is not without precedent in Jewish literature. His calling of men and women to radical commitment to God, in view of the inbreaking of the Kingdom, has certain affinities with the teachings of both John the Baptist and Qumran. Yet, on the whole, Jesus appears to be a unique and sometimes radical reformer of the views of women and their roles that were commonly held among His people.

How then did the post-Easter community react to the initiatives of Jesus for women? Note that it is the *later* material from the first century (Luke – Acts and the Fourth Gospel) which argues most strongly for the viability of new roles for women in the early Church. Further, Paul, like Jesus, affirms a transformed vision of the old patriarchal schema coupled with an affirmation of women's new roles in the community of faith.

The tension between the family of faith and the physical family is maintained by the Evangelists. The First Evangelist has more emphasis on a somewhat revised traditional orientation, and Luke's agenda places more stress on the new roles and possibilities for women. However, not one of the Evangelists neglects either side of the tension. Deliberate neglect of women and their roles along with a reassertion of Old Testamental patriarchalism is not found before some of the second-century Christian literature. None of the relevant New Testament material fits neatly into either of our modern patriarchal or feminist categories. Such stereotypes do not do justice to the evidence, and do not advance the discussion of this complex subject.

What sort of societal and community pressures prompted the balancing of tensions we have seen in our study? What were the forces that led to a reformed patriarchal orientation?

In examining the *external* pressures, as R. L. Wilken has shown, early Christians lived under the suspicion that they were practitioners of a "superstition," i.e. a religion which not only was foreign in origin but also undermined the social and civic order and the very foundation of Roman society. Romans valued religion largely because of its usefulness in sustaining the Roman commonwealth, and Christianity did not fit this description. According to Wilken,

Given this [Roman] attitude that religion is a patrimony from the past which sustains the life of the state, it was inevitable that the piety of the persecutors would conflict with the new movement that had begun in Palestine. The Christians were seen as religious fanatics, self-righteous outsiders, arrogant innovators, who thought that only their beliefs were true.[1]

Both the exclusive claims of Christianity and its perceived lack of support for any nation's institutions or culture, placed Christianity in a very bad light in the eyes of most Romans.

Secondly, as W. L. Meeks has suggested, first-century Christianity was mainly a lower- and working-class phenomenon with some notable exceptions.[2] All indications are that Christianity was *perceived* as a religion largely supported by women, slaves, and even minors. If we take at face value Paul's reminder in 1 Cor. 1.26 that not many in his audience were powerful or of noble birth, then we see that Paul and probably the other New Testament authors mainly addressed a group of people who had most to gain by a change in their status. This being the case, in an environment where Paul was concerned that Christianity present no scandal but the scandal of the Gospel, it is not surprising to hear exhortations to support the governing authorities, for wives to submit to their husbands, or even for slaves to remain in their socio-economic state. What is surprising is that Paul believes there is a theological rationale for such exhortations. Perhaps one should conclude that societal pressures provided the occasion and impetus for such exhortations, but not the rationale for them.

Thirdly, early Christianity was largely an urban phenomenon, and Paul was writing to Christians who had not withdrawn from the world like the Qumran community. Thus, advice on how to live in and with the societal pressures and norms of the day is to be expected. Indeed, Paul did not want Christians to withdraw from society, but to be witnesses to the dominant culture. Instructions for transformation, rather than capitulation, to societal models had to be urged, and this had to be done in a context where Christianity would be perceived as a viable option for urban pagans and Jews. A process of adopting and adapting ideas and practices (whether Jewish or pagan), as well as generating new uniquely Christian ones, was the order of the day. Christians were but a tiny minority in the Roman Empire, and that minority status could not help but affect the way Christians viewed their behavior, since they were also people who believed fervently in witnessing. The apparently widespread effort by New Testament authors to balance the old and new, traditional and non-traditional, is understandable because Christianity was from the outset a world affirming, yet world transforming, religion. Since Christianity was evangelistic by nature, it did not wish to be perceived as a revolutionary group so far as political, economic, and (to some extent) social matters were concerned. This meant that a process of sifting the values of the dominant culture was in order, along with the creation of some new values as well.

But how could early Christians demonstrate that it was not their purpose to undermine the fabric of Roman society? How could they allay suspicions that they might be the sort who would lead a slave revolt or burn the capital city of Rome? How could they live in the world without being of it and still make a positive impression on their potential converts? Certainly one way of doing this was to participate in the ordinary activities and common social life of the Empire. To some extent this was possible, and there are indications that

Christianity was perceived as another "club," similar to those which met for meals, social functions, and religious activities including burial rituals. It was only natural that members of the dominant culture would draw this conclusion about The Way, a group whose members largely met in private homes and had no public shrines. Yet, though Christianity resembled various other groups in the Empire, this did not place it above suspicion so far as those in power were concerned.

Christianity operated at distinct disadvantages first because it was not associated with a particular nation, shrine, religious location, season, or function of nature, and secondly because it appeared to deliberately distance itself from its nearest "relatives" – Palestine and Judaism. To make matters worse, Christians refused to recognize the legitimacy of other people's religious practices. This had definite social, economic, and political ramifications. Minucius Felix was not the first or only one to complain about Christians: "You do not go to our shows, you take no part in our processions, you are not present at our banquets, you shrink in horror from our sacred games."[3]

Thus, it was imperative for Christians to appear to be good citizens in the few areas where they could endorse the values of the society, i.e. in obedience to governing authorities and the endorsement of traditional family values. The surprise, then, is not that some traditional values were strongly asserted by Christian writers both during and after the New Testament era, but that new roles for women and new evaluations of slaves were also developed. I can only conclude that both the old and new roles for women in the Christian community must have been considered *essential* to early Christianity, for the pressure to conform to other religious and social groups was considerable, especially on a proselytizing religion that refused to withdraw from the urban environment and dominant culture.

But what of the *internal* forces which prompted the balancing of the old and new in regard to women and their roles in the Christian community? What internal pressures were at work to cause or resolve the conflict between cultural norms and community values? Answers to these questions seem harder to come by.

It has become common to argue that the loss of belief in an imminent Parousia caused a gradual process of accommodation by the Church to the values of the dominant culture. In fact, Käsemann once defined early Catholicism as "that transition from earliest Christianity to the so-called ancient Church, which is completed with the disappearance of the imminent expectation."[4] Now I do not deny that there were various early Christians who believed in an imminent Parousia in the first century, and that this number likely diminished as the first century came to a close. I maintain, however, that it is difficult to demonstrate that the concept of the imminent Parousia was the main factor causing New Testament theology and ethics to develop in the ways they did, much less to prove that this concept explains why the post-New Testament, Ante-Nicene Church seems so different from what we find depicted in the New Testament.

It seems to me that a much more significant shift within the Church's thinking that affected views of women and their roles is the shift from a balanced "already-not yet" eschatology to an "over-realized" eschatology. "Already/not yet" eschatology holds that God in Christ has *already* acted in history and has begun to transform humanity, a process that is *not yet* completed but will be completed at the end of time. Over-realized eschatology is vertical in approach; it looks up to heaven as the final state, rather than outward toward the horizon for a new state of affairs here on earth, a new earth. This shift, I believe, adequately, explains the growing dualism, other-worldly orientation, and world-denying character of early Christianity. Also, it explains why certain more ecstatically oriented groups, who affirmed that "the future so far as life on the earth is concerned is now" allowed women to have significant roles in their communities (Corinth, for example). Further, it explains why other groups, with a different sort of realized eschatology, saw the importance of developing Church institutions and structures which would "incarnate" the Kingdom on earth. Whether the structures were thought not to matter *or* were seen to be of paramount importance, both of these approaches reflect a replacement of a future eschatology with a realized one.

On one hand, vertical eschatology was capable of being world-denying and dualistic, insisting that flesh and spirit were inherently at odds with each other. On the other hand, vertical eschatology was capable of insisting on the essential goodness of creation, believing that the spirit could be incarnated in the flesh, and even in human

institutions. For those who affirmed the former type of realize
eschatology, all sorts of social, economic, and political matter
became of no importance; for those who affirmed the latter, suc
matters could be seen as of paramount importance for the advanc
of Christianity in the Roman Empire. The former approach woul
lead to a more private, if not separatist, approach to Christianity
while the latter would opt for a public approach to Christianit
involving both culture and cult.

In both subtypes of vertical eschatology, it is the nature of thei
realized eschatology, not their view of the timing of the end, whic
determines their orientation. As a careful reading of the Ante-Nicen
Fathers shows, it was possible for exponents of either approach t
believe in an imminent Parousia. This should not surprise us sinc
we find this same phenomenon in the New Testament. On the on
hand the author of Revelation takes a rather world-denying approac
to religion and prays for the imminent return of Christ to right al
wrongs and to remedy the suffering of the saints. On the other hand
Paul counseled about earthly matters and relationships, the natur
of marriage and government, etc., precisely because he did no
believe they were matters of indifference, even though 1 Thess. !
shows he could believe that the end might be near. Not the timing
but the nature of the eschatological approach is what is crucial
Further, how the creation and so-called creation order fits into one':
eschatology (or total theology of redemption) will significantly affec
one's view of women and their roles in the Christian community
The way creation and redemption interact in one's eschatology
will in large measure determine one's view of social roles and
relationships.

Richard Longenecker has put the matter as follows:

At the heart of the problem as it exists in the Church is the question of how
we correlate the theological categories of creation and redemption. Where
the former is stressed, subordination and submission are usually emphasized
– sometimes even silence; where the latter is stressed, freedom, mutuality,
and equality are usually emphasized. What Paul attempted to do in working
out his theology was to keep both categories united – though, I would insist,
with an emphasis on redemption. Because of creation there are differences
between the sexes which exist for the blessing of both men and women and
for the benefit of society ... yet Paul also lays emphasis on redemption

in such a way as to indicate that what God has done in Christ transcends what is true simply because of creation.[5]

Now, it seems to me, that Longenecker errs at precisely the crucial juncture. Surely, for Paul, it is not a matter of transcending creation, but of transforming it in Christ. Whatever is done in Christ is a fulfillment, not an abolition, of God's original purposes in creation and His renewed purposes in the work of redemption. This is precisely because Paul believed in the redemption, not the replacement, of creation.

Käsemann is much nearer the truth when he says:

Paul did not take over the present eschatology of the enthusiasts but set over against it eschatological reserve and apocalyptic. He is unable to assent to the statement that the Christian has only to demonstrate his heavenly freedom because the powers and principalities have already become subject to the Christ ... Present eschatology by itself, and not comprehended within a future eschatology – that would be for the Christian pure glorying in the flesh, such as [sic] enthusiasm has certainly sufficiently demonstrated in every epoch. It would be illusion and not reality. It is precisely the apocalyptic of the apostle which renders to reality its due and resists pious illusion. The Christian Church possesses the reality of sonship only in the freedom of those under temptation – the freedom which points forward to the resurrection of the dead as the truth and the completion of the reign of Christ.[6]

Later, Käsemann affirms:

The new age is not suspended in mid-air: it takes root on this our earth to which Christ came down. It does not create for itself there an island of the blessed as the Corinthians believed: it creates the possibility of the kind of service which can no longer be universal and alive if it is not carried out in the midst of the old, passing world, thus declaring God's rightful lordship over this earth; that is, preserving the world as divine creation. According to Paul, it is none other than the Spirit who imposes himself on the everyday life of the world as being the *locus* of our service of God.[7]

This is the vision of Paul, the dominant figure of New Testament theology, and it adequately accounts for his attempt to balance the "already/not yet," the present and future aspects of eschatology, the old roles of women in the physical family with their new roles in the family of faith. Paul espouses a theology of creation affirmed but reformed in redemption. It would appear that few were able to follow Paul in preserving the various tensions between old and new, and some, such as the authors of Matthew and Luke – Acts, had to place more stress on one side or the other of the tension probably because of the problems their communities faced in adjusting to life in the dominant culture.

A brief word is in order concerning the implications of these conclusions for modern discussions about women's roles in the Church. Nothing in this book suggests that women did not assume, or should not assume, a variety of roles in the Church – teaching, preaching, prophesying, providing material support, hostessing church functions, etc. The question of women's ordination is not discussed or dismissed in the New Testament, but there is nothing in the material that rules out such a possibility. If the possibilities for women in the earliest churches, as evidenced in the New Testament, should be seen as role models for Church practice in subsequent generations, then it should be seen that women in the New Testament era already performed the tasks normally associated with ordained clergy in later eras. These roles seem to be clearly supported by various New Testament authors.

At the same time, note that there is no evidence of any sort of radical repudiation of the traditional family structure. Such structures are revised and reformed in the Christian community. Headship comes to mean head servant, or taking the lead in serving, but this is not quite the same as some modern notions of an egalitarian marriage structure. It is possible to argue that the New Testament material, even if it involves imperatives, is no longer normative for Church teaching on marriage today. However, this raises the problem of using a selective hermeneutic, or of having some standard external to the biblical material itself as the final authority or arbiter of what is appropriate in matters of faith and practice.

One can also argue that it is the direction the New Testament data is pursuing, its trajectory, not its position, that is normative for the Church of subsequent eras. At this point one might suggest an analogy between the New Testament teaching on slavery and on women and their roles. If the direction of the New Testament data is the reformation of patriarchy coupled with the affirmation of women's new roles, then could this not lead to a stage in which the

Church has reformed itself into a state beyond patriarchy? If the cry of the New Testament authors is "always reforming," does there come a point where reformation entails abandonment or a point where reformation is no longer necessary? Whatever conclusions one draws on these issues or their implications for modern Church practice, surely the starting point for such discussion should be the careful, historical exegesis and study of the biblical material itself.

It appears that the case for new and more open attitudes toward women had still to be argued when the Evangelists wrote their Gospels. Perhaps this is the very reason why the Third and Fourth Evangelists take pains to present various women as religious models for their audience. What then was the effect of these new attitudes about women and their roles on the women who participated in the community of Jesus? What was the community of Jesus offering women in terms of status and roles in comparison to what was offered them in Judaism?

It is probable that Jesus' teachings attracted women in part because of the new roles and equal status they were granted in the Christian community. There were many cults in Greece and Rome that were for men only or, at best, allowed women to participate in very limited ways. Further, it is easy to see why women who were on the fringe of the synagogue community became Christian converts. Judaism offered women proselytes a circumscribed place at best, for they were faced with the Jewish restrictions that limited their participation in religious functions. While women were not allowed to make up the quorum necessary to found a synagogue, nor to receive the Jewish covenant sign (circumcision), these limitations did not exist in the Christian community. The explanation of why Christianity differed from its religious mother, Judaism, is that Jesus broke with both Old Testament and Jewish traditions that restricted women's roles in religious practices, and He rejected attempts to devalue the worth of a woman and her word of witness. Thus, the community of Jesus, both before and after Easter, granted women *together* with men (not segregated from men as in some pagan cults) an equal right to participate fully in the family of faith. This was a right that women did not have in contemporary Judaism or in many pagan cults. Jesus' teaching on the priorities of discipleship, His willingness to accept women as His disciples and traveling companions, and His teaching on eunuchs and what defiled a person, effectively paved the way for women to play a vital part in His community. *Anyone* could have faith in and follow Jesus – He did not insist on any other requirements for entrance into His family of faith.

In regard to the roles women could and did assume in Jesus' community, Luke particularly shows us that a variety of tasks were assumed by women, especially in the post-Easter community. The Third Evangelist suggests that women often simply resumed their traditional roles of providing hospitality or material support, though now it was in service to the community of Jesus. Such roles were acceptable so long as they did not hinder a woman from choosing or learning more about the "one thing needful" (Lk. 10.38 – 42). It is interesting that the major female figures in the Gospels are depicted as being in the process of becoming full-fledged disciples, a process which involved learning how to reorient their traditional roles so that the priorities of the family of faith were heeded. Thus, we saw Mary learning to be a mother *as* a disciple, Martha learning to be a hostess *as* a disciple, and Mary Magdalene and others providing material aid *as* they followed Jesus. In the post-Easter community we find women being portrayed as assuming a greater variety of roles (even as prophetesses), some of which would have been forbidden to a Jewish woman (e.g. being a teacher of men, Acts 18.24 – 6). The Lukan material in Acts only corroborates what we have seen in Paul and this suggests that Luke was likely drawing on some valuable historical material, especially in the case of Priscilla and Aquila, when he presented his portraits of different women.

While the teaching and community of Jesus was perhaps more easily embraced by Gentile women than by Jewish women, it offered Jewish women more in terms of status and roles than it did to Gentile women. For a Jewish woman, the possibility of being a disciple of a great teacher, of being a traveling follower of Jesus, of remaining single "for the sake of the Kingdom," or even of being a teacher of the faith to persons other than children, were all opportunities that did not exist prior to her entrance into the community of Jesus. Nonetheless, the Christian faith and community offered Gentile women a great deal also. As well as the roles mentioned above, the offer of salvation from sin, of starting life with a new self-image and purpose, of actively participating in a community whose Master had directed His mission especially to the oppressed, were offers that appealed greatly to Gentile, as well as Jewish women. This new status and these new roles are factors which explain the influx of women into the community of faith.

The implications of this study lead us to conjecture that Paul's appeal to the creation order in his discussion of matters involving men and women is a technique that he may have derived from the teaching of Jesus. Further, Paul's belief that singleness for the Kingdom was not only a legitimate but also a preferable option to being married may well be derived from the attitude and teaching of Jesus about "eunuchs" for the Kingdom. Paul's concept of continent singleness and fidelity in marriage as a gift seems to echo Mt. 19.11. Paul openly states that his teaching about the indissolubility of marriage is derived from "the Lord" (1 Cor. 7.10 – 11). This leads one to suppose that the exceptive clauses are the First Evangelist's editorial expansion on the words of Jesus. Note also that structurally 1 Cor. 7 is a grand exercise in male – female parallelism on a scale and to a degree that even Luke did not pursue. In all these matters Jesus and Paul stand together and in contrast to their own Jewish backgrounds. The precedent set by Jesus of allowing women to travel with Him, to hear and heed His words, and to serve the community may also have borne fruit in Paul's ministry, for there were several women whom he considered his co-workers.

If we are right that Jesus was attempting to reform, not reject, the patriarchal framework of His culture, then it is understandable why Paul and other New Testament authors sought to redefine, not reject, the concept of male headship and leadership in light of Christian or biblical ideas. Paul may be encouraging women to exercise their spiritual gifts in a way that did not involve the violation of their husband's headship. It is possible that the tensions in Paul's thought between the concept of male headship and his willingness to allow women to exercise new roles in the Christian community are tensions that were inherent in the attitudes and teachings of Jesus, and do not reflect, as some have suggested, tensions between ideas drawn from Paul's non-Christian Jewish past and theological concepts that he had learned since becoming a Christian.

The effects of Jesus' teachings and attitudes also appear to be in evidence in Luke's two-volume work. Luke especially seems determined to drive home his point about the equal place and new roles of women in the community of Jesus by utilizing the techniques of male – female parallelism, male – female role reversal, and by giving space to stories about women not found in the other Gospels. Luke's five stories in Acts presenting women assuming various roles in the primitive Christian community must not be passed over as though they were only descriptive accounts of history. Their choice, position, and content reveal a deliberate attempt on the author's part to indicate how things ought to be. Further, both Luke and the Fourth Evangelist wished their audiences to know that the tensions between the claims of the physical family and the family of faith on a woman could be resolved so long as the physical family allowed itself to be defined and directed by the dictates and priorities of the family of faith. Thus, in their own way, they present episodes in the life of Jesus' mother to reveal the difficulties of hearing and heeding the call to discipleship faced by a mother, and how these difficulties could be successfully overcome as Mary learns to become a mother *as* a disciple. The stories about Mary and Martha also reflect this theme. Notable is the Fourth Evangelist's presentation of Martha's confession as, to some extent, a model for his audience.

Another motif that comes to light in the Gospels is the presentation of women as valid witnesses of the truth about Jesus, and especially about His death, burial, empty tomb, and appearance as the risen Lord. It is significant that a crucial part of the Christian Creed is based on the testimony of Jesus' female followers. It is to the credit of the Evangelists that, to different extents, they highlighted the role of women in the Passion and Resurrection narratives. Worthy of special mention is Luke's way of revealing the validity of the testimony of Jesus' female followers by showing that it was confirmed by the Apostle Peter. Whatever the historical value of the Resurrection narratives, they tend to bear witness to the effect of Jesus' attitudes toward women on the Christian community.

The purpose of this book has been to present to lay persons especially the New Testament material which deals with women and their roles in the context of the movement Jesus began. We have focused on the passages that tell us something about the attitudes of Jesus and Paul toward women and their roles, in particular how

NOTES

1 Women in Judaism

1. While the Mishnah comments mainly on legal matters relating to Jewish religious practice (feasts, holy things, laws of cleanness, etc.) the Talmuds (Jerusalem and Babylonian) comment on a wide variety of topics ranging from sayings of the rabbis, to scriptural matters, to everyday life. Midrashes can be found in a variety of Jewish writings. The midrashic technique attempts to comment on Scripture (interpretation), and relate it to current situations (application), much as preachers today try to make the Scriptures relevant for today's living.

2. Mishnah Nedarim 9.10, most conveniently found in *The Mishnah*, ed. Herbert Danby (London: Oxford University Press, 1933), 277.

3. S. Lowy, "The Extent of Jewish Polygamy in Talmudic Times," *Journal of Jewish Studies* 9 (1958), 115–25; Mishnah Yebamoth 3.10, in Danby, *Mishnah*, 324, 326.

4. Babylonian Talmud Yebamoth 62b, Nashim I, Yebamoth I, most conveniently found in *The Babylonian Talmud*, ed. I. Epstein (London: Soncino Press, 1935–52), 419ff.

5. Mishnah Yebamoth 6.6, in Danby, *Mishnah*, 227; and Babylonian Talmud Yebamoth 65b, Nashim I, Yebamoth I, in Epstein, *Babylonian Talmud*, 436ff. The belief in an obligation to procreate and thus the duty to marry was one shared by Jews, Greeks, and Romans. See D. Daube, *The Duty of Procreation* (Edinburgh: T. and T. Clark, 1977).

6. Hillel and Shammai, both Pharisees, taught during the time of Herod the Great and became the two best-known scholars of their day. Hillel favored a more open approach instilling a new spirit into the laws. Shammai favored a conservative approach to tradition and had the larger following. See George F. Moore, *Judaism*, vol. 1 (New York: Schocken Books, 1971), 72–82.

7. See R. Yaron, "Aramaic Marriage Contracts – Corrigenda and Addenda," *Journal of Semitic Studies* 5 (1960), 66–70; P. Sigal, "Elements of Male Chauvinism in Classical Halakhah," *Judaism* 24

251

(2, 1975), 226–44; B. Cohen, "Concerning Divorce in Jewish and Roman Law," *Proceedings of the American Academy in Jewish Research* 21 (1952), 3–34.

8. The quotation is from a midrash on Gen. 2.18 most conveniently found in Moore, *Judaism*, vol. 2 (1971), 119.

9. Mishnah Tanhuma Wayyishlah sec. 36, most conveniently found in C.G. Montefiore and H. Loewe, *A Rabbinic Anthology* (New York: Schocken Books, 1974), 508, num. 1434.

10. Torah refers to the Jewish Scriptures, primarily the teaching on the Law as found in the Pentateuch (first five books of the Old Testament).

11. "Women," *Encyclopedia Judaica*, vol. 16, col. 626. H. Freedman, in Epstein, *Babylonian Talmud*, Nashim VIII, 141, n. 1, says that R. Eliezer's statement probably refers to advanced Talmudic education only, because women had to have some instruction in Torah to properly say their prayers.

12. Mishnah Sotah 3.4 and Mishnah Nedarim 4.3, Danby, *Mishnah*, 296, 269. In the latter statement, the Mishnah is giving permission to teach someone else's sons and daughters. The implication of this text may be that they could be taught Scripture but not Mishnah, etc.

13. R. Loewe, *The Position of Women in Judaism* (London: S.P.C.K., 1966); Montefiore and Loewe, *Anthology*, 510–11; L. Swidler, *Women in Judaism: The Status of Women in Formative Judaism* (Metuchen, NJ: Scarecrow Press, 1976), 97–104; A. Goldfield, "Women as Sources of Torah in the Rabbinic Tradition," *Judaism* 24 (2, 1975), 245–56; "Women, Rights Of," *Jewish Encyclopedia*, vol. 12 (ed. I. Singer; New York, 1906), 556–9.

14. The Seleucids came to power following the battle of Panium in 198 B.C. and zealously forced Hellenic culture upon the Israelites. First Maccabees records that the Seleucid reign finally ended in 170 as a result of the Maccabean revolution.

15. Moore, *Judaism*, vol. 2, 46, 130 for differing opinions on the matter of women's galleries. Also, J. Jeremias, *Jerusalem in the Time of Jesus* (Philadelphia, PA: Fortress Press, 1969), 363, 365, 374, n. 78; E.L. Sukenik, *Ancient Synagogues in Palestine and Greece* (London: Oxford Press for the British Academy, 1934), 47–8. One must also ask why women were originally separated from men in the Temple and in the synagogue. The separation may not have implied anything negative originally about a woman's nature or religious rights.

16. Note the famous benediction recited by a Jewish man each day thanking God He has not made him "a heathen, a woman, or a brutish man" (Babylonian Talmud Menahoth 43b). It may be that this blessing was

said because a normal man, unlike any of these other groups, had the privilege of fulfilling all the positive ordinances of the law and of full participation in the cult.

2   Women in Hellenistic settings

1. F. W. Cornish and J. Bacon, "The Position of Women," in *A Companion to Greek Studies*, ed. L. Whibley (Cambridge: Cambridge University Press, 1931), 615–16.
2. A. W. Gomme, "The Position of Women in Athens in the Fifth and Fourth Centuries B.C." in his *Essays in Greek History and Literature* (Oxford: Oxford University Press, 1937), 89–115; M. B. Arthur, "Early Greece: The Origins of the Western Attitude Toward Women," *Arethusa* 6:1 (1973), 7–58.
3. Thucydides, *History of the Peloponnesian War* 2.45.2 (Loeb Classical Library; London: Wm. Heinemann, 1935), 340–1.
4. K. J. Dover, "Classical Greek Attitudes to Sexual Behavior," *Arethusa* 6:1 (1973), 59–73; Cornish and Bacon, "Position of Women," 610–17; D. C. Richter, "The Position of Women in Classical Athens," *Classical Journal* 67 (1971), 1–8.
5. G. E. M. de Ste. Croix, "Some Observations on the Property Rights of Athenian Women," *Classical Review* 20 n.s. (1970), 273–8.
6. Diogenes Laertius, *Thales* 1.33, *Lives of Eminent Philosophers* (Loeb Classical Library; London: Wm. Heinemann, 1925), 34–5.
7. Robert Flaceliere, *Love in Ancient Greece* (London: F. Muller, 1962), 115ff.; H. Licht, *Sexual Life in Ancient Greece*, ed. L. H. Sawson (London: George Routledge, 1932), 339–63, 395–410.
8. James Donaldson, *Woman: Her Position and Influence in Ancient Greece and Rome, and Among Early Christians* (London: Longmans, Green and Co., 1907), 59.
9. *Ibid.*, 26.
10. Plutarch, *Sayings of Spartan Women* 242.23, *Moralia* (Loeb Classical Library; London: Wm. Heinemann, 1931), 3:466–7.
11. *Harper's Dictionary of Classical Literature and Antiquities*, ed. H. T. Peck (New York: Harper and Bros., 1897); Licht, *Sexual Life in Ancient Greece*; Gerhard Delling, *Paulus' Stellung zu Frau und Ehe* (Stuttgart: Kohlhammer, 1931).
12. L. R. Farnell, *The Cults of the Greek States*, 5 vols. (Oxford: Oxford University Press, 1896–1909); Martin Nilsson, *A History of Greek Religion* (Oxford: Clarendon Press, 1925); *The Dionysiac Mysteries of the Hellenistic and Roman Age* (Lund: C. W. K. Gleerup, 1957); and *Greek Folk Religion* (New York: Harper and Row, 1961).

13. Pseudo-Demosthenes, *Against Neaera* 122, *Private Orations* III (Loeb Classical Library; London: Wm. Heinemann, 1939), 444–7.
14. W. W. Tarn and G. T. Griffith, *Hellenistic Civilisation*, 3rd edn (London: Edward Arnold, 1952), 98.
15. G. H. Macurdy, "Queen Eurydice and the Evidence for Woman Power in Early Macedonia," *American Journal of Philology* 48 (1927), 201–14, shows there is no evidence to prove that before Eurydice women mingled in political affairs, and there are no traces of matriarchy anywhere in Macedonia.
16. Tarn and Griffith, *Hellenistic Civilisation*, 98.
17. Donaldson, *Woman*, 124.

3 Women in Roman settings

1. J. P. V. D. Balsdon, *Roman Women: Their History and Habits* (London: Bodley Head, 1962), 45; James Donaldson, *Woman: Her Position and Influence in Ancient Greece and Rome, and Among Early Christians* (London: Longmans, Green and Co., 1907), 77–147; Sarah Pomeroy, *Goddesses, Whores, Wives, and Slaves* (London: Robert Hale, 1975), 149–226. For a summary of a Roman woman's legal status, see R. Villers, "Le Statut de la Femme à Rome jusqu'à la Fin de la République," 177–89, and J. Gaudemet, "Le Statut de la Femme dans L'Empire Roman," 191–222, both in *Recueils de la Societe Jean Bodin*, vol. 11: *La Femme* (Brussels: Editions de la Librairie Encyclopédique, 1959).
2. Balsdon, *Roman Women*, 282.
3. See J. Carcopino, *Daily Life in Ancient Rome* (London: George Routledge, 1941); F. H. Marshall, "The Position of Women," in *A Companion to Latin Studies*, ed. J. E. Sandys (Cambridge: Cambridge University Press, 1910); Pomeroy, *Goddesses*, 198–230.
4. Livy 34.2.11–12 (Loeb Classical Library IX; London: William Heinemann, 1935), 416–17.
5. F. Altheim, *A History of Roman Religion* (London: Methuen and Co., 1938).

4 Teachings on family and single life

1. V. R. Mollenkott, *Women, Men, and the Bible* (Nashville, TN: Abingdon Press, 1977); K. Stendahl, *The Bible and the Role of Women* (Philadelphia, PA: Fortress Press, 1966); J. Leipoldt, *Die Frau in der antiken Welt und im Urchristentum* (Leipzig: Koehler and Amelang, 1955); A. Grassi, "Women's Liberation: The New Testament Perspective," *Living Light*

8 (2, 1971), 22–34; C. F. Parvey, "The Theology and Leadership of Women in the New Testament," in R. R. Ruether, *Religion and Sexism, Images of Women in the Jewish and Christian Tradition* (New York: Simon and Schuster, 1974), 117–49; S. Terrien, "Toward a Biblical Theology of Womanhood," *Religion in Life* 42 (1973), 322–33.

2. Vincent Taylor, *The Gospel According to St. Mark*, 2nd edn (New York: St. Martin's Press, 1966), 339.

3. J. D. M. Derrett, *Studies in the New Testament*, vol. 1 (Leiden: E. J. Brill, 1977), 112–17; J. Bligh, "Qorban!" *Heythrop Journal* (1964), 192–3.

4. O. Oepke, "Child," *Theological Dictionary of the New Testament*, 10 vols. (Grand Rapids, MI: Wm. B. Eerdmans Publishing Co., 1964–76), 5:640.

5. Alfred Plummer, *A Critical and Exegetical Commentary on the Gospel According to S. Luke* (Edinburgh: T. and T. Clark, 1922), 421.

6. This is not to say that children were considered the ultimate divine blessing by Jesus, as they seem to have been by some Jews (see Lk. 11.27–8). Jesus also saw that in the Day of Judgment what would normally be a blessing would become a curse (Lk. 23.29).

7. J. D. M. Derrett, "'Eating up the Houses of Widows': Jesus's Comment on Lawyers?" in *Studies in the New Testament* I (Leiden: E. J. Brill, 1977), 118–27. F. W. Danker, *Jesus and the New Age, According to St. Luke* (St. Louis, MO: Clayton Publishing House, 1972), 208, argues that the scribes were seizing the widows' property because they could not pay their debts.

8. K. Haacker, "Der Rechtssatz Jesu zum Thema Ehebruch (Mt. 5.28)," *Biblische Zeitschrift* 21 (1, 1977), 113–16. "In his heart" is perhaps awkward in this interpretation, nevertheless, Jesus is talking about the initial act, the sinful gazing, which amounts to the man leading the woman astray to adultery in his heart (even if the act is never carried out). Jesus was not shy of speaking of a man's adultery (Mt. 5.32b, Lk. 16.18).

9. J. D. M. Derrett, "Law in the New Testament: *Si scandalizaverit te manus abscinde illam* (Mk IX.42) and Comparative Legal History," in *Studies in the New Testament* I, 25–6.

10. H. J. Cadbury, "A Possible Case of Lukan Authorship," *Harvard Theological Review* 10 (1917), 237–44, esp. 243, n. 12; C. K. Barrett, *The Gospel According to St. John*, 2nd edn (London: S.P.C.K., 1978), 590.

11. In Lk. 16.18 also, it is the male who is the subject of the action, but here he is called the adulterer, a more radical statement for its day than Mt. 5.32a (and there is no exceptive clause in Luke). Luke has juxtaposed this statement with one about the Law not passing away,

and thus Lk. 16.18 is intended to indicate Jesus' intensification of the eternally valid Law. It does not appear that Mt. 5.32 implies that divorce itself is adultery; rather, the adultery that the woman is forced to commit comes if she remarries. Adultery is associated only with a further marriage union in Lk. 16.18. Mt. 5.32b and Lk. 16.18b are both more radical statements than the rabbis were willing to make, since marrying a divorcee was frowned on but not prohibited in early Judaism.

12. J. Murray, *Divorce* (Philadelphia, PA: Presbyterian and Reformed Pub. Co., 1975); J. A. Fitzmyer, "The Matthean Divorce Texts and Some New Palestinian Evidence," *Theological Studies* 37 (2, 1976), 197–226; W. B. Powers, "Marriage and Divorce: The Dispute of Jesus with the Pharisees, and its Inception," *Colloquium* 5 (1, 1971), 34–41.

13. "Q" refers to a source or collection of the sayings of Jesus common to the First and Third Gospels, but apparently not available to Mark.

14. Ben Witherington, "Matthew 5.32, 19.9: Exception or Exceptional Situation," *New Testament Studies* 31:4 (1985), 571–6.

15. J. Blinzler, "eisin eunochoi – Zur Auslegung von Mt. 19.12," *Zeitschrift für die neutestamentliche Wissenschaft* 48 (1957), 254–70.

16. J. Blenkinsopp, *Sexuality and the Christian Tradition* (London: Sheed and Ward, 1970), 91.

5 Women in the parables and judgment sayings

1. A. M. Hunter, *The Parables Then and Now* (London: SCM, 1971), 5.

2. T. W. Manson, *The Sayings of Jesus* (London: SCM, 1957), 282.

3. C. F. Parvey, "The Theology and Leadership of Women in the New Testament," in R. R. Ruether, *Religion and Sexism, Images of Women in the Jewish and Christian Tradition* (New York: Simon and Schuster, 1974), 139.

4. J. D. M. Derrett, "Law in the New Testament: The Parable of the Unjust Judge," *Studies in the New Testament*, vol. 1 (Leiden: E. J. Brill, 1977), 32–47, is right in saying that it was common for Jews to go to civil courts because, unlike religious courts, they could act without trial, witnesses, or evidence, and thus they were used commonly to gain illegal advantage of another person.

5. God's people are often characterized as one or another sort of woman depending on whether Jesus is present (bride, bride-to-be, or even bridesmaid, see Mt. 25.1–13), or absent (widow). If it is true that the role of the community of faith is characteristically feminine, then

perhaps women's roles and natures are better models for Jesus' disciples than men's.

6. Joachim Jeremias, *The Parables of Jesus*, 2nd rev. edn (New York: Charles Scribner's Sons, 1972), 133.

7. Hunter, *Parables*, 12; C. H. Dodd, *The Parables of the Kingdom* (New York: Charles Scribner's Sons, 1961), 93.

8. R. W. Funk, "Beyond Criticism in Quest of Literacy: The Parable of the Leaven," *Interpretation* 25 (1971), 149–70.

9. W. D. Ridley, "The Parable of the Ten Virgins," *Expositor*, 5th ser. 2 (1895), 342–9, here 343.

10. Hunter, *Parables*, 102, notes that in modern Palestinian weddings, once the bridegroom arrives and the door is shut, latecomers are not admitted. Perhaps this was the rule in Jesus' day as well. Theologically, closing the door means that all opportunities for participation in the Kingdom are over.

11. H. Flender, *St. Luke – Theologian of Redemptive History* (London: S.P.C.K., 1967), 10.

12. William Manson, *The Gospel of Luke* (London: Hodder and Stoughton, 1930), 200.

13. The OT background for the term "daughter of Jerusalem" is found in Song of Songs 1.5, Isa. 37.22, and Zeph. 3.14.

6 Stories of help and healing

1. I. H. Marshall, *The Gospel of Luke, A Commentary on the Greek Text* (Exeter: Paternoster Press, 1978), 310.

2. G. W. MacRae, *Faith in the Word – The Fourth Gospel* (Chicago, IL: Franciscan Press, 1973), 38.

3. *Ibid.*, 39.

4. R. A. Harrisville, "The Woman of Canaan. A Chapter in the History of Exegesis," *Interpretation* 20 (1966), 274–87.

5. There is no hint that her disease was life-threatening. We read in Mishnah Yoma 8.6: "Whenever there is doubt whether life is in danger this overrides the Sabbath."

6. Marshall, *Luke*, 195.

7. David Daube, *The New Testament and Rabbinic Judaism*. Jordan Lectures in Comparative Religion (London: Athlone Press, 1956), 170–83, esp. 181–2.

8. See Lk. 13.1–5. Jesus rejects this thinking and removes all excuses for discriminating against the sick by treating them as outcasts. Marshall, *Luke*, 559, suggests that perhaps this woman was being denied her status

as a descendant of Abraham because her long sickness was taken as a sign of sinfulness.

9. E. Earle Ellis, *The Gospel of Luke* (Greenwood, SC: Attic Press, 1974 rev. edn), 186.
10. I. Brennan, "Women in the Gospels," *New Blackfriars* 52 (1971), 291–9, here 296–7.

7 Women in the ministry of Jesus

1. Vincent Taylor, *The Gospel According to St. Mark*, 2nd edn (New York: St. Martin's Press, 1966), 235.
2. *Ibid.*, 249.
3. E. Stauffer, *Jesus and His Story* (New York: Alfred A. Knopf, 1974), 138.
4. Raymond E. Brown, ed., *Mary in the New Testament* (Philadelphia, PA: Fortress Press, 1978), 212.
5. Even their marital status is a non-issue which implies they have an important identity apart from marriage and strongly suggests they were not married. Jesus' teaching on eunuchs (Mt. 19.10–12) may have already had the effect of allowing women to have a choice in regard to marriage. Mary and Martha, presuming they were single, could then be models of the single life for Luke's audience.
6. R. Bultmann, *The Gospel of John: A Commentary* (Oxford: B. Blackwell, 1972), 402.
7. Raymond Brown, *The Gospel According to John, I–XII* (Garden City, NY: Doubleday and Co., 1966), 429.
8. *Ibid.*, 433.
9. C.K. Barrett, *The Gospel According to St. John* (London: S.P.C.K., 1955), 345.
10. D. Flusser, "The Crucified One and the Jews," *Immanuel* 7 (1977), 34.
11. W. Bauer, W. Arndt and F.W. Gingrich, *A Greek–English Lexicon of the New Testament*, 4th edn (Chicago, IL: University of Chicago Press, 1952), 791.

8 Women and the physical family

1. F. Scott Bartchy, *MALLON XPHEAI: First Century Slavery and the Interpretation of 1 Corinthians 7:21*, SBL Dissertation Series 11 (Missoula, MT: University of Montana Press, 1973); D.R. Cartlidge, "1 Corinthians 7 as a Foundation for a Christian Sex Ethic," *Juridical Review* 55 (1975), 220–34, esp. 221–2.
2. *Ibid.*, 164.

3. J.K. Elliott, "Paul's Teaching on Marriage in 1 Corinthians: Some Problems Considered," *New Testament Studies* 19 (2, 1973), 219–25.
4. D.J. Doughty, "The Presence and Future of Salvation in Corinth," *Zeitschrift fur die neutestamentliche Wissenschaft* 66 (1975), 61–90, here 67.
5. J.J. von Allmen, *Pauline Teaching on Marriage* (London: Faith Press, 1963), 53, who rightly points out that a marriage ended by natural death is a marriage ended by God in His providence. See also D.E.H. Whiteley, *The Theology of St. Paul* (Philadelphia, PA: Fortress Press, 1972), 217.

9 Paul and the household tables

1. D.L. Balch, *Let Wives Be Submissive: The Domestic Code in 1 Peter*, SBL Monograph #26 (Chico, CA: Scholars Press, 1981).
2. W. Lillie, "The Pauline House Tables," *Expository Times*, 86 (1975), 179–83, here 183.
3. C.F.D. Moule, *Epistles to the Colossians and to Philemon* (Cambridge: Cambridge University Press, 1968), 127–8.
4. Ralph Martin, *Colossians and Philemon* (London: Oliphants, 1974), 117–18.
5. G.E. Cannon, *The Use of Traditional Materials in Colossians* (Macon, GA: Mercer University Press, 1983), 131.
6. G. Delling, "Submit," *Theological Dictionary of the New Testament*, 10 vols. (Grand Rapids, MI: Wm. B. Eerdmans Publishing Co., 1964–76), 8:45.
7. Marcus Barth, *Ephesians 4–6* (New York: Anchor, 1974), 647.

10 Women and the family of faith

1. See H.D. Betz, *Galatians* (Philadelphia, PA: Fortress Press, 1979), 182ff. For detailed information on this passage, see Ben Witherington, "Rite and Rights for Women – Galatians 3.28," *New Testament Studies* 27:5 (1981), 593–604.
2. G. Theissen, *The Social Setting of Pauline Christianity* (Philadelphia, PA: Fortress Press, 1982); W.A. Meeks, *The First Urban Christians* (New Haven, CN: Yale University Press, 1984).
3. J. Painter, "Paul and the Pneumatikoi at Corinth," in *Paul and Paulinism. Essays in Honor of C.K. Barrett*, ed. M.D. Hooker and S.G. Wilson (London: S.P.C.K., 1982), 237–50, here 245.
4. C.M. Galt, "Veiled Ladies," *American Journal of Archaeology* 35 (1981), 373–93.

5. H. Licht, *Sexual Life in Ancient Greece*, ed. L. H. Sawson (London: George Routledge, 1932), 357.
6. S. Bedale, "The Meaning of Kephale in the Pauline Epistles," *Journal of Theological Studies* n.s. 5 (1954), 211–15.
7. W. M. Ramsay, *The Cities of St. Paul* (Minneapolis, MN: James Family Christian Pub., reprinted, n.d.), 202ff.
8. M. D. Hooker, "Authority on her Head: an Examination of 1 Cor. XI.10," *New Testament Studies* 10 (1963–64), 410–16.
9. J. D. G. Dunn, *Jesus and the Spirit* (Philadelphia, PA: Westminster Press, 1975), 212–300; D. H. Hill, *New Testament Prophecy* (London: Marshall, Morgan and Scott, 1979).
10. K. L. Schmidt, "Church," *Theological Dictionary of the New Testament*, 10 vols. (Grand Rapids, MI: Wm. B. Eerdmans Publishing Co., 1964–76), 3:506.

11 Paul and his female co-workers

1. W. A. Meeks, *The First Urban Christians* (New Haven, CN: Yale University Press, 1984), 75.
2. *Ibid.*, 76.
3. Allan Chapple, "Local Leadership in the Pauline Churches" (Ph.D. dissertation, University of Durham, England, 1985), 74.
4. R. Scroggs correspondence with Wayne Meeks as recorded in Meeks, "The Image of the Androgyne: Some Uses of a Symbol in Earliest Christianity," *History of Religions* 13:3 (1974), 165–208, here 203, n. 153.
5. C. E. B. Cranfield, *A Critical and Exegetical Commentary on the Epistle to the Romans*, vol. 2 (Edinburgh: T. and T. Clark, 1975), 781–2.

12 The Pastoral Epistles

1. J. B. Hurley, *Man and Woman in Biblical Perspective: A Study in Role Relationships and Authority* (Leicester, UK: Inter-Varsity, 1981), 199.
2. R. M. Lewis, "The 'Women' of 1 Timothy 3.11," *Bibliotheca Sacra* 136:542 (1979), 167–75.

13 Women and the Third Evangelist

1. H. Flender, *St. Luke – Theologian of Redemptive History* (London: S.P.C.K., 1967), 10.
2. F. W. Danker, *Jesus and the New Age, According to St. Luke* (St. Louis, MO: Clayton Publishing House, 1972), 11.

3. W. Grundmann, "Humble," *Theological Dictionary of the New Testament*, 10 vols. (Grand Rapids, MI: Wm. B. Eerdmans Publishing Co., 1964–76), 8:21.

4. Alfred Plummer, *A Critical and Exegetical Commentary on the Gospel According to S. Luke* (Edinburgh: T. and T. Clark, 1922), 71.

5. Raymond E. Brown, ed., *Mary in the New Testament* (Philadelphia, PA: Fortress Press, 1978), 161–2.

6. D.W. Riddle, "Early Christian Hospitality: a Factor in the Gospel Transmission," *Journal of Biblical Literature* 57 (1938), 141–54.

7. *Ibid.*, 152.

8. E.E. Ellis, "The Role of the Christian Prophet in Acts," *Apostolic History and the Gospel* (Grand Rapids, MI: Wm. B. Eerdmans Publishing Co., 1971), 55–6.

9. Ernst Haenchen, *The Acts of the Apostles, A Commentary* (Philadelphia, PA: Westminster Press, 1971), 533.

10. *Ibid.*, 539.

11. Homily XL of John Chrysostom in G. B. Stevens, *Nicene and Post Nicene Fathers*, vol. 11 (Grand Rapids, MI: Wm. B. Eerdmans Publishing Co., 1975 repr.), 245.

14 Women and the Evangelists Matthew, Mark, and John

1. E.L. Bode, *The First Easter Morning – The Gospel Accounts of the Women's Visit to the Tomb of Jesus* (Rome: Biblical Institute, 1970), 5.

2. Raymond Brown, *The Birth of the Messiah* (London: Geoffrey Chapman, 1977), 50.

3. M.D. Johnson, *The Purpose of Biblical Genealogies with Special Reference to the Setting of the Genealogies of Jesus* (London: Cambridge University Press, 1969).

4. Raymond Brown, "Roles of Women in the Fourth Gospel," *Theological Studies* 36 (4, 1975), 688–99, here 692.

Conclusions

1. R.L. Wilken, *The Christians as the Romans Saw Them* (New Haven, CN: Yale University Press, 1984), 63.

2. W.A. Meeks, *The First Urban Christians* (New Haven, CN: Yale University Press, 1984), 9ff.

3. As quoted in Wilken, *Christians as the Romans Saw Them*, 31.

4. E. Käsemann, *New Testament Questions of Today*, trans. W.J. Montague, *et al.* (Philadelphia, PA: Fortress Press, 1969), 237.

5. R. N. Longenecker, *New Testament Social Ethics for Today* (Grand Rapids, MI: Wm. B. Eerdmans Publishing Co., 1974), 92.
6. Käsemann, *New Testament Questions of Today*, 136–7.
7. *Ibid.*, 211–12.
8. B. Witherington, *Women in the Earliest Churches* (Cambridge: Cambridge University Press, 1988).

SELECT BIBLIOGRAPHY

Allworthy, T. B. *Women in the Apostolic Church. A Critical Study of the Evidence in the New Testament for the Prominence of Women in Early Christianity.* Cambridge: W. Heffer and Sons, 1917.

Balch, David Lee. *The Domestic Code in 1 Peter.* Chico, CA: Scholars Press, 1981.

Balsdon, J. P. V. D. *Roman Women.* New York: John Day, 1962.

Bilezikian, Gilbert. *Beyond Sex Roles.* Grand Rapids, MI: Baker Book House, 1985.

Bloesch, Donald. *Is the Bible Sexist?* New York: Cornerstone, 1982.

Bode, E. L. *The First Easter Morning, The Gospel Accounts of the Women's Visit to the Tomb of Jesus.* Rome: Biblical Institute, 1970.

Boldrey, Richard and Joyce. *Chauvinist or Feminist? Paul's View of Women.* Grand Rapids, MI: Baker, 1976.

Brooten, B. J. *Women Leaders in the Ancient Synagogue: Inscriptional Evidence and Background Issues.* Chico, CA: Scholars Press, 1983.

Carmody, Denise Lardner. *Feminism and Christianity: A Two-Way Reflection.* Nashville, TN: Abingdon, 1982.

Clark, Stephen B. *Man and Woman in Christ: An Examination of the Roles of Men and Women in Light of Scripture and the Social Sciences.* Ann Arbor, MI: Servant, 1980.

Danielou, J. *The Ministry of Women in the Early Church.* Leighton Buzzard, UK: Faith Press, 1974.

Donaldson, J. *Woman: Her Position and Influence in Ancient Greece and Rome and in the Early Church.* New York: Gordon, 1973.

Fiorenza, E. Schussler. *In Memory of Her.* New York: Crossroad, 1983.

Foh, S. *Women and the Word of God. A Response to Biblical Feminism.* Philadelphia, PA: Presbyterian and Reformed Pub. Co., 1979.

Goodwater, L. *Women in Antiquity: An Annotated Bibliography.* Metuchen, NJ: Scarecrow, 1975.

Gryson, R. *The Ministry of Women in the Early Church.* Collegeville, MN: Liturgical Press, 1976.

Heine, Susanne. *Women and Early Christianity, a Reappraisal.* Trans. by John Bowden. Minneapolis, MN: Augsburg Publishing House, 1988.

Hurley, James B. *Man and Woman in Biblical Perspective.* Grand Rapids, MI: Zondervan Pub. Co., 1981.

Man and Woman in 1 Corinthians. PhD Dissertation Cambridge University, 1973.

Jewett, Paul K. *Man as Male and Female.* Grand Rapids, MI: Wm. B. Eerdmans, 1975.

The Ordination of Women. Grand Rapids, MI: Wm. B. Eerdmans, 1980.

Knight, G.W. *The New Testament Teaching on the Role Relationship of Men and Women.* Grand Rapids, MI: Baker Book House, 1977.

Lightfoot, N.R. *The Role of Women: New Testament Perspectives.* Memphis, TN: Student Association Press, 1978.

Loewe, R. *The Position of Women in Judaism.* London: SPCK, 1966.

McHugh, John. *The Mother of Jesus in the New Testament.* London: Darton, Longman, and Todd, 1975.

Mollenkott, Virginia R. *Women, Men, and the Bible.* Nashville, TN: Abingdon Press, 1977.

The Divine Feminine: The Biblical Imagery of God as Female. New York: Crossroad, 1983.

Pomeroy, Sarah B. *Goddesses, Whores, Wives, and Slaves; Women in Classical Antiquity.* New York: Schocken, 1975.

Ruether, Rosemary R., ed. *Religion and Sexism, Images of Women in the Jewish and Christian Traditions.* New York: Simon and Schuster, 1974.

Ryrie, Charles. *The Place of Women in the Church.* New York: Macmillan, 1958.

Sampley, J.P. *And the Two Shall Become One Flesh.* Cambridge: Cambridge University Press, 1971.

Sayers, Dorothy. *Are Women Human?* Downers Grove, IL: Inter-Varsity Press, 1978.

Stagg, E., and F. Stagg. *Women in the World of Jesus.* Philadelphia, PA: Westminster Press, 1978.

Stendahl, Krister. *The Bible and the Role of Women: A Case Study in Hermeneutics.* Trans. by Emilie T. Sander. Philadelphia, PA: Fortress, 1966.

Swidler, Leonard. *Biblical Affirmations of Women.* Philadelphia, PA: Westminster Press, 1979.

Women in Judaism: The Status of Women in Formative Judaism. Metuchen, NJ: Scarecrow Press, 1976.

Women and Ministry in the New Testament. Ramsey, NJ: Paulist Press, 1980.

Tavard, George H. *Women in Christian Tradition.* Notre Dame, IN: University of Notre Dame Press, 1973.

Theissen, G. *The Shadow of the Galilean. The Quest of the Historical Jesus in Narrative Form*. Philadelphia, PA: Fortress Press, 1987.

The Social Setting of Pauline Christianity. Philadelphia, PA: Fortress Press, 1982.

Thrall, Margaret E. *The Ordination of Women to the Priesthood*. London: SCM, 1958.

Trible, Phyllis. *God and the Rhetoric of Sexuality*. Philadelphia, PA: Fortress Press, 1978.

Williams, Don. *The Apostle Paul and Women in the Church*. Ventura, CA: Regal Press, 1977.

Witherington, Ben. *Women in the Ministry of Jesus*. Cambridge: Cambridge University Press, 1984.

Women in the Earliest Churches. Cambridge: Cambridge University Press, 1988.

INDEX OF SCRIPTURE CITATIONS

Index of modern authors